AF560304

CRISIS IN THE WESTERN HIMALAYAS
REPORTS OF J.D. CUNNINGHAM
1841-1842

CRISIS IN THE WESTERN HIMALAYAS

Reports of J.D. Cunningham

1841-1842

Edited by

C.L. Datta

Surinder Singh

CRISIS IN THE WESTERN HIMALAYAS
Reports of J.D. Cunningham, 1841-1842
edited by C.L. Datta and Surinder Singh

First Published 2015

ISBN 978-93-5002-357-0

Published by
AAKAR BOOKS
28 E Pocket IV, Mayur Vihar Phase I, Delhi 110 091
Phone : 011 2279 5505 Telefax : 011 2279 5641
aakarbooks@gmail.com; www.aakarbooks.com

Printed at
Sapra Brothers, Delhi 110 092

Contents

1

Introduction

I

Joseph Davey Cunningham's *History of the Sikhs* is a well known work on the subject.[1] It was first published in 1849. The last two chapters of this book dealing with the post-Maharaja Ranjit Singh period, present a comprehensive account of the momentous developments pertaining to the years 1839-1846. Perhaps that is why the book has run into many editions.[2] Here a few words about Cunningham's association with the Punjab affairs may not be out of place. At the young age of twenty-

1. For a brief sketch of his career, see the Biographical Note by H.L.O. Garrett in J.D. Cunningham, *A History of the Sikhs: From the Origin of the Nation to the Battle of the Sutlej*, S. Chand & Co, Delhi, (Reprint), 1955, pp. xix-xxi.
2. It is another matter that the book caused immense damage to his illustrious career, as he was dismissed from the Political Service which he had served with distinction for twelve years. The Court of Directors poured unqualified condemnation for the spirit pervading the work, besides containing statements and inferences affecting the reputation and honour of the British government and army. The punitive action was based on the charge that he had used official documents without permission. His efforts to secure restoration in service ended in a failure. He died on 28 February 1851 in Ambala at the young age of thirty-nine. S.S. Bal, 'Cunningham's Attempt to Get Himself Rehabilitated in the Political Service,' in Harbans Singh and N. Gerald Barrier, (eds.), *Essays in Honour of Dr. Ganda Singh*, Punjabi University, Patiala, 1976, pp. 215-233.

five, he was appointed Assistant Political Agent, North West Frontier Agency, Ludhiana in 1837. He lived among the Sikhs for a period of eight years during a crucial phase of their history. At that time Colonel (afterwards Sir) Claude Martin Wade was the Governor General's Agent, North West Frontier Agency and envoy to the Sikh court. He was also officer-in-charge of the British relations with the chiefs of Afghanistan. In 1839, when George Russel Clerk succeeded Wade, Cunningham worked under him. Cunningham was given many important assignments. He took steps to build a cantonment at Ferozepur, then an important British frontier post near the Sikh kingdom. In 1838, he was present at the interview which took place between Maharaja Ranjit Singh and Governor General Lord Auckland. At that time, plans to restore Shah Shuja, the deposed ruler of Afghanistan, on the throne of Kabul were maturing. In 1839, Cunningham was with Wade and the British army when it forcibly took possession of the Khyber Pass and laid open the road to Kabul. In 1840, he was given the administrative charge of Ludhiana district, which at that time was another important frontier post of British India. It was from here that Shah Shuja's court-in-exile worked. Further, after its occupation by the British in 1809, Ludhiana became an important centre where deserters, spies and malcontents from the Punjab, Afghanistan and many hill states, used to gather.[3] However in 1841, Cunningham was

3. Shah Shuja, the former ruler of Afghanistan, failed to recover his kingdom and took shelter in the Mubarak Haveli at Lahore. Forced to surrender the Kohinoor diamond to Ranjit Singh and suffer numerous indignities, he escaped from Lahore and rushed to Jammu. He made an abortive attempt to occupy Kashmir with the help of the chief of Kishtwar and, on reaching Ludhiana, received British protection. During 1826-31, he had unsuccessful negotiations with Ranjit Singh so as to recover his kingdom. Finally he signed a treaty with Ranjit Singh on 12 March 1833. Having raised a considerable force, he succeeded in defeating the Amirs of Sindh, but met with a disaster in Qandhar. He wandered aimlessly in Herat and Sindh before returning to Ludhiana. Armed with an ambiguous tripartite treaty with Ranjit Singh and the British, he was restored to the throne of Afghanistan, but was murdered during an uprising in 1841. Bikrama Jit Hasrat, *Life and*

appointed on a political mission to West Tibet about which more will be said in the second part of this Introduction.

Very little is known about Cunningham's contribution when he was appointed on a political mission to West Tibet in 1841-42. During these years, Wazir Zorawar Singh, (the brave general of the Dogra ruler Raja Gulab Singh, the feudatory of the Lahore Durbar) after annexing Ladakh and Baltistan, was fighting in West Tibet. Cunningham's reports, which were submitted by him during his year's stay on the frontier, are quite revealing. These are being published for the first time in this book. The duties assigned to Cunningham by his government, inter alia, included reporting about Zorawar Singh's incursions into Ladakh and Baltistan. Therefore, it is considered advisable to give a brief conspectus of these Dogra conquests. This will enable the reader to understand the various issues, which have been discussed in the reports, in a historical perspective.

Maharaja Ranjit Singh (r.1799-1839), the powerful ruler of the Punjab, employed many soldiers and adventurers, who conquered several territories and rendered useful services to him. One such person who joined his service about 1810 was Mian Gulab Singh, a Dogra Rajput of Jammu. Born in 1792, he was the descendant of a collateral branch of the ruling family of Jammu. He was a brave soldier who impressed Ranjit Singh by his obedient conduct. After some years, he was given the command of a small force and was chiefly employed not only during revolts in the hills around Jammu which the Maharaja had conquered in 1800-1801, but also for conquering new territories in the Jammu sector and western Punjab. After being impressed by his faithful services, the Maharaja conferred on Gulab Singh the *jagir* of Jammu in 1820 and, two years later, also granted him and his successors the hereditary title of the 'Raja.' He was also authorized to raise and maintain his own army. The Raja, quite ambitious as he was, raised a large army, mainly consisting of the doughty warriors, the Mian Rajputs of the Jammu hills. With the help of this army, he conquered many

---

Times of Ranjit Singh: A Saga of Benevolent Despotism, V.V. Research Institute, Hoshiarpur, 1977, pp. 116-118, 126-130, 163-176.

new territories such as Riasi, Sambha and Dalpatpur. He also subdued Behandrate and Chaneni in 1822, and the fort of Samarth in 1825. He made all these conquests ostensibly for the Maharaja, but actually these were meant for himself. Meanwhile, Gulab Singh conquered Kishtwar, whose Muslim chief Raja Tegh Singh had given asylum to Shah Shuja, the erstwhile ruler of Kabul who had escaped from Sikh captivity. Tegh Singh was made prisoner and sent to Lahore. In addition to acquiring territories, Gulab Singh held large tracts in the Punjab plains and also obtained monopoly of the salt mines of Pind Dad Khan.[4] In short, according to Hutchison and Vogel, by 1834 Gulab Singh, after Maharaja Ranjit Singh, came to be considered 'the greatest chief in the Punjab.'[5]

Raja Gulab Singh called to Lahore his younger brothers, Dhian Singh and Suchet Singh, where they were also employed by the Maharaja. They impressed their royal patron with their devotion and hard work. The Dogra brothers played an active role with the Sikh army in many conquests. Being an accomplished courtier, Dhian Singh was appointed Minister-in-Waiting (Deodiwala) in 1819 and nine years later he was elevated to the position of the Prime Minister. This made him one of the most powerful nobles in the Lahore Durbar and further enhanced the influence of the Dogra brothers. The three Dogra brothers made a common cause at the Lahore Durbar. Dhian Singh looked after the interests of Gulab Singh at Lahore, while the latter attended to the concerns of his brothers in the Jammu Hills. With the passage of time, the Dogra brethren emerged as a powerful element in the Durbar.

Raja Gulab Singh, for running the administration and keeping under his effective control such large areas as he now possessed, had employed many talented people who mainly consisted of the inhabitants of the hills.[6] One such person was

---

4. J. Hutchison and J. Ph. Vogel, "History of Jammu State," *Journal of the Punjab Historical Society*, Vol. VIII, No. 2, p. 134.
5. K.M. Pannikar, *The Founding of the Kashmir State: A Biography of Maharaja Gulab Singh, 1792-1858*, Allen & Unwin, London, 1953, p. 37.
6. J. Hutchison and J. Ph. Vogel, 'History of the Jammu State,' *Journal of the Punjab Historical Society*, Vol. VIII, No. II, p. 34.

Zorawar Singh, a Rajput who belonged to the Kahluria Mians. According to the Lahore Durbar Records, Zorawar Singh joined service as a private soldier in one of Raja Gulab Singh's battalions. The former received training in military weapons and horse riding and went on to render many useful services to his master. About 1815 he successfully defended the fort of Riasi when it was attacked by Mian Dewan Singh, another contender for the possession of the jagir of Riasi. Soon thereafter, Zorawar Singh was appointed Inspector of Commissariat Supplies in all the forts north of Jammu, which had been conquered by Raja Gulab Singh. About 1823 Zorawar Singh was appointed Governor of Kishtwar and Kussal and soon thereafter he was also given the title of Wazir. He spent the next few years in strengthening his position in and around Kishtwar. Here he introduced many revenue reforms. He got the land measured and fixed the state share at half of the produce. He also renovated the fort of the former Kishtwari rulers, garrisoned it with his own troops and stored there a large quantity of provisions. Rugged terrain and high mountains surrounding Kishtwar were used for imparting rigorous military training to his soldiers.[7] He used Kishtwar as a base for his military operations for the conquest of Ladakh and Baltistan.

---

7. A division of Udhampur district, Kishtwar was bounded on the north by Kashmir and Maru Wardwan valley, on the south by Badhawar, on the east by Chandra Bhaga river and on the west by the districts of Ramban and Banihal. The Rajput Rajas of this principality converted to Islam along with their followers, probably in the wake of their submission to the Delhi Sultans. They received land grants in Kashmir from the Mughals, which they possessed till the time of the Sikhs. After its occupation by Raja Gulab Singh of Jammu, its revenue was reduced by Sikh oppression to a paltry sum of Rs. 3,000 in 1850. Rich in the cultivation of a variety of fruit, it had intimate trade relations with Ladakh and Punjab. Quarter Master General (Intelligence Branch), ed., *Gazetteer of Kashmir and Ladak*, Vivek Publishing House, Delhi, Reprint, 1974, (First published in 1890 by Superintendent of Government Printing, Calcutta), pp. 503-505.

II

Ladakh, with its capital at Leh, is a rugged and elevated table land which is situated on the Indus. In its north are the Kuen Lun range and the slopes of the Karakoram range, while in the west, it has Kashmir and Baltistan. To its south are situated Chamba, Kullu and Kinnaur and on its east and south east, beyond the international boundary, are the Tibetan district of Rudok, Gartok and Chumurty. Ladakh's area was about 48,000 square kilometres. This area, however, shrank in 1846 when its southern districts—Lahaul and Spiti—were snatched from it by the British and annexed with their newly acquired territory of Kangra district. In 1834 Tsepal Namgyal (c. 1790-1834) was the last Gyalpo (king) of Ladakh. He was a weak and indolent ruler. He had alienated the Leh officialdom and, internally,[8] the administration of the country was disintegrating and centrifugal forces were gaining momentum. The Gyalpo had also failed to defend the country against aggressive neighbours from Baltistan, Chamba, Kullu and Bashahr who were nibbling at his territories. Thus, the Ladakhi kingdom appears to have earned a name for being an easy prey to conquerors.

---

8. The polity of Ladakh has been characterized as a mild despotism under a king known as Gyalpo. In running the central government, he was assisted by a council comprising three grades of officers—chief ministers (Kahlons), ministers (Lonpos) and elders (Gangsum). The actual administration was entrusted to a prime minister (Bangki Kahlon) whose office was hereditary and restricted to a single family of district governors (Kahlons). The administration of towns and districts was in the hands of hereditary chiefs who had been earlier autonomous rulers. They also served as commanders (Kharpons) of forts and raised local levies for military service. The village headmen (Gobas), while being subordinate to local chiefs, exercised revenue and judicial powers in their petty jurisdictions. For details, see Alexander Cunningham, *Ladakh: Political, Statistical and Historical*, Sagar Publications, New Delhi (Reprint), 1970, pp. 257-260; C.L. Datta, *Ladakh and Western Himalayan Politics*, Munshiram Manoharlal, New Delhi, 1973, pp. 32-38.

Zorawar Singh took full advantage of this situation. After adequate preparation, he invaded Ladakh for the first time in July 1834. His first target was the western extremity of Ladakh towards Kashmir and Baltistan, known as Purig which comprised the districts of Purig, Suru and Dras. After fighting many battles at places such as Sanku, Langkartse, Kartse, Pashkyum and Sod, he established control over a large tract of Ladakh. But his march towards Leh was checked, as it was reported that Doctor Henderson, said to be an agent of the English East India Company, was staying with the Ladakhi king. Zorawar Singh suspended his operations and reported the matter to Raja Gulab Singh who, in turn, wrote to Maharaja Ranjit Singh. The latter addressed C.M. Wade, the British Agent at Ludhiana, who assured the Maharaja that the doctor had crossed the Sutlej in direct violation of the orders of his Government and that the Company did not want to interfere in the Maharaja's conquests on the north. In the wake of this explanation and having suspended his operations for three months, Zorawar Singh resumed his offensive. But, by then, winter had set in and an advance towards Leh was considered inadvisable. He made an offer to the Ladakhi ruler Tsepal Namgyal that if he paid war indemnity of Rs. 15,000, the invaders would retreat. The Ladakhi authorities, however, did not agree and, on the contrary, mobilized the war potential of the country. They encircled the Dogra army at Malbe. Here a pitched battle was fought in which the invaders were defeated. Many Dogra soldiers were killed and one of their brave leaders Uttam Padhiar was seriously wounded. After this setback, Zorawar Singh was forced to fall back on Kishtwar.

During the winter of 1835, Zorawar Singh invaded Ladakh for the second time. Perceiving a strong Ladakhi resistance on the Kishtwar-Suru-Leh route, which he had followed during the previous year, Zorawar Singh adopted the direct though difficult route via Zanskar, which passed through the glaciers. The Ladakhis were defeated and the Gyalpo paid war indemnity and some additional expenses. He was deposed and, in his place, Ngorub Stanzin (who was married to the Gyalpo's sister) was raised to the throne. Zorawar Singh built a fort at Leh which was garrisoned by 300 Dogra soldiers. After taking with him some influential Ladakhis as hostages and for the better conduct of the new ruler, Zorawar Singh returned to Jammu in early March 1836. Soon after, Prime Minister Dhian Singh and Raja Gulab Singh presented to Maharaja Ranjit Singh a document containing the agreement of the new Ladakhi ruler with the Maharaja. A tribute of Rs.30,000 and many presents were offered to the Sikh ruler. In this manner, Ranjit Singh accorded recognition to Gulab Singh's conquest of Ladakh.

Sohan Lal Suri, who was Maharaja Ranjit Singh's court vakil and historian, tells us that on 15 March 1836 Zorawar Singh met the Maharaja at the town of Jandiala Sher Singh and presented him with some 'Gont' horses and forty Ladakhi cows. The Wazir said that the country of Tibet extended over a distance of 500 *kos* and its boundary was contiguous with China. He continued that, if the Maharaja be pleased to give an order to him, then he was ready to conquer that country for the Maharaja. The latter however, remarked that "the king of China had 12 lakhs of soldiers. How could possession of that country be established?"[9] These remarks of Ranjit Singh show that he was far more realistic than Zorawar Singh who, in his endeavour to conquer West Tibet, perished along with his army in 1841.

During the winter of 1836 and the summer of 1839, Zorawar Singh led two more expeditions to quell rebellions in the different parts of Ladakh. The Gyalpo, Ngorub Stanzin, was found to be conspiring with the rebels. However, his machinations did not bear any fruit. The revolt was suppressed with a heavy hand. The Ladakhi ruler was deposed and, in his place, the aged Tsepal Namgyal was restored to the throne. Raja Gulab Singh appears to have adopted a dual form of government, i.e. the king was the titular head while he himself was the de facto ruler. This arrangement ended in 1842 when the Ladakhi ruler was removed and his state annexed.

9. Sohan Lal Suri, *Umdat-ut-Tawarikh*, Dafter III, English Translation, V.S. Suri, S. Chand & Co., New Delhi, 1961, pp. 316-317.

III

Meanwhile, after his conquest of Ladakh, Zorawar Singh turned his attention towards Baltistan. With its capital at Skardu and having an area of about 18,200 square kilometres, Baltistan is situated in the Indus Valley to the west of Ladakh and north of Kashmir. The kingdom was divided into eight subdivisions or districts which were under the control of different hereditary chieftains, who owed fealty to Ahmad Shah, the powerful ruler of Baltistan. After the Sikh conquest of Kashmir in 1819, the Balti ruler apprehended that his state would also be invaded and, in order to prevent such an eventuality, he tried to cultivate the friendship of the British. When William Moorcroft,[10] the British traveller, was in Ladakh during 1820-1822, Ahmad Shah sent some presents to him and proferred his help by providing porters and provisions, besides letters of introduction to the Muslim chieftains on the road to Badakhshan and Kokand. Moorcroft did not accept all this, yet he wrote an ambiguous letter to Ahmad Shah, holding out promises of British support. Thereafter, the Balti ruler continued to expect British assistance. Visits of some Englishmen such as Dr. Henderson, G.T. Vigne and Dr. Falconer to Baltistan in the 1830s, to some extent enabled

---

10. William Moorcroft, a veterinary surgeon in the Bengal Army, was deputed by the British to Turkistan to procure horses for improving the breeds in British provinces, to explore possibilities of British trade with trans-Himalayan regions and possibly to gather intelligence about the Russian interest in the area. He was granted two years leave, certificates of introduction and presents for local chiefs. Accompanied by a surveyor George Trebeck and an agent Mir Izzatullah Khan, he travelled in a caravan comprising sixty mules and other beasts of burden. After passing through the hills of Kumaun and Nahan, he advanced across Mandi, Kullu, Lahaul and Kangra. In the plains of Punjab, he visited Hoshiarpur and Amritsar on his way to Lahore, where he had an audience with Ranjit Singh. He stayed for two years in Ladakh (September 1820 to September 1822), leaving behind an accurate description of the kingdom and signing a commercial agreement with it on behalf of the British. Subsequently, he marched through Kashmir, Peshawar, Kabul and Kunduz, ending his journey at Bukhara.

Ahmad Shah to postpone the evil day. Yet, an internal feud in the Balti ruling family paved the way for the Dogra invasion. Ahmad Shah was having differences with his eldest son Muhammad Shah, whom he proposed to pass over in favour of a younger son from another wife in fixing the succession. Muhammad Shah sought help from Zorawar Singh, who allowed him to stay at Leh for some time. But in 1839 the Balti ruler, with the connivance of Tsepal Namgyal, took away Muhammad Shah forcibly to Baltistan. This offended Zorawar Singh who invaded Baltistan in November 1839. It was a casus belli, but in reality Zorawar Singh, by conquering Baltistan, intended to encircle the Kashmir valley from the north, which his master Gulab Singh wanted to occupy.

Having made appropriate preparations and taking with him the old Ladakhi king and his militiamen, Zorawar Singh marched towards Baltistan. He divided his army into two columns. The first one, which comprised mainly of the Ladakhis under a Dogra officer, entered Baltistan over the Chorbat La. Later marching along the right and then on the left side of the river Shyok, a tributary of the Indus, and passing through Khapalu, it descended into the Skardu district. Heading the second column himself, Zorawar Singh marched from Kargil towards Marol, but had to encounter many difficulties on the way, owing to heavy snowfall and intense cold. At long last and after immense suffering, the Dogras, with the help of Ali Sher Khan, the chieftain of Kharmang and some local people, who acted as their guides, crossed the Indus near the Wanko Pass. Once on the road to Sakardu, the assailants fought some battles and defeated the Baltis. Near Gol, the other column which had been sent over the Chorbat Pass, joined the main army without doing any fighting on the way. The invaders then moved towards Skardu, where Ahmad Shah had gathered a large force and had fortified his citadel. The Dogras besieged the fort and cut off its water supply. The Baltis were defeated in a well-contested military action. Ahmad Shah was deposed and, in his stead, Muhammad Shah was installed as the new king who became a vassal of Raja Gulab Singh and agreed to pay an annual tribute of Rs. 7,000. From the Skardu fort, the Dogras acquired a vast booty which comprised a rich treasure, a large quantity of provisions, matchlocks, swords and other implements of war. Zorawar Singh constructed a new fort at Skardu and garrisoned it with a strong contingent under Bhagwan Singh Kishtwaria.

After the conquest of Skardu, Zorawar Singh took steps to subdue those feudatories of Ahmad Shah who had actively assisted the Gyalpo and still held out. First was the turn of Shigar, which is situated to the north of Skardu. It was conquered without much difficulty. Then Zorawar Singh paid attention to Rondu, which is situated on the Skardu-Gilgit line. At first, Raja Ali Khan of Rondu offered a stiff resistance but, when hard pressed, he agreed to pay a war indemnity of Rs. 5,000 and accepted to become a vassal of the Dogras. Thereafter the assailants moved towards Astor or Hasora, which is an important halting station on the Srinagar-Gilgit road. Though the ruler of Astor, Raja Jabbar Khan, submitted, yet after opposition from Colonel Mihan Singh, the Sikh Governor (*nazim*) of Kashmir, the Dogras were forced to withdraw from that principality. This opposition of Colonel Mihan Singh checked the Dogra expansion in the direction of Gilgit. Thereafter the Dogras returned to Skardu.

After staying at Skardu for some time, Zorawar Singh ordered Ahmad Shah and his prominent chieftains to assemble their armies and march with him back to Leh, whence soon after they were to assist the Dogras in their invasion of Western Tibet. Zorawar Singh returned to Leh in the middle of 1840. Tsepal Namgyal, being unable to bear the exertion of the campaign, died on the way. The Dogra General, on reaching Leh, installed the eight-year-old grandson of the deceased as the new nominal ruler of Ladakh. Zorawar Singh stayed in Leh for about a year during which he reorganized his army as well the troops of the vassal chiefs. He replenished his resources and contemplated the conquest of more territories. Before proceeding with our narrative, we may point out that the Doctor Henderson incident mentioned earlier, reveals that the British were not interested in Ladakh and did not want to check the Lahore Durbar's expansion in that direction. The British attitude vis-à-vis the Dogra conquest of Baltistan was similar.[11] However, when the Dogras invaded Western Tibet, there was a change in the British policy. They prevailed upon Maharaja Sher Singh to ask Zorawar Singh to withdraw and appointed J.D. Cunningham on a special mission to oversee the withdrawal of the Dogras. This was due to a clash of interests. These details are discussed in the following pages.

The conquest of Ladakh and Baltistan resulted in adding an area of about 64,000 square kilometres to the Sikh kingdom and extended its boundaries on the north to its geographical limits. As if the acquisition of this vast territory was not enough, Zorawar Singh was now ready for fresh conquests. As mentioned earlier, his movement in the direction of Gilgit having been checked by the Sikh Governor of Kashmir, his only avenue of expansion lay north and north-east of Ladakh, i.e. towards Yarqand and West Tibet. He first thought of conquering Chinese Turkistan for which there was an ostensible reason. The British were then fighting the First Opium War (1839-1842). The Ching Emperor understood that the British and the Sikhs were friends and, therefore, ordered his Governor in Yarqand to confiscate and destroy the entire stock of opium belonging to the Punjab traders that was valued at about eight lakhs of rupees. George Russel Clerk, the British Agent for the affairs of Punjab and the North-West Frontier, wrote to the Supreme Government that Raja Gulab Singh was inciting the Maharaja to the effect that the seizure and destruction of opium of his subjects should not be allowed to go unpunished. In these circumstances, Zorawar Singh could teach the Chinese a lesson and was capable of conquering Yarqand. But, because an amicable settlement over the Opium War was in sight, Clerk recommended to the Maharaja to ask "Raja Gulab Singh to desist from his designs on Yarqand." Under these circumstances, Zorawar Singh turned his attention to the conquest of West Tibet, which was comparatively easy of access.

---

11. For details regarding the visits of the British and other European travellers to Baltistan and Raja Ahmad Shah's endeavours to enter into an alliance with the British Government, see, C.L. Datta, *Ladakh and Western Himalayan Politics*, pp. 119-121.

IV

Tibet has been divided into several large and vaguely defined areas. Its western part was known as West Tibet or Na-ris. It consists of the area between the Mayum Pass on the east and the Ladakh border on the west. On the north, it is bounded by the Chang Thang and in the south it touched the then state of Bashahr (which formed a part of the Simla Hill States), Kumaun and Garhwal (then part of the North West Province with headquarters at Agra). To its further east-west it touches Nepal. In 1841-1842, when the Dogras invaded West Tibet, it was under the control of Central Tibet, with its capital at Lhasa. Gartok or Garo, situated at a distance of about 200 miles from Leh, was the main centre of the government. For the administration of West Tibet, the Governor (Garpon) of Gartok was responsible to the authorities in Lhasa. Other important places in this area were Rudok, Chaprang, Daba and Taklakot, which were under the administrative control of different officials.

As mentioned earlier, after the conquest of Baltistan, Zorawar Singh stayed at Leh for about a year and reorganized his army and refurbished his resources. Additional Dogra troops from Kishtwar and Jammu were asked to join the army. Many Pathan soldiers from the Peshawar sector also joined him. The contingent was presumably sent by Raja Gulab Singh who, at that juncture, was fighting in that sector. Ahmad Shah, the deposed Balti ruler and his vassal chiefs converged at Leh along with their contingents and auxiliaries. Similarly, the erstwhile Ladakhi chieftains and their forces were ordered to join his army, which was now prepared to invade the western part of Tibet. He revived the old claims of Ladakh over the Tibetan territory that lay to the west of the Mayum Pass.[12] In April 1841, the Dogra army moved into West Tibet and by the

---

12. This territory known in Tibetan as mNa-ris sKor-gSum and having important districts such as Rudok, Gartok and Taklakot, was ceded to Ladakh by Tibet during the reign of Tse-bratan rNam-rGyal (1780-90). For details see L. Petech, 'Tibetan Ladakhi Moghul War of 1881-83,' *Indian Historical Quarterly*, Vol. XXIII, September 1947, pp. 169-199.

end of September, it overran the entire area lying to the west of the Mayum Pass. Some of the important places in this tract, where fortresses were constructed, were Rudok, Gartok, Churit, Chumurti, Kardam, Tirtha Puri and Taklakot. The last mentioned place was conquered by the Dogras on 6 September 1841. T.C. Robertson, the Lieutenant- Governor of the North-West Province, in his Minute dated 28 September 1841, observed that Zorawar Singh was increasing his force every day at Taklakot and "evidently intends to winter there having collected from the stores of the people of the country grain enough" to support his army for many months.[13] His party at this post has increased to about seven or eight hundred Sikhs.[14] The garrison was placed under the control of Mehta Basti Ram. This officer constructed a fort there which was supplied with water and provisions. He took further steps to fortify the stronghold. With this, the Dogra conquest of West Tibet was complete.

As the de facto ruler of the newly acquired territories, Zorawar Singh initiated measures to consolidate his position. Local Tibetan functionaries were taken into service and were asked to collect taxes as per the old practices and pacify the people. Orders were issued to sell shawl-wool as it was customary to Ladakhis only. The Bhotias, the British subjects of Kumaun and Garhwal, who traded with West Tibet, were also taxed as in the past. The Bhotias felt alarmed at the Dogra conquest.[15] In order to allay their fears, Colonel Basti Ram held

---

13. See, Minute by the Lieutenant Governor, North-West Provinces, 28 September 1841, *FDS Proceedings*, 11 October 1841, No. 50.
14. Ibid.
15. The Dogra invasion of West Tibet had an adverse impact on the livelihood of traditionally mercantile communities like the Bhotias and Hunias. The Bhotias, who were the inhabitants of Kumaun and Garhwal, engaged in trade as the only source of income. Since they had made purchases for their annual trips to the Tartary across the Himalayas, they sank into immense privations owing to the cancellation of their deals and the grave risks posed by the disturbed conditions. Hunias, the counterparts of the Bhotias in West Tibet, were forced to abandon their homes and flee to the neighbouring territories including the British protected hill states.

a meeting (8 October 1841) with G.T. Lushington, the Commissioner of Kumaun, at Kala Pani which was a small village about ten miles from the Tibetan frontier, inside the British territory. Basti Ram told Lushington that Zorawar Singh was keen to do everything to place the commercial traffic of the British subjects on its former footing. From all this, it appears that Zorawar Singh had no intention of vacating the newly conquered territories and, like Ladakh and Baltistan, he wanted to make West Tibet also a part of the Dogra dominions. The acquisition of West Tibet may be considered as the apogee of Zorawar Singh's conquest and what followed was in the nature of an anti-climax.

The Dogras were not allowed to digest their gains in West Tibet. The Tibetan functionary General Pishi's requests for reinforcements were promptly attended by the authorities in Lhasa. The latter collected a force of about 10,000 and immediately dispatched it to the front to expel the 'Shenpas.'[16] The commander of this army was Kalon Surkhang and it had a strong park of artillery. With the help of the local people and the Tashilhunpo monastery, provisions which could last for nearly nine months were requisitioned from military post warehouses and were transported to the front on hundreds of yaks and donkeys.[17]

When Zorawar Singh heard about the arrival of this army, he sent for reinforcements from his commanders stationed at different military posts. Basti Ram moved along with his followers towards Do-yo near the Mansarovar Lake, where Zorawar Singh was fighting, but owing to heavy snowfall and

---

Some Dogra invaders even entered pargana Byans of Kumaun and extorted dues from the Bhotias which they had earlier been paying to the Tibetan authorities. C.L. Datta, *Ladakh and Western Himalayan Politics*, pp. 161-162.

16. 'Shen-pa' or 'Sen-pa' literally meaning 'the Singh people' was a term used by the Ladakhis, Tibetans and Chinese to refer to both Sikhs and Dogras. See, M. Fisher, W.M. Rose and R.A. Hattenback, *Himalayan Battleground: Sino-Indian Rivalry in Ladakh*, Frederick A. Praeger, New York and London, 1963, Appendix, p. 155.
17. Ibid.

the presence of the Tibetan army, he could not reach him. Basti Ram tells us that Mian Awtara Kishtwaria, who was in charge of the Kardam post, was killed along with his soldiers.[18] Mian Dullu Singh moved from Spiti along with his soldiers, but due to heavy snowfall, it became difficult for him to cross the Boot Pau Pass. Mian Magna Ram, Zorawar Singh's bother-in-law, advanced from Leh with his troops. But owing to the long distance, heavy snowfall and extremely inclement weather of mid-winter, he also failed to render any help to Zorawar Singh. The latter was surrounded by a strong Tibetan army, and died fighting on 12 December 1841.[19]

V

The Dogra conquest of West Tibet, unlike the occupation of Ladakh and Baltistan, was considered quite detrimental to the interests of the East India Company and was fraught with many dangers. Firstly, the trade of the British protected hill states received a serious setback. Secondly, it was found that another object of Zorawar Singh's invasion was to enter into a friendly alliance with Nepal, which at that time was in search of anti-British alliances. In August 1841, Lord Auckland, the Governor General, wrote to George Russel Clerk, his Agent at Ludhiana, that by the proceedings of the Dogras in the trans-Himalayas, an excitement had been caused at Kathmandu which it was desirable to check.[20] Thirdly, the British were anxious to avoid any interference of the Ching Emperor in favour of Tibet, then a Chinese protectorate. At that time, the First Opium War was going on between the United Kingdom and China and it was feared that the Chinese Emperor would confound the

18. For details, see, 'Basti Ram's Disclosures to Lushington,' *FDSC*, No. 106, 7 February 1842.
19. For a detailed account of Zorawar Singh's conquest of West Tibet, see, C.L. Datta, *General Zorawar Singh: His Life and Achievements in Ladakh, Baltistan and Tibet*, Deep & Deep Publications, New Delhi, 1984, pp. 63-83.
20. Government to Clerk, 16 August 1841, *FDSC*, 16 August 1841, No. 39.

independent Sikhs with the English, and create additional difficulties in the way of pending and probable negotiations.[21] B.H. Hodgson, the British Resident in Nepal, had already cautioned his Government that if it did not desire that the attention of China be drawn to this quarter then, "the sooner these wanton encroachments of the Jammu family upon the states and districts contiguous to Ladakh are discountenanced the better."[22]

Clerk had addressed the Lahore Durbar several times soliciting information regarding Zorawar Singh's objectives and movements in West Tibet,[23] but the usual reply which he always got was that the Sikh Government had not received any intelligence from that quarter. Clerk wrote to the Supreme Government that the reports of the Durbar in this case were dictated by the Prime Minister Raja Dhian Singh and would continue to be so till the Maharaja was alarmed at the prospect of the consequences of the dissatisfaction of the British Government.[24] Clerk, therefore, suggested that "some perfect system of intelligence of passing events" on the eastern side of the Himalayas should be instituted. He observed that such a system was that a competent British agent should go to the area and see things with his own eyes, his presence would interrupt "political intrigues should Zorawar and his master have conceived in that quarter, detrimental or embarrassing to the interests of the British Government or its allies."[25]

In pursuance of this advice, J.D. Cunningham, who, as mentioned earlier, was well acquainted with the affairs of the Lahore Durbar, was considered competent to do the job.

---

21. J.D. Cunningham, *History of the Sikhs*, p. 218.
22. Hodgson to Maddock, 30 July 1841, *FDSC*, 16 August 1841, No. 41.
23. Clerk to Maharaja Sher Singh, 27 August 1841, *FDSC*, 20 September, 1841, No. 65, Enclosure No. 1; *FDSC*, 27 September 1841, No. 42.
24. Clerk to Government, 9 September 1841, *FDSC*, 27 September 1841, No. 69.
25. Clerk to Government, 10 August 1841, *FDSC*, 30 August 1841, No. 89.

Cunningham was asked to travel up to the Sutlej to a point near the Tibetan frontier where active hostilities were going on between the Dogras and the Tibetans. The point chosen by Cunningham was the remote Shalkhar village in the Kinnaur district in the north eastern part of Bashahr, where the boundaries of Ladakh and West Tibet meet.[26] With a view to enable Cunningham to discharge his duties effectively, he was accredited by the Lieutenant Governor, North-West Province, to the Raja of Bashahr.[27] The latter was asked to provide guides and other assistance which the British Commissioner might demand. The service of one Havaldar and twelve soldiers from 'Nusseerie Battalion' was also requisitioned for Cunningham.[28]

Instructions issued to Cunningham were quite detailed and his duties were manifold. He was asked to enquire about the intentions of Wazir Zorawar Singh or his subordinates in advancing to or towards Rudok and subsequently moving down upon Gartok and Lake Mansarowar, the number and description of his troops, his tenure of the districts conquered by him, the cause or pretext of those encroachments and "the nature and ramifications of the trade which for sometime past seems to have been a bone of contention on the one hand between Yarkand and Ladakh, and on the other between Bashahr and Ladakh."[29] Also it was an essential part of

---

26. According to a recent official survey, the village of Shalkar (Hadbast No. 35/1) possesses an area of 329 hectares and a population of 357 persons who are spread over 83 households. With reference to land use, culturable waste includes 279 hectares, while 9 hectares are irrigated and 8 hectares are unirrigated. An area of 33 hectares is not available for agriculture. In addition to an elementary school up to the fourth class and a primary health sub centre, the village has been provided with a post office and bus stop. Approached by a pucca road, Shalkar is situated at a distance of 171 kilometres from the nearest town of Rampur. *District Census Handbook, Himachal Pradesh, Part XII, A & B, Census of India, 1991*, pp. 50-51.
27. *FDSC*, 27 September 1841, Nos. 42-44.
28. Ibid.
29. Clerk to Cunningham, 25 September 1841, *FDSC*, 22 November 1841, No. 28.

Cunningham's duties to watch narrowly the progress of the Dogras not only in Western Tibet, but also in Skardu and Gilgit, and "to endeavour to arrive at an understanding of the designs of those chiefs of Jammoo east and west of Cashmere."[30] The Supreme Government further desired Cunningham to be a witness to the evacuation of the western part of Tibet by the Dogras."[31]

Cunningham stayed on the frontier for about a year (September 1841- September 1842) and remained for most of the time at Shalkhar (present name) village, which is very near the boundary line with West Tibet and Ladakh. He spent some time at Chango village which is thirty kilometres downward journey from Shalkhar.[32] He did spend some time at Nako and Leo villages also (which are not very far from Chango) from where he sent a few reports to his Government. He also stayed for some time at Reckong Peo which is at present the administrative headquarters of Kinnaur district of Himachal Pradesh. Towards the end of November 1841, Cunningham moved to Churit, a village in West Tibet, about fifteen miles to the north-west of Shalkhar. At one time Cunningham even determined to go to the camp of Zorawar Singh who, at that time, was wintering near the Lake Mansarowar, but because of inclement weather he could not do so and returned to Shalkhar in Kinnaur. Though the climate was extremely hostile, yet Cunningham devoted all the energies of his body and mind to write very detailed reports to his Government.

---

30. Ibid.
31. Government of India to Clerk, 8 October 1841, *FDSC*, 11 October 1841, No. 47.
32. When the election for electing a member of the Lok Sabha from the parliamentary constituency of Mandi in Himachal Pradesh was held on 29 June 2013, the condition of this stretch of 30 kilometres of road from Chango to Shalkhar was quite bad. The narrow road had been broken at several places by 'recent heavy rain and snowfall.' If this was the condition of the road in the recent summer of 2013, one can well imagine the condition 173 years ago in the cold season when Cunningham traversed the area and stayed there during winter when the snowfall was the heaviest. *Sunday Times*, 30 June 2013, p. 2, cols.3-6.

The following is a brief description of some salient aspects of Cunningham's reports:

Zorawar Singh's army and its movements attracted Cunningham's immediate attention. The strength of the army was about 6,000 out of which nearly 3,000 were the Dogras of Kishtwar and Jammu hills and the rest were Ladakhis and Baltis.[33] The former, mostly armed with matchlocks, formed the nucleus of the army and constituted the fighting force, whereas the Ladakhis and Baltis served as auxiliary troops. In addition, the local population was conscripted for carrying of provisions, tents and accoutrements. The Dogras also had about six *jingals* or small guns, which could be carried by men or mules.[34] Zorawar Singh also took with him some important dignitaries both from Ladakh and Baltistan. Inter alia, these included Ahmad Shah, the dispossessed ruler of Skardu; Gonpo, the steward of the powerful Hemis monastery in Ladakh; Nonu Sunnum, the brother of the former Raja of Ladakh and Ghulam Khan, the son-in-law of Rahim Khan, the Qiladar of Spiti district.[35]

The Dogra attack on Tibet was three-pronged. The first contingent, which was led by Ghulam Khan, entered Rupshu and, passing through Hanle, the headquarters of Rupshu district in Ladakh, ran over the Tibetan posts of Churit, Chumurty, Tsaparang and Tholing. After establishing pickets at all important places conquered by him, Rahim Khan joined with the main column and, taking the middle route, conquered Tashigong. Zorawar Singh himself led the third column. With nearly 3,000 soldiers and following the route to the south easterly direction, he sacked Gartok, where the other two columns also joined him. The invaders then conquered other places around Lake Manasarowar and Taklakot, the last important post in West Tibet which is located about fifteen miles from the border of Nepal. By September 1841, the Dogras became the masters of all territory to the west of the Mayum Pass. Zorawar Singh's conquest of West Tibet was complete.

33. *FDSC*, 1 November 1841, No. 37-38.
34. Cunningham to Clerk, 21 October 1841, *FDSC*, 28 November 1841.
35. Ibid.

In order to further strengthen their position in West Tibet and not depending on the only Leh-Gartok supply route, the Dogras started widening and repairing the road from Dunkur, the chief town in Spiti to Bootpau Pass. They also started clearing the pathways and other internal roads. All this was done to facilitate easy movement of troops and transport supplies to their main army. Cunningham wrote to Clerk that the Sikh Thanadar of Spiti, Mian Dullu Singh, was personally supervising this work.[36]

Besides the details of Zorawar Singh's army, Cunningham was keen to know whether the Dogra General invaded West Tibet to quench his thirst for more territory, or whether there was some other objective behind this move. It was alleged that another purpose could be to enter into an alliance with Nepal against the British. This was considered a very grave problem which was frequently discussed by the British Government with its Resident in Nepal, its Agent at the Lahore Durbar and other officers posted at the frontier. While serving as the Assistant Political Agent at Ludhiana, Cunningham had keenly watched the developments at the Lahore Durbar. He knew that after the death of Maharaja Ranjit Singh in June 1839, the real power was wielded by his capable grandson, Kanwar Naunihal Singh.[37]

---

36. Cunningham to Clerk, 8 November 1841, *FDSC*, 20 December 1841, No. 40.
37. The grandson of Ranjit Singh and son of Kharak Singh from Chand Kaur, Naunihal Singh was endowed with courage, intelligence and discretion. He participated in military operations in Peshawar, Dera Ismail Khan and Multan. During the short reign of Kharak Singh, he assumed the reign of power at the age of eighteen. He joined hands with Dhian Singh and other nobles in putting an end to Chet Singh Bajwa. He succeeded in establishing administrative control on the provincial governors and Afghan tribes on the north-west frontier. By deft political moves, he curtailed the power of the Dogra brothers as well as the pretensions of Sher Singh. His relations with the British were strained, owing to the latter's interest in Afghanistan and contacts with recalcitrant elements in the Lahore kingdom. His life was cut short in an accident while returning from the funeral of his father.

The latter, acting with the help of the Dogra brothers, organized a strong party and was the protagonist of a forward policy. He was anxious to counter the British policy of encirclement by entering into an alliance with Nepal and other powerful Hindu states. All this was quite disconcerting to the British Government. The latter was keen to prevent the approximation which was being 'accomplished of the Jammoo dominion to the Nepal frontier.' That is why Cunningham was directed to report if one of the objectives of Zorawar Singh's invasion of West Tibet was to build a chain of forts from Ladakh to the border of Nepal on the other side of the Himalayan axis and, thus, to effectuate the much desired alliance with Nepal, still a desideratum.[38]

The British Resident in Nepal and other functionaries also sent detailed reports on this subject to the Government.[39] But here we are concerned with what Cunningham reported. On 5 January 1842, he wrote to Clerk that he did not think "any particular view of connecting the Sikh and Nepal dominions to our eventual detriment suggested the expectation. The chief men in either country have of late been too much occupied in maintaining their influence at home to give their time or inclination for combining to deprive us of any of our provinces, though vague schemes of future aggrandizement may amuse their fancy."[40] Five days later Cunningham again wrote that he "did not suppose Zorawar Singh's chief or even secondary object in taking Garoo was to propose to the Pandeys (the then ruling clique in Kathmandu) to drive us into the sea."[41] With the advantage of hindsight, one may remark that this was a very correct assessment of the problem.

---

38. G.T. Lushington, Commissioner of Kumaun to Secretary to the Government, North West Province, 25 August 1841, *FDSC*, 13 September 1841, No. 20.
39. For a detailed discussion on this subject, see, C.L. Datta, *Ladakh and Western Himalayan Politics*, pp. 169-177.
40. Cunningham to Clerk, 5 January 1842, *FDSC*, 21 March 1842, No. 84.
41. Cunningham to Clerk, 10 January 1842, *FDSC*, 21 March 1842, No. 64.

Cunningham also made a close study of the complex and anomalous interrelationship of the Himalayan states. When he reached Kinnaur on 8 October 1841, the Raja of Bashahr complained to him that for about the last sixty years, he had been receiving a tribute of thirty 'Punkhees' or pieces of woollen cloth from Peri, a village in the Manning Parganah—a subdivision of Spiti under Ladakh.[42] But for the year under review, he did not receive the pieces of woollen cloth. Cunningham, on further enquiries, found the statement of the Raja correct,[43] but he was surprised to know that the Raja, who enjoyed British protection, collected revenue from a village in Ladakh, which was under Sikh paramountcy. The case of village Gheo,"situated at a good day's journey," to the north-west of Churit in West Tibet was similar. From this village the Bashahr Raja received annually a trifling amount of Rupees seven and a half, and for the year 1841 this sum too remained unpaid.[44] Yet another anomaly which Cunningham noticed in this connection was that the ruler of Bashahr, a British tributary, used to send presents to the Tibetan Governor of Gartok once in every three years.[45] The Raja was afraid that if he did not send the same, his subjects would incur the displeasure of the Tibetan rulers and consequently their trade would suffer. It was also observed that, when a new Raja of Bashahr took the Gaddi, he received presents from the Governor of Gartok.[46]

Thus all this was a complex situation where "multiplicity of relations" and "divisions of allegiance" existed. In Western political parlance it was not clear as to who was the sovereign of whom and who was the paramount power? Cunningham informed his Government that the time had come to remodel the relations of the hill states under British protection with the

42. Cunningham to Clerk, 21 October 1841, *FDSC*, 22 November 1841, No. 40.
43. Cunningham to Clerk, 8 November 1841, *FDSC*, 20 December 1841, No. 40.
44. Ibid.
45. Cunningham to Clerk, 3 August 1842, *FDSC*, 7 September 1842, No. 28.
46. Ibid.

border states under the Chinese rule. He observed, "The consolidated empires of England and China have met one another along the Himalayan mountains and it is time that the doubt should be at an end. It is not for us to share with others the allegiance of petty princes, nor should we desire that our dependents should have claims upon the territories of foreign states. Our territories should have no political connection with strangers although we may allow them to interchange friendly letters and even visits with their neighbours under the rule of others. The presence of the Chinese collector in our territory—[is] I think extremely objectionable and our traders should only pay the usual customs duties at the usual places of collection beyond our own boundary."[47]

While staying in Kinnaur, Cunningham also highlighted its strategic importance. In a Memorandum dated 20 June 1842 addressed to Clerk, he wrote that the best place of encampment was Chango, about two miles below Shalkur, where water was abundant, the place open and the ground tolerably level. Here a fort might be constructed. Since Kinnaur offered the "simplest or easiest road into India from Tibet," to check the enemy, a small mud fort might be built here with advantage and kept garrisoned by one or two companies of men with a "detail of artillery to work some small field pieces and mortars." This fort could be built by the Sappers Corps at no great expense. Both the Sikhs and Chinese had frontier posts, the former at Dunkur in Spiti and the latter at Churit or Shaktud on the Para river, but the British fort of Shalkur was such only in name.[48] Clerk, while sending the Memorandum to the Government remarked that there may seem to be no occasion for forwarding the same, nevertheless, "the document may as well be in the Government office, as it may be useful, should there at any future time be a necessity for making a demonstration by moving a corps into Kinnaur."[49] Importance of these observations becomes obvious in the context of modern developments.

47. Ibid.
48. *FDSC*, 20 July 1842, No. 60.
49. G.R. Clerk to Secretary, Government of India, 14 June 1842, *FDSC*, 30 July 1842, No. 59.

After the Chinese aggression on India in 1962, China is still in illegal occupation of about 90,000 square kilometres of Indian territory both in the western sector (Ladakh) and eastern sector (Sikkim and Arunachal Pradesh). These sectors are becoming volatile again as the Chinese infiltrations have become a frequent occurrence. The middle sector in which Kinnaur is situated has not witnessed any fighting between China and India. Who can say that this middle sector, which is of easy accessibility and quite vulnerable, and where the Indian army is facing the People's Liberation Army (PLA), would remain dormant for ever?

Another problem which Cunningham discussed in great detail was the export and import trade of Bashahr. But before going into the details of these matters, we would do well to consider his observations on the roads of this area.[50] He felt that improvement in the lines of communication was highly desirable for the promotion of trade of Bashahr. The then narrow road linking Rampur with Shipki La, especially its upper part, was quite difficult to traverse. It was barely kept passable by the Raja. It ran high up the precipitous ravines of the Sutlej and, in crossing the petty streams falling into it, frequent side long ascents and descents was rendered necessary. "Thus going up merely to make a turn to the left, is most wearisome in every way, and after a laborious journey the traveller may perhaps

50. G.C.L. Howell, the Assistant Commissioner of Kullu during 1907-10, discovered an ancient trade route in Kullu. It was found that since ancient times, Tibetans had been crossing the passes and, making inroads into Kullu, formed settlements at the head of ravines leading into the main valleys. These sites represented advanced posts of Tibetan influence flanking the ancient trade route from Ladakh and Tibet to Rampur Bashahr. Avoiding Hamta and Rohtang Passes, this route followed the Baralacha Pass and left bank of River Chandra. At Patseo in Lahaul, the Tibetan traders met their counterparts from Kinnaur. The Tibetans returned with their packs to Rudok or Leh, while the Kinnauris marched across the Parbati Valley towards the Sutlej and Rampur, where they met traders from the plains. J. Hutchison and J. Ph. Vogel, *History of the Panjab Hill States*, Low Price Publications, New Delhi (Reprint), 2008, Vol. II, pp. 447-450.

see the place he left some five miles behind him." He recommended that the road should be found almost in the very bed of the Sutlej and its irregular course in general carefully followed. In this manner, a road which was moderately undulating and not very winding would be obtained. He pointed out that the principal financial outlay would be in cutting or blasting where the river ran between walls of rocks. Another expenditure would be that of bridges across the streams joining the Sutlej and occasionally on that river itself. For constructing the bridges timber was available in plenty until near the junction of the Spiti river.[51]

In the end Cunningham observed that the Raja of Bashahr, who would directly benefit by the opening of this new route, might be required to defray at least half of the original expense of the road through his own territories and also to keep it in repair out of the duties he levied on goods brought to Rampur.[52]

With the passage of time, extension of this road from Rampur to Kalka via Simla became a very important line of communication. It may be mentioned that during the period of Lord Dalhousie, the Governor General (1848-1856) who spent three consecutive summers in 1849-51 at Simla, took a personal interest in the matter. The construction of this road from Kalka to Simla and later on its extension up to the Indian border with Tibet, was given the name of Hindustan-Tibet road. Dalhousie suffered from gout and, as such, the damp climate of Simla during the rains did not suit him.[53] During the monsoons, his

---

51. Cunningham to Clerk, 13 November 1841, *FDS Proceedings*, 13 December 1841, No. 42.
52. Ibid.
53. The youngest Governor General of India, Lord Dalhousie aimed at completing and consolidating Britain's Indian empire. He brought a large number of territories under British rule by conquest, annexation and abolition of titles. To begin with, he annexed Punjab and established a three-member board for its administration. He concluded a peace treaty with Amir Dost Muhammad of Afghanistan, but undertook military action in Sikkim and Burma. By applying the Doctrine of Lapse, he achieved the annexation of a number of states, viz. Satara, Nagpur, Jhansi, Udaipur, Balghat, Sambhalpur, Jaitpur, Carnatic and Tanjore. He

favourite resort was Chini, the climate of which was dry and cold and which was situated in Kinnaur, at a distance of about 240 kilometres from Simla on the Hindustan-Tibet road. However, after the departure of Dalhousie, the work of building was not undertaken with much vigour. Its completion was met with many difficulties. There were frequent landslides and rock-slides. In addition, many legal disputes arose among the individuals, the chiefs of Simla Hill States and the British Government.[54] However, it was after the departure of the British in 1947 that the work of widening and tarring of this road was taken up in the right earnest. During the Chinese aggression in 1962, it received special attention from the Government of India. The Border Roads Organization was entrusted with the work of widening and tunnelling the road and a stretch of land is now under its control. In a nutshell, the development of this highway from narrow shawl wool and salt trade route to a black top all weather road, took about a century and a half and it was really an uphill task. Now it is considered a remarkable piece of engineering in one of the highest mountain ranges of the world.[55]

Cunningham also submitted detailed reports on the import and export trade of Bashahr. Ram Pur in Bashahr was quite a busy trade mart where fairs were held every year. In the first half of the nineteenth century, when the inhabitants of Kashmir, due to the oppression of the Afghan and Sikh rulers, left that valley and settled in the Indian plains, these fairs became quite

---

annexed Oudh on the ground of misgovernment. While reforming the administration and army, he formulated a plan for a railway network. He also undertook the construction of roads and canals, besides instituting a modern postal system and electronic telegraph. He contributed to fundamental changes in governance, economy, social outlook and concept of Indian unity. His actions appeared to trigger unrest which manifested in the revolt of 1857. Parshotam Mehra, *A Dictionary of Modern Indian History 1707-1947*, Oxford University Press, Delhi, 1985, pp. 175-179.

54. For details regarding the manner in which this and other roads in this area were built, see, C.L. Datta, *The Raj and the Simla Hill States*, ABS Publications, Jalandhar, 1994, pp. 22-49.
55. Ibid., p. 28.

important.[56] Now the traders from Ladakh, West Tibet, Kumaun, Bashahr and the Indian plains visited these fairs and exchanged their commodities.[57] Churrus or opium, till the then prohibitive regulations of the Chinese Government, was an important item of export to Yarkand. But the most important and lucrative item was shawl-wool, which was brought to Ram Pur from Rudok and other districts of West Tibet.[58] Cunningham diligently collected the statistics of imports and exports of Bashahr during the years 1837 to 1841, and pointed out that if the British wished to improve the trade of their Hill States with West Tibet, "a road should be carried from the table-land of Tibet to the plains of India and the transport of merchandise be simplified and rendered secure." Such measures, Cunningham suggested, will induce the merchants of Delhi and Amritsar to come forward with their large means and to embark in the trade of the Chinese provinces and to secure among other advantages the continued manufacture of shawls in the plains.[59]

Another matter which Cunningham commented upon and acquainted his Government with was the ignorance of the Himalayan states about the laws of war and behaviour of the belligerents towards the neutrals. After the defeat and death of Zorawar Singh, when the Tibetan army swooped down upon Ladakh and besieged Leh, one Ladakhi and his wife fled from their country and took refuge in Kinnaur. The Oomzud (Tibetan local authority) of Tashigong asked Cunningham to surrender these persons to the Tibetan authorities of the neighbouring post of Churit, as they were Tibetan subjects. Cunningham refused to surrender them on the ground that they had taken shelter in a state which was neutral.[60] But his reply irritated Kalon

56. Cunningham to Clerk, 22 October 1841, *FDSC*, 26 October 1841, No. 96.
57. *FDSC*, 13 December 1841, No. 42.
58. For a detailed discussion on the manner in which trade of shawl-wool affected political developments, see, C.L. Datta, 'Significance of Shawl-Wool Trade in Western Himalayan Politics,' *Bengal: Past and Present*, Vol. LXXXIX, Part I, Serial No. 167, pp. 16-28.
59. *FDSC*, 13 December 1841, No. 42.
60. *Foreign Secret Proceedings*, 7 September 1842, No. 23.

Surkhang, the Tibetan commander, who wrote to Cunningham that if not at present, at least after the cessation of hostilities, those persons should be surrendered, "otherwise it may cause differences between the two Governments."[61] Cunningham, while pointing out this ignorance of the 'half barbarous Asiatics' about the laws of war and principles of international law, observed that the 'domineering tone' of the Surkhang's letter "further affords an additional reason for modifying the relationship of our subordinate principalities with Lassa, and for coming to an explicit understanding with the Peking Commissioner about these relations and about some of the more obvious points of international law."[62]

It may be noted that Cunningham's mission led to a closer acquaintance of the British with the Western Himalayas. His suggestions and recommendations greatly influenced the future course of the British policy towards the Himalayan states.[63] His doctrine that the British feudatories should not be allowed to

---

61. Zoorkang (Surkhang) to Cunningham, 10 August 1842, *FDSC*, 26 October 1842, No. 91.
62. Cunningham to Clerk, 20 August 1842, *FDSC*, 26 October 1842, No. 96.
63. The Gurkha expansionism in the hill states created conditions for British intervention in the region. The Gurkhas could not make much headway against Kangra and Bashahr, but their substantive presence in the hill states of the cis-Sutlej tract and encroachments in the plains of Punjab attracted British military action. In the ensuing Anglo-Nepalese War (1814-16) the Gurkhas were defeated and relinquished all claims to Kumaun Garhwal and Punjab hills, which passed under the control of the British. With a view to establish its paramountcy, the British restored the displaced rulers, punished recalcitrant chiefs, retained some localities and garrisoned strategically located forts. In return for British protection, the hill states undertook a number of obligations, e.g. to allow free passage to British merchants, to furnish labourers for constant attendance, to construct 12 feet wide roads in their domains, to pay tributes of varying amounts and to supply war contingents when summoned. C.L. Datta, *The Raj and the Simla Hill States: Socio-Economic Problems, Agrarian Disturbances and Paramountcy*, pp. 2-15.

pay any kind of tribute except religious in nature to any other power, was first put into effect in the case of Spiti in 1846.[64] This very principle governed the settlement of Burma in 1886 and of Sikkim in 1890 and led the Indian Government to examine with interest and some anxiety the tributary status of Nepal to the Chinese Empire.[65] In consonance with Cunningham's other suggestions, transit duties in Bashahr were abolished in 1847 and,[66] as mentioned earlier, the work of constructing a road linking the Indian plains with West Tibet via Simla and Chini, later popularly known as the Hindustan Tibet Road, was taken up in the 1850s.

Cunningham's reports on the developments after the defeat and death of Zorawar Singh and expulsion of the Dogras from West Tibet are also quite revealing. Here it may not be inappropriate to mention some of the important points raised by him. By April 1842, the victorious Tibetan army moved towards Ladakh. They even talked of invading Kashmir and felt happy at the prospects of plunder and revenge. Cunningham, in one of his reports, remarked that hordes of 'Kalmaks', the inhabitants of Sinkiang who were Chinese subjects, were likely to help the Ladakhis in their war against the Sikhs.[67] Gonpo, the steward of the powerful Hemis monastery in Ladakh and a great favourite of the old king, Tsepal Namgyal, who fell into the hands of the Tibetans about the time of Zorawar Singh's death, was now sent to Leh to rouse the Ladakhis against the Dogras. Gonpo issued a call to his countrymen that Zorawar Singh was dead and his remaining soldiers were leaving, being pursued by the Tibetan army and that the time had come for Ladakhis to prepare for war. As a consequence, people revolted everywhere and all the Dogra garrisons, except the one at Leh, were put to the sword.

Thanedar Magna Ram and Commandant Pehlwan Singh, leaders of the Dogra garrison at Leh, had taken steps to fortify

64. *FDSC*, 26 December 1846, No. 1335.
65. Alastair Lamb, *Britain and Chinese Central Asia: The Road to Lhasa 1767 to 1905*, Routledge & Kegan Paul, London, 1961, p. 80.
66. Cf. *Imperial Gazetteer of India*, Oxford, 1908, Vol. VII, pp. 94-95.
67. Cunningham to Clerk, 5 August 1842, *FDSC*, 7 September 1842, No. 29

their strongholds. The latter strengthened a stable of the Ladakhi kings as a defensive post and established links with Magna Ram, who occupied the fort which, some years ago, had been constructed by Zorawar Singh. Magna Ram had also converted some enclosed ranges of stables near the fort into a defensive post. In addition to about fifty of his own soldiers, the Thanedar also had three hundred Pathans under his command.[68] Further, he had also collected large quantities of ammunition and provisions. The Dogra soldiers, who had fled from various posts in West Tibet such as Hanle, Tholing and Churit, also joined their compatriots in Leh. This resulted in swelling the number of the garrison to about 1,000.[69]

Ahmad Shah, the ex-king of Baltistan, who was held in some kind of honourable durance by the Tibetans, was asked to foment trouble in Baltistan. He sent his confidants to Skardu and asked the chiefs and people to revolt against the Dogras, who had oppressed them. All the chiefs, except Muhammad Shah, the then Balti king and a vassal of Raja Gulab Singh, revolted. The chiefs of Rondu, Khapalu and Shigar gathered a large army and imprisoned the Dogra garrison in Skardu. Ghulam Hussain, the ex-minister of Ahmad Shah, along with a Balti force, marched towards Leh to help the Ladakhis in beating down the Dogra garrison there.[70]

Rigorous attempts were made to capture the Dogras, but Magna Ram and Pehlwan Singh resorted to a sally from the fort and killed many of their enemies. This greatly demoralized the latter and enabled the Dogras to set matters in order in the fort. About the last week of April 1842, a strong Tibetan detachment under the command of General Pishi also arrived in Leh. A combined force—comprising Ladakhis, Baltis and Tibetans—made a vigorous assault and succeeded in battering an outer tower of the fort, but the Dogra garrison bravely held out.[71]

At the time of the death of Zorawar Singh, Raja Gulab Singh

---

68. Cunningham to Clerk, 3 May 1842, *FDSC*, 6 July 1842, No. 6.
69. Cunningham to Clerk, 3 May 1842, *FDSC*, 6 July 1842, No. 6.
70. *FDSC*, 6 July 1842, No. 42; also see, Hashmatullah Khan, *Tarikh-i-Jammu*, Lucknow, 1939, p. 396.
71. Cunningham to Clerk, 19 May 1842, *FDSC*, 14 September 1842, No.50; *FDSC*, 22 June 1842, No. 40.

was directing an expeditionary force at Peshawar, which had been sent to help the British who then were against the Afghans. He appears to have sent an urgent message to his younger brother Prime Minister Raja Dhian Singh, who raised a relief army of about 5,000 hill soldiers. This reinforcement was well equipped to endure the cold and also armed with some pieces of artillery. In February 1842, this Dogra division, which was led by Diwan Hari Chand and Wazir Ratnu, moved towards Ladakh via Kashmir. It may not be out of place to mention that hitherto all the Dogra armies that invaded Ladakh, moved from Kishtwar, either via the Suru Valley or Zanskar. This was due to the opposition of the strong Sikh Nazim of Kashmir, Colonel Mihan Singh, who would not let the Dogra army pass through the Kashmir territory. Mihan Singh was killed in 1841. His successor Shaikh Ghulam Muhiuddin was a puppet of the Dogra brothers. Anyway, this Dogra expeditionary force, advancing with forced marches, reached the environs of Leh in May 1842, encountering numerous difficulties and not without fighting a few actions on the way. On hearing of the arrival of this army, most of the Ladakhis and Baltis dispersed to their homes, while the Tibetan army, having raised the siege, pulled back along the Indus and halted at a place near Chimri about 60 kilometres from Leh. Gonpo and the young Ladakhi king also fled with the Tibetans. The latter started strengthening their new positions with more reinforcements coming from Gartok and provisions floating down the Indus. On the other hand, Diwan Hari Chand and Wazir Ratnu, after resting for a while, started in pursuit of the enemy and set up their camp a few miles away from the Tibetans. A pitched battle was fought in which both sides suffered losses. The Tibetans lost one of their leaders, namely Pun Aghim. Ultimately, the Lhasa force was defeated and, after this reverse, retreated towards Pangong Lake and encamped near Chushul.

Simultaneously with the dispatch of the expeditionary force to Ladakh, the Dogras also suppressed revolts in Zanskar, Nubra, Spiti and Baltistan. Baba Lachhman Singh, at the head of 200 soldiers, marched from Kangra to Spiti via Kulu.[72] Order

72. Cunningham to Clerk, 28 August 1842, *FDSC*, 12 October 1842, No. 84; *FDSC*, 7 September 1842, No. 29.

was restored in all the far-flung districts of Ladakh. Wazir Lakhpat Rai, another high ranking Dogra officer, was deputed to restore peace in Baltistan.[73] At the head of 3,000 soldiers, he marched from Kishtwar to Skardu via Kargil. He fought many actions on the way. Ali Sher Khan, the chief of Khartaksho, who had helped the Dogras when they invaded Baltistan for the first time, again helped them. Advancing with forced marches, Wazir Lakhpat Rai reached Skardu and punished the rebels, many of whom were killed. Muhammad Shah and the Dogra garrison were freed. The former was restored to his previous position on the old terms and a strong Dogra garrison was stationed at Skardu. After making these arrangements and, taking with him many arch rebels of Baltistan and Purig, Wazir Lakhpat Rai returned to Kishtwar.[74]

In Ladakh, both the contestants remained encamped in the Pangong Lake area for some days. The Dogras realized that if they wanted to turn the tables on the Tibetans, then they had to force them to fight before the advent of winter. But the Tibetan camp was situated in the lower part of a narrow valley and storming it would have meant a great loss of life on the part of the Dogras. However, the fighting started soon and raged indecisively for about two weeks. Diwan Hari Chand's men ultimately dammed up a channel and flooded the Tibetan camp. Finding himself in trouble, Kalon Surkhang sued for peace. The Dogras first demanded the surrender of the Ladakhi king, Gonpo and Ahmad Shah. This having been done, the Tibetans emerged from their camp. A pitched battle was fought in which most of the latter were killed, while the survivors fled from the field. Surkhang, Pishi, two Kalons and many other Tibetan officers and soldiers were made prisoners. Regarding this action, Cunningham remarked that this victory was due "to the superior military arrangements of the Sikhs."[75]

---

73. Cunningham to Clerk, 31 August 1842, *FDSC*, 12 October 1842, No. 86.
74. Hashmatullah Khan, *Tarikh-i-Jammu*, pp. 413-414
75. Cunningham to Clerk, 27 September 1842, *FDSC*, 9 November 1842, No. 61.

VI

At this juncture, it would be appropriate to consider the Tibetan side of the above story. Six years after his first invasion of Ladakh, Zorawar Singh led another incursion into the kingdom and reversed the earlier arrangement regarding the occupancy of the throne. As a consequence, the facilities of accommodation and transport, which were hitherto provided to the Tibetan government traders, were stopped. At the same time, Zorawar Singh (accompanied by the Ladakhi ruler, the Sikh and Ladakhi troops) entered West Tibet. In the fighting that took place at Ngari Korsum, Zorawar Singh defeated an ill-equipped Tibetan force, which was commanded by two generals, Dapon Shatra and Dapon Surkhang. The victors advanced as far as Taklakot in Purang. Large Tibetan reinforcements, which were led by the council minister Kalon Pallhun, poured into the scene of conflict. Fighting continued for several months. As the winter approached, Kalon Pallhun intensified his efforts and drove out the invaders from Taklakot. The Tibetans gained the upper hand over the Sikhs who were unaccustomed to conditions of heavy snow. During the course of a close encounter, Zorawar Singh (while mounting his horse) was recognized by platoon commander Migmar, who accurately aimed a spear at Zorawar Singh. He brought down the Dogra general to the ground and, having severed his head, took it to the Tibetan camp. Of the Sikh army, 3,000 soldiers were killed and 700 were made captive along with two Ladakhi ministers. The remnants of the defeated army, who fled towards Ladakh, were pursued by the Tibetans as far as Leh. The pursuing Tibetan contingent halted at Dumra and remained there for a year.

Continuing the narrative of the Tibetan version, we learn that Gulab Singh sent a Sikh force of 8,000 into Ladakh under Dewan Hari Chand and Wazir Ratnu. The Tibetan generals Dapon Shatra and Dapon Surkhang, along with sixty soldiers, were captured and taken to Leh. As the party reached Leh, a representative of Kalon Pallhun opened negotiations with Dewan Hari Chand. Under a temporary treaty, it was agreed that the Tibetan troops would withdraw from Dumra, that neither party would violate the other's territory, that prisoners wishing to return to their country would be allowed to do so and that a comprehensive treaty would be drawn up later. The two Tibetan generals and their subordinates were repatriated. Interestingly, one third of the Sikh and Ladakhi prisoners decided to remain in Tibet. "The Sikhs were settled in the warmer regions of Southern Tibet by the government and many of them married Tibetan girls. The Sikhs are known to have introduced the cultivation of apricots, apples, grapes and peaches into the country." The Tibetan records indicate that the Dogras were equipped with firearms and cannon, whereas the Tibetans were armed with conventional weapons like swords spears, bows and a few primitive muskets. Therefore, they did not hesitate to attribute their victory to heavy snow. The Tibetan government rewarded those who distinguished themselves in the war. Kalon Pallhun was honoured, the two generals Dapon Shatra and Dapon Surkhang were included in the ministerial council (Kashag) and Migmar was promoted along with a small estate.[76]

The Tibetan version enables us to understand the circumstances in which the peace treaty was signed by the contending parties. Kalon Surkhang was directed to join Dapon Peshi (the Tibetan general operating in West Tibet) and to proceed to Leh in order to negotiate the final treaty with Ladakh. After a meeting of the two delegations, Tibetan and Ladakhi, two different letters were drafted so that each side sealed and signed its own letter. These documents affirmed everlasting friendship between Tibet and Ladakh, the recognition of respective ancient boundaries, continuation of trade between the two kingdoms and revival of free accommodation and transport for the Tibetan traders in Ladakh. A perusal of the texts of the two agreements, which were exchanged between Tibet and Ladakh, brings out a few significant points. What is most noteworthy, the Chinese authorities were conspicuous by their absence. The letters did not even mention the name of the Chinese emperor as one of the dignitaries. This omission must

76. Tsepon W.D. Shakabpa, *Tibet: A Political History*, Yale University Press, New Haven and London, 1967, pp. 177-178.

be read with the fact that the Chinese imperial troops were not involved in the war against the Dogras. This absence was quite understandable. On the one hand, China could not spare its troops to fight in Western Tibet, as it was engaged in the Opium War. On the other hand, the small garrison of Sino-Tibetan troops (sons of Chinese soldiers and Tibetan mothers) at Lhasa had suffered deterioration in terms of quality and discipline. As such, it was only the Tibetan army, fighting under the command of a Kashag minister, which brought about the defeat of the Dogras. Moreover, the Tibetan delegates at the negotiations duly received the approval from Lhasa, as the two Tibetan generals (Dapon Shatra and Dapon Surkhang) were released before signing of the final treaty and had returned to Lhasa, where they were included in the ministerial council.[77]

Further, it was equally significant that the treaty was negotiated in the name of two sovereign powers, the Maharaja of the Lahore kingdom and Dalai Lama of Tibet, the fact being formally recorded in the two letters. Gulab Singh, who ordered the Dogra invasion of Ladakh, Baltistan and West Tibet, was duly recognized as an independent ruler, but none of his representatives had put his signatures on the agreement.

VII

Having considered the Tibetan version of the war, we will revert to our discussion. It was observed that after suffering a military defeat, the Tibetans appear to have abandoned the cause of the Ladakhis. They had already expelled the Dogras from West Tibet and thought it inadvisable to carry on this unprofitable war. The Dogras also nurtured a lurking fear that the tragedy of the previous year might not be repeated. Thus both the parties were willing to come to terms. The peace treaty, which took the form of an exchange of documents embodying the undertakings given by each side to the other, was concluded at Leh on 17 September 1842. Diwan Hari Chand and Wazir Ratnu signed the document as representatives of Raja Gulab Singh, while

77. Ibid., pp. 179-180.

Kalon Surkhang and Bakshi Shajput signed it on behalf of the Lhasa ruler. After some time, a treaty, which was binding on the sovereigns of the two sides, was concluded between the Governor of Kashmir (representing the Lahore Durbar) and the Lhasa officials on behalf of China. Before discussing the terms of the treaty, a few words might be said about the return of the victorious Dogra army. This expeditionary force, being commanded by Diwan Hari Chand and Wazir Ratnu, was keen to return to Kishtwar as the winter had set in. However, the passage from Leh to Srinagar and then from the latter place to Kishtwar and Jammu, was beset with numerous difficulties. Ferocity of weather and heavy snowfall took a heavy toll of the fatigued soldiers. Hundreds of them perished in snow, while many lost their limbs and sustained serious snow bite wounds. Nevertheless, the successful return of the remnants of the victorious army back to the place of their departure must be considered a great landmark in the annals of the Western Himalayas.[78]

In order to understand the provisions of the above mentioned treaty, it is necessary to look at both the Persian and Tibetan documents, because the Dogra treaty lists only the restrictions imposed on the Tibetans, which is conversely true of the Tibetan version. The Tibetans guaranteed that 'we shall neither at present nor in future will have anything to do or interfere at all with the boundaries of Ladakh and its surroundings as fixed from ancient times and will allow the annual export of wool, shawls and tea by way of Ladakh according to old established customs.'[79] The Tibetan document containing the guarantees given by the Dogras stated that in future perpetual friendship shall prevail between the Dogras and Tibet. The Ladakhi king and his family were permitted to stay in Ladakh provided they did not 'indulge in any intrigue'

---

78. G.R. Clerk to T.A. Maddock, 11 December 1842, *FDSC*, 11 January 1843, No. 88.
79. C.U. Aitchison, *Treaties, Engagements and Sanads Relating to India and Neighbouring Countries*, Vol. XIV, Central Publishing Branch, Government of India, Calcutta, 1933, p. 15.

against the Dogras.[80] The Ladakhi king, if he so desired, was allowed to send the annual gifts to the Dalai Lama and his ministers.

Cunningham wrote to Clerk that on the night of 5 October 1842, just before leaving Shalkur for Simla, he heard that the peace had been concluded between the Dogras and the Tibetans.[81] The Raja of Bashahr informed the British authorities that a peace treaty had been signed between the Chinese and the Sikhs, copies of which in the Bhoti and Bedechuree characters were procured by his agents who had gone to the Garpon of Garo for paying the customary yearly presents. The treaty was signed on behalf of the suzerain powers of the contestants. This was a simple document of six articles and agreed with the Persian and Tibetan versions.[82] With the signing of this treaty and cessation of hostilities, Cunningham's political mission to West Tibet also came to an end.

From all that has been discussed above, Cunningham wrote most of his reports while staying in Kinnaur and West Tibet during the months when winter was at its peak. Often it was snowing outside his tent and in the sub-zero temperature, there was numbness in his fingers and hands due to which it was difficult to write. Yet, he produced quite comprehensive reports, giving details about the armies, actions fought by them and conflicting interests of various powers who were involved in fighting. While writing his reports about the import and export trade of Bashahr and the adjoining areas, he took great pains in compiling statistics and analysed the causes of increase and decrease in the volume of commerce involving various articles.

In the performance of his duties, Cunningham employed the residents of Bashahr, Kumaon and Garhwal on spying missions. They disguised themselves as traders and religious mendicants (Gosains). They succeeded in reaching very near the Dogra and Tibetan camps, where fighting was in progress.

80. Ibid.
81. Cunningham to Clerk, 19 October 1842, *FDSC*, 11 January 1843, No. 41.
82. For details, see, *FDSC*, 24 May 1843, No. 62.

They informed Cunningham about the latest developments on the scene of action. That is why the information provided by him was comprehensive as well as authentic. In a word, Cunningham worked under extremely inhospitable circumstances and at a great personal risk. He acquitted himself quite creditably and his mission may be rated as a great success. One may conclude in the words of H.L.O. Garret, "Cunningham was never a dilettante; on the other hand, he was an expert and an authority."[83]

83. H.L.O. Garret, 'Biographical Note,' J.D. Cunningham, *History of the Sikhs*, p. xx.

2

Reports of J.D. Cunningham

FDSC No. 23 of 22 November 1841

Subject: Cunningham's Intelligence about Zorawar Singh

From J.D. Cunningham | To G.R. Clerk
Surabu Camp
21 October 1841

1. I arrived at Surabu, the summer and autumn residence of the Raja of Bassahir.[1]
2. In my intercourse with the Raja and his Vezeer, they expressed generally their apprehensions of the Sikhs and complained:

   (i) that the portion of revenue due to them from the village of Manning in the Purgunnah of Dunkur in

1. Endowed with an area of 3,820 square miles, Bashahr was the most extensive of the Simla Hill States. It was bounded on the north by Spiti, on the east by West Tibet, on the south by Tehri Garhwal and Keonthal and on the west by Jubbal, Kotkhai, Kumharsain and Kullu. It was 84 miles long, with maximum breadth of 62 miles on the eastern side and minimum breadth of 12 miles on the western side. Besides the two principal rivers, the Sutlej and Pabar, the state was formed of a great mass of mountain ranges, between which were enclosed narrow ravines or small rivers with sheer banks. The state was divided into three tahsils viz. Rampur, Rohru and Chini. *Gazetteer of the Simla Hill States 1910*: *Bashahr State Gazetteer*, Indus Publishing House, New Delhi, Reprint, 1995, p. 3.

Spiti had recently been refused, as they believed, at the instigation of the Sikhs.

(ii) that certain inhabitants of Kumaun proceeding on the annual journey to the neighbourhood of Garoo to purchase wool etc. had been plundered and murdered by the Sikhs at Tholing and also at another place near Bootpoo Pass between the Indus and Sutlej.

(iii) that the Sikh messengers by name Jeewan Singh and Ganesh had arrived at Ram Pore, with, as they heard later from Raja Dhian Singh or Goolab Singh, demanding a daughter of the Raja's (Mohinder Singh) in marriage for one of their sons and threatening in case of refusal to seize the trans-Sutlej possessions of Bussahir.

(iv) that their agents at Shealkur had reported that Zorawar Singh had given out that the Kunawar district as far as Cheenee, was properly a part of Ladakh and that it would be occupied by the Sikhs.

3. I assured him that since his possessions are under our protection,[2] he will not be a loser. I told him he should refrain as far as possible, on his part, from intimate relations with the Sikhs, as especially with the Jammoo Rajas. The Wezeer and Raja thereafter said they would only reply to the communications of the Sikhs on consultation with Erskine.

---

2. From 1803 to 1815 Bashahr was under the control of the Gurkhas who, in 1815, were expelled by the British. By a notification (*sanad*) of 6 November 1815 Raja Mohinder Singh, then a minor, was confirmed in possession of all his territories, except Rawin and Kotgarh along with three forts which were retained by the British. Under the terms of the notification, the ruler was required to join the British army with his armed retainers and hill porters when called upon to do so and to construct roads within his territory. The annual tribute of Rs. 15,000, which had been imposed by the notification, was reduced in 1847 to Rs. 3,945 as compensation for the abolition of transit duties. C.L. Datta, *The Raj and the Simla Hill States: Socio-Economic Problems, Agrarian Disturbances and Paramountcy*, ABS Publications, Jalandhar, 1997, pp. 156-157.

4. I told Raja, the demands in question of the Jammoo Rajas and of Zorawar Singh rested on foundations too uncertain to require our present notice.
5. With respect to the Raja's claim on the village of Manning, I may here mention that he says, he has derived revenue from it for 60 years. He added that his predecessors wrested Spitti from Kooloo about that time since, but that Ludakh two years afterwards seized all the districts with the exception of a part of the land of Manning from which village he regularly received thirty pieces of woolen cloth as tribute or revenue.
6. In my conversation with the Raja, Vezeer and others, I have ascertained following circumstances relating to the progress of the Sikhs in Thibet, but of course that can not be implicitly relied on as correct.

   (i) After the conquest and settlement of the affairs of Iskardo, the district of Rodokh was invaded and the first taken about the beginning of last June. Chooret and other places then fell and in July 1941 Garoo was occupied. The Sikhs are now in possession of Tuklakot to the south of the Mantullao. They allege that they occupy these countries as part of the kingdom of Ludakh which extends as far as (they say) the valley of Marghil, four or five marches to the east of the Lakes.

   (ii) The Sikhs have small posts at Rudok, Chooret, Tashigong, Garroo and Tukla Kot, the parties stationed in Chaprung and Tholing are said to have been removed towards the Lakes. Chooret is one march only to the North of Shalkur. It is in the Purgunna of Sumghil and the Purgunna Chomoorta which has been mentioned as including Chooret, appears to be beyond Sumghil towards the Indus.

   (iii) Zorawar Singh has 4 or 5000 men in all with him chiefly Kishtwarees, Ludakhees and men of Iskardo. He has also it is said 5 or 6 small guns, probably jingals,[3] which can be carried by men or on mules.

(iv) He is said to have with him the present Vezeer of Ludakh; the dispossessed Raja of Iskardo; the brother of the Raja placed by the Sikhs on the Ludakhee guddee and Golam Khan, the son-in-law of Ruheem Khan, the Kiladar of Dunkur in Spiti. This Golam Khan is probably the same as mentioned by the Commissioner of Kumaun in his letter of 25 August 1841 to the Government; and at present I make out that Ruheem Khan managed Spitti under the native Ludakh Government.

(v) All trade especially in shawl wool to the Company's provinces is at a stand still or has been prohibited.

(vi) Zorawar Singh himself is now in the Purgunna of Proontz near the Lakes; he has the Governor of Garoo and the Kiladars of Chuprung and of Proontz itself prisoners in that fort.

---

3. Associated with jazair, jazail and janjal, the word jingal was applied to a weapon which was a wall piece or swivel gun, partaking the character of both a firearm carried by a combatant and artillery. A long matchlock, it possessed a substantial barrel of 7 or 8 feet. It could fire a ball which, according to different reports, weighed from a few ounces to two pounds. Its range could be as long as 1,000 yards. Since it was too heavy to use without rest, many were provided with an iron prong about a foot in length, which was fixed on a swivel or pivot not far from the nozzle and this, when placed on a wall or ground or bush, served as a support. It was commonly employed in the defence of forts, as the besieged could hit the target with great accuracy even from great distance. Its use by the Afghans in 1842 has been described by Col. Thomas Seaton. William Irvine, *The Army of the Indian Moghuls: Its Organization and Administration*, Eurasia Publishing House, New Delhi, (Reprint), 1962, pp. 109-111.

FDSC No. 45 of 8 November 1841

Subject: Withdrawal of Zorawar Singh

From G.R. Clerk — To J.D. Cunningham
20 October 1841 — Camp Bussahar

1. I am transmitting to you copy of instructions from Government dated 8 October 1841, and also a copy of letter which I have in consequence this day addressed to Maharaja Sher Singh.
2. You will observe that the 10th December next is the date beyond which, it is intended that the Sikh or Jammoo rulers shall not retain Zorawar Singh or any troops in advance of the Ludakh border with impunity.
3. It is not to be expected that at this season you can yourself speedily reach the scene of Zorawar Singh's late encroachments, but you will adopt every means in your power to supply timely information of the measures that may be taken by the Sikhs in Thibet consequent upon this demand made upon the Maharaja for the withdrawal of Zorawar Singh, and the relinquishment of his recent conquests

FDSC No. 25 of 22 November 1841

Subject: Report on Shawl Wool Trade at Ram Pore Fair

From J.D. Cunningham To G.R. Clerk
Camp Turrenda
22 October 1841

1. As the traffic carried on by means of the fair held at Ram Pore in Bassahar, bears intimately on my present deputation it may not be uninteresting to briefly state such information as I have gathered regarding it.[4]
2. Three fairs appear to have been held in Ram Pore from time immemorial, but none became of any importance until the oppressions of the Afghans and Sikhs in Cashmere and subsequently a severe famine, drove many of the inhabitants of that valley to the plains of India. This emigration very much extended the manufacturing of shawl in our North Western Provinces, but chiefly in the Punjab, and the trade in wool became in part diverted from Cashmere and the construction of tolerable road from the plains to Ram Pore seem to have determined it in a measure to that place and after the impulse given about 21 years ago by Captain Gerard's successive purchases of large quantities of sheep and goat's wool on account of Government, the fair held at Ram Pore in

4. Rampur was the capital of the state of Bashahr. It stood at the base of a lofty mountain, overhanging the left bank of the Sutlej, 138 feet above the stream and 3,300 feet above the sea level. Cliffs surrounded the town and confined the air, so that during summer the radiation from the rocks rendered the heat intolerable. The houses, which were made of stone, rose in tiers. The royal place, which was located at the north eastern corner of the town, consisted of several buildings with carved wooden balconies exhibiting traces of Chinese style. The Gurkhas inflicted much damage to the town and its trade during their supremacy, but it was recovered under the British protection. *Imperial Gazetteer of India, (Provincial Series): Punjab*, Vol. II, Superintendent of Government Printing, Calcutta, 1908, pp. 373-374.

November has been much frequented and the price of shawl wool as it has been permanently raised.

3. The articles brought from distant Hill States or from Thibet to the fair consist chiefly of 'Pushum' or shawl wool, sheep's wool, coarse manufacture of 'Pushum', various woollens, Borax (unrefined), musk, tea and silver ingots, all of which are exchanged for the productions of the plains or of the Lower Hills, opium until recently having formed a considerable item. The traders from the North West are chiefly Kumaonees, Bhotias and people of Kooloo, but woollens are brought for sale by the inhabitants of every petty hill state on either side of the Sutlej. The purchasers are chiefly the Cashmerees from Ludhiana, Nur Pur and Amritsar, but the wool is also taken to Delhi and even to Lucknow, as it is much superior to that which can be purchased at the fairs held in Kumaon.[5]
4. Shawl wool is now the chief article of traffic in the fair. The value of that brought for sale has of late averaged about 80,000 rupees per year, and the Raja farms the duties levied at this fair, principally on shawl wool for 60,000 rupees but as the produce frequently much exceeds that sum, he only continues the contract at that rate on the presentation of a suitable 'Nuzzur' by the farmers at the period of its expiration.
5. The purchaser of wool pays a duty of one rupee per maund cutcha (about 16 seers) while the seller pays one pice per rupee on its sale price; no other duties are levied

---

5. The town of Rampur was famous for producing fine shawls which were known as the Rampur Chadars. This industry has undergone a decline of late years. Though shawls of good quality were still made at Rampur, yet they were regarded as inferior to those woven at Subathu, Ludhiana and Amritsar with the wool brought from Bashahr and Tibet. Rampur was the only mart in the state of Bashahr as shops elsewhere were scarce. All shopkeepers in the Rampur tahsil were native of Ambala, Hoshiarpur or Kangra districts or of the Patiala state. *Gazetteer of the Simla Hill States 1910: Bashahr State Gazetteer*, p. 60.

whether on the frontier or in the interior of the Bassahar territory. The whole of the white wool is sold at one rate and also the whole of the black, which rate are agreed on by the Raja in case of a difference of opinion. Later the white wool appears to have sold at from 5 to 8 rupees per 'buttee' of 2 seers (each of 80 Tolas) and the black wool for about half that sum.

6. The best wool brought to Ram Pore fair comes from the neighbourhood of Rudok and inferior from the districts to the south and east of that place as far as and even beyond the Manasarowar Lake.[6]
7. Owing to the recent operations of the Sikhs in Thibet it is not expected that above 1/5 of the ordinary quantity of wool will be brought to the fair to be held. The Cashmeree brokers, indeed of Simla, believed that Raja Goolab Singh had levied a rupee from every goat herd's house in Ludakh and the adjacent districts and had given permission to traders to go where they pleased, but this does not agree with what I have heard from various sources since I left Simla.

---

6. Situated on the western extremity of Nari (Western Tibet), Rudok possessed the most wild and dreary landscape in the world. It lay near the plateau which was spread behind the massive range of Kuen Lun mountains touching the dreary desert of Chang in the north. It was known for the cultivation of barley and abundance of salt, while the surrounding country was famous for horses which fetched a high price in the market. Central Asian caravans, which travelled from Leh to Lhasa, passed through Rudok or via Gartok past Lake Mansarovar. The road from Leh to Gartok, which was a distance of 200 miles, passed through Rudok, going via Tashigong and Demchok on the Indus. The distance between Rudok and Gartok was covered in eight or ten days. The Tibetan traders carried the produce of Western Tibet to Leh, with whom they had excellent relations. Rudok and other places in Western Tibet also attracted traders from Lahaul, a part of the principality of Kangra. All inhabitants of Lahaul traded with Tibet from earliest times and were familiar with the Tibetan language. Charles A. Sherring, *Western Tibet and the Indian Borderland*, Cosmo Publications, New Delhi, Reprint, 1974, p. 156-157, 310.

FDSC No. 26 of 22 November 1841

From Secretary to GOI To G.R. Clerk
2 November 1841

GG in Council approves that Cunningham having turned his attention to this subject and will be happy to receive all the information, which that officer may be able to collect relative to the foreign trade of Bassahar, and the affect which may have been produced upon it by the late proceedings of Zorawar Singh in the territories which adjoin that district on its northern and eastern frontiers.

FDSC No. 40 of 20 December 1841

From J.D. Cunningham
Camp Shalkur

To G.R. Clerk
8 November 1841

1. About the Sikhs I have learnt that the road from Dunkur in Spitee as far as at least the Bootpau Pass, towards Garoo, is being put in order as Zorawar Singh is shortly expected in this neighbourhood, but I do not place much confidence in the report, and would rather infer that the road is being repaired, to expedite the transport of supplies to the Sikh camp.
2. Since writing the above, I have heard that 200 Gurkhas joined Zorawar Singh near the lakes at the same time that two English officers arrived on the frontier, concerning which you will learn authentically from Lushington.
3. About the trade to our provinces, I learn that the Sikhs have strictly prohibited the export of shawl wool and borax to Bassahar, but that they allow salt, common wool etc. to be taken on the payment of a duty, while they also demand a percentage on grain and other articles brought from Kumaon to be exchanged for these commodities. It would further appear that they have stopped the traders from the northward at Chooret with the view of making our subjects resort to that place, so as to secure to themselves the duties both on exports and imports.
4. On my way hither, I met parties of 'Kampas' itinerant traders, who usually frequent the Ram Pore fair in considerable numbers, but who on account of the duties demanded by the Sikhs had been unable to affect their ordinary purchases this season, and were consequently proceeded to the southward to graze their flocks during the winter, taking with them some few seers of salt only. I also took the opportunity during my journey of securing some of the principal Kumaonee traders; they too had been unable to lay in their usual investment and several indeed had not attempted to make any purchases whatever, and they stated in reply to my inquiries that

their losses would amount to from one to three hundred rupees each. Notwithstanding however the prohibition with regard to shawl wool, the persons to whom I spoke seemed to think that perhaps 200 or 250 maunds would be smuggled to the Ram Pore fair this season.

5. With regard to the complaint of the Bassahar Raja about the withholding of his portion of revenue from village of Manning in Spitee as stated in the 2nd paragraph of my letter of the 21st ultimo, I found on more particular inquiries here, that the 30 pieces of cloth are really due from the Purgunna of Peri, a subdivision of Spitee but were usually received through Ludakh functionaries resident in Manning. I have further learnt that the sum of Rs. 7½ received annually by the Bassahar Raja from the Chinese village of Gheo, situated a good day's journey to the north west of Chooret, had also been withheld this season by order of the Sikhs. Concerning both these points, I would on the 4th instant write to the Sikh commander of Chooret, Mean Doola Singh.
6. I can have no authentic intelligence regarding the Kunnawaree traders said to have been killed by the Sikhs in Tholing. The Sikhs are said to have excused themselves at one time, by alleging that they joined the inhabitants in resisting their authority; and at another that they were killed by some Iskardo soldiers who were ignorant of their being British subjects. The Raja's people however admit that these traders had some shawl wool with them, which circumstances may have caused a dispute and afterwards a fight. I appear to have been misinformed regarding the murder of other Kunnawarees near the Bootpau Pass, also mentioned in the second para of my letter of the 21st ultimo. Two men really sent as spies by the Raja's Agent here were indeed detained for 10 or 12 days in Chooret by the Sikhs, but they suffered no further molestation.
7. The Chinese authorities between this place and the lakes appear to have fled or else to be in the hands of the Sikhs and in my journey, I may wish to make to the eastward, they cannot at present either assist me or throw

difficulties in my way, which the Sikhs themselves will scarcely attempt to forcibly oppose my going in whatever direction I may find it advisable to proceed. My real difficulties in moving about will arise from the severity of the season and the great scarcity of carriage and supplies in districts naturally sterile and now much impoverished by the exertions of the invaders. I conceive however that I can best fulfill the wishes of the Government as conveyed to me in your letter of the 20th ultimo by keeping near Vezeer Zorawar Singh and accordingly propose to move towards the lakes by the road of Tholing as soon as I can make arrangements for carriage and supplies. I will inform the Lamas of that place, the chief of whom not now present however, is the Chinese agent for the surrounding country as far as Tashigong, of my intentions, so that I may not be considered as unnecessary regardless of authority in abeyance—for should the Sikhs precipitately retreat in consequence of the demand of our Government and it is not improbable that the Chinese jealousy of Englishman may return in full force in spite of the plain meaning of our proceedings.

8. Should I be able to reach Tholing the people of the country will,[7] I hope, come forward of themselves with carriage and grain and I may then be able to follow Zorawar Singh and see him evacuate place after place from Tukla Kot to

---

7. Tholing (or Chugaon), a large thickly populated village in parganah Rajgaon and tahsil Chini (in the state of Bashahr), contained a handsome temple of the village god or Maheshras the third, the first and second Maheshras being in Shungra or Grosnam and Kathgaon or Gramang in parganah Bhaba respectively. It is said that Banasur, who was a demon and who ruled in Sarahan at a very remote period, was slain by Sri Krishna. His three sons and a daughter were also slain, and so the first son became the Maheshras of Shungra, the second of Kathgaon, the third of Chugaon (Tholing), and their sister Ukha became the goddess of Nalhar. The three temples of these Maheshras were beautifully built and that of Ukha was also picturesque. *Bashahr State Gazetteer*, (*Gazetteer of the Simla Hill States 1910*), p. xii.

Rudok or else ascertain in person, whether he can argue any reasonable excuse for not withdrawing his troops without delay—should I not be able to proceed beyond Tholing, I consider that I shall be better placed for gathering news than at Shalkur.

9. As I move about, I think I may with propriety freely invite people to accompany me for the purposes of trade and assure them that no duties shall be claimed except by the Chinese authorities if any were ever levied and in the meantime I should like to be informed of the views of Government with respect to compensations to individuals and to public bodies such as the establishments of the Lamas etc. for losses sustained at the hands of the Sikhs by direct plunder or otherwise.
10. Though unable to give you most recent intelligence of the Sikhs in this quarter, yet in continuation of my letter of the 21st ultimo, the narrative of what I have since heard of their early or less recent proceedings, may not be uninteresting. I must premise, however as before that, as the ignorance of the people of these countries is surprising, all that I say cannot be relied on as accurate which remark is particularly applicable to dates.
11. Last year perhaps after the conquest of Iskardo,[8] Zorawar

---

8. As principal place in Baltistan, Skardu lay on the left bank of the Indus. Occupying a nearly level plain of fine alluvial clay, it extended from one of the two isolated rocks which overhung the Indus towards the mountains on the south side of the valley. The neighbourhood of this 1,000 feet high rock was selected as the site of the town, owing to the advantages it afforded for defence. The palace of the ruler, which stood at the edge of the plateau, was dismantled during the Dogra invasion. Of the two forts, the ancient one was in ruins. The other one was a square structure with bastions at the corners, besides sheds for troops and stores along inside of the walls. The usual garrison consisted of two regiments and 20 or 30 artillery men. Two small streams flowed on the right and left of the rocky hill on which the town stood. The cultivated land was irrigated by artificial canals issuing from the streams. Quarter Master General in India in Intelligence Bureau, Ed., *Gazetteer of Kashmir and Ladakh*, Vivek Pubishing House, New Delhi, (Reprint), 1974, pp. 758-760.

Singh sent an agent to Garoo to demand cession of Rudok, as an old dependency of Ludakh, and to require that the trade in shawl wool should all pass though that city as heretofore. The alternative being an appeal to the sword. The Chinese Governor replied that the wool could only be sold as usual to the highest bidders—that they themselves were the servants of the Great King, and could not give away his possessions at the bidding of any one, and that if the Sikhs wished to fight, let them not come like thieves in the dark, but name a day and place and they should be fairly met in arms. To deliver these replies the Gorpun sent an Agent with the Sikh Vakeel on his return, but I do not learn any further correspondence took place.

12. Early this season the Sikhs moved from Leh in three bodies.[9] First Goolam Khan with 300 men marched on Chooret, which he took without opposition on the 1 April 1841; he remained there for 18 days and having made a detour to the northward, he occupied Tholing and Chuprung, the Chinese authorities flying before him. In the fort of Chuprung, he found a large quantity of grain,

---

9. The capital town of Ladakh, Leh was situated three miles from the right bank of the Indus and at the apex of a triangular shaped valley. Lying 1,000 feet above the river, the town surrounded the base of a low spur on the east of the valley, while the centre and the west were occupied by extensive tracts of cultivation, which were irrigated by rills drawn from a stream flowing down from the centre of the valley. The most conspicuous building was the royal palace of the Gyalpo, which was 250 feet in length and several stories in height. About a mile southwest of the town was a fort built by the Dogras on the banks of the Leh rivulet. Surrounded by two boundary walls and a ditch, its bastions had openings for small guns. The town served as an entrepot for foreign commerce, as it was meeting point of routes from Yarqand, Chinese Tibet, Kashmir and Punjab. The population of Leh varied greatly as the trading season (July to November) attracted merchants from different regions. Inside the town, the streets were found in irregular patterns, while a good bazaar has been built by the Dogras. *Gazetteer of Kashmir and Ladakh*, pp. 562-563.

two jingals, some ammunition and other stores and public property. The Governor of Chuprung was on leave of absence, but his brother acting for him in the interim period, met Goolam Khan at Shongphoo on the road to Garoo about the end of June. The Chinese were defeated and their leader slain, and soon after, Goolam Khan without further opposition joined Zorawar Singh in Garoo. Parties of men were left in Chooret, Tholing and Chuprung.

13. Nonoo Sunnum, the brother of the Raja first placed by the Sikhs on the Ludakh guddee, moved with about 300 men on Tashigong, which he reached in May and occupied after a short resistance during the night after the action. The Sikhs plundered the place, not excepting the Thakoordwaras or Lama Temples. Nonoo Sunnum appears to have awaited Zorawar Singh's arrival at Tashigong, and then to have gone with him to Garoo.
14. Zorawar Singh with 2500 infantry, 500 cavalry and 6 or 7 jingals (guns) marched to Rudok, which he captured on the 5th June after a short resistance making the Governor prisoner and securing a large quantity of ammunition. He reached Garoo early in August, and found the place evacuated. The Gorpuns or Governors had however assembled a force of 200 men and gave Zorawar Singh battle at Dogpoo Burwah, west of the Lakes. The Chinese were defeated and one of the Gorpuns killed. The Sikhs lost 40 men and the Vizier of Ludakh was severely wounded in a personal encounter with the Chinese of rank. The surviving Gorpun with the other principal men fled to Tukhlagher, which place the Sikhs contrived to take by surprise ten days afterwards, making the authorities prisoner. A very large quantity of tea is said to have been found in Tukhlagher.[10]

---

10. Situated in the valley of River Karnali, Taklakot (Purang) stood at a height of 13,300 feet and was distinct from the adjoining main plateau which has achieved an elevation of 15,000 feet. It stood at the immediate foot of Gurla Mandhata and at the junction of three rivers. It enjoyed a commanding position, with cliffs descending

15. The Pan Aghimor chief of the Jukkpas escaped from the field of battle and one Dewa Peshee, on his way from Lhassa to report on the proceedings of the Sikhs also returned when he heard of the issue of the fight. The Jukkpas of Chukk Pass are bands of mounted robbers, at whose depredations the Lhassa ruler is accused of conniving, but who appears to have been taken with the pay of Government and partially organized when the Sikhs invaded the country. Dewa Peshee it is said is now bringing up a considerable force to expel the Sikhs.
16. The Sikhs now occupy the country, as far as the pass of Marghil, which I take to be on the watershed line of the Indus and Burram Putra and which is now described to me as much nearer the Lakes than is mentioned in the 6th para of my letter of the 21st ultimo. Zorawar Singh it is said gave out that he will proceed to Lhassa next year, but this may be the inference of any one as well as the proposal of the Sikh leader. I hear generally that he levied contributions in four of our Purgannas, Neetee, Doomnies, Kumaon and Shoho, but I cannot learn anything regarding the foray in Beans reported by Lushington. Possibly Doones may be another name of that district as Beans according to any pronunciation, I can give it is unknown as its whereabouts, are not known.
17. In July or in early August 140 Putans with two jingals joined Zorawar Singh from Leh and Raja Goolab Singh who is in Cashmere, appears to have sent 500 men Putans,

---

on three sides for 500 feet, making it difficult for assault in the past. The surrounding country was extremely fertile, while the streams flowed from hamlet to hamlet, irrigating the crops like barley, mustard and peas. The district comprises thirty seven villages that are located on the banks of streams. A distinctive feature was the construction of substantial dwelling houses with stone, mud and sun dried bricks. The market served as a flourishing trade centre owing to existence of storage facilities and wool production east of the Mansarovar Lake. Its extensive Buddhist monastery, known by the Hindu name of Shivling, was quite rich and lodged 60 monks and 40 nuns. Sherring, op. cit., pp. 168-170, 184-188, 200, 206, 259.

also to Ludakh to reinforce the Vizier if necessary, but I have not heard that they have yet to proceed to join him.

18. The troops with Zorawar Singh draw their supplies at firstly chiefly from Ludakh itself and from the Spittee Valley;[11] now they have the last cooperation but until grain ripened they were much straitened for provisions and in Garoo I hear the allowance to each fighting man was for sometimes half a seer. Zorawar Singh forces the people of the country to carry all the grain they possess, along with his camp at their own expense and without fixing any scale for its sale. But notwithstanding their free quarters the troops are said to be dissatisfied nor can it be otherwise in a cold and barren country, which scarcely bears a mark of the improving hand of man.

---

11. The district of Spiti, having an area of 2,155 square miles, was hemmed in by lofty mountain ranges of an average elevation of 18,000 feet or more. These mountains separated it from Rupi and Lahul in Kullu tahsil on the west, from the state of Rampur Bashahr on the south, from Tibet on the east and from Ladakh in the north. From the main ranges, transverse lines of mountains penetrated far into the valley, leaving in many cases only a narrow passage for the Spiti river. The mountain ranges hindered easy access to the area, besides excluding it from the monsoon and making the cultivation dependent on irrigation from small seasonal streamlets. The main valley, which might have been originally a plain, has been largely carried way by the river. Natural vegetation was scanty. Two or three willows and poplars were planted in every village to meet the needs of fuel and fodder. It was only below the elevation of 11,500 feet that the trees were numerous, enabling proprietors to sell timber. Banks of water channels and slopes between fields offered grass that was converted into hay. *Gazetteer of the Kangra District: Kulu, Lahul and Spiti, 1897*, Indus Publishing House, New Delhi, Reprint, 1994, pp. 71-73.

F.D. Secret Proceedings No. 41 of 13 December 1841

From G.R. Clerk	To T.A. Maddock
Agent to the G.G., NWFA	Secretary to
29 November 1841	Government of India

I have the honour to transmit a copy of a Trade Report from Lieutenant Cunningham at Shalkur dated 13th instant.

F.D. Secret Proceedings No. 42 of 13 December 1841

From J.D. Cunningham To G.R. Clerk
Camp Shalkur 13 November 1841

1. Having gained, since I wrote to you on the 22nd ultimo, some further information regarding the trade carried on by the line of the Sutlej between Tibet and our provinces, and as I do not think that I shall be able to add much to it for some time, it seems proper that I should tell you at once, what I have already learnt. My remarks will chiefly relate to the nature of the import trade, as it will be sufficient to allude to all but a few articles of export, while the exact value of the traffic carried on can only be learnt by careful enquiry among individuals concerned in it and an examination of such documents as the Bassahar Raja may possess connected with the Ram Pore fair.
2. The principal articles of import are shawl wool, sheep, woollens, sheep wool, borax and salt, but many other articles of luxury use or curiosity such as chowries, felts, silks, tea, leather, sulphur, musk, zedoary, Chinaware, coral, amber etc. are brought to the fair held at Ram Pore. Our exports are chiefly mules, wooden cups, cotton piece goods, grain, dried fruits, brass pots and spices; but similarly as with imports, indigo, madder, horse shoes, broad cloth, kimkabs, sugar, tobacco, medicinal seeds and Bassahar tea, are carried to Ludakh or the Garoo fair. Opium was until the recent regulations of the Chinese government by far the most considerable article of export and was taken to Ludakh from the Yarkand market and in the former city also, our traders usually disposed of their indigo, but the consumption of that article is not one fifth of what it was before the invasion and exactions of the Sikhs; they have greatly impoverished the county and as another reason for the reduced demand, I hear today from two traders just returned from Leh that they scarcely realized any profit and a small investment of country indigo, as the Yarkandees said they now got it from the other side meaning no doubt through Bokhara.

3. The balance of trade is entering on the side of Thibet owing to the large quantity and great value of shawl wool bought from that country, but the demand from opium might probably in the end have given us the advantage, had not the trade been suddenly put an end to. This attention however would not have directly affected the medium of exchange in the trade in shawl wool as that is chiefly carried on at Garoo, while the opium was exported to Ludakh as before maintained. We now as hitherto, buy nearly all our wool with coined money, while we sold our opium for the silver ingots of China. These ingots, I may here add, bear the Government stamp and the metal is of great purity. They usually weigh about two seers or 160 rupees and sell in Ram Pore for 10 Rs. more than their weight. I would roughly estimate that we import 80,000 Rs. worth of goods annually from Thibet, and that more than two-thirds of our purchases are made with cash.
4. Although the trade in shawl wool to Ram Pore is comparatively new as stated in my letter of the 22nd ultimo, yet I hear that until within the last 40 or 50 years, the Kashmiris had been in the custom of purchasing the wool in Garoo and of selling it in their own villages to Cashmiris who came at appointed times to receive it. The graves of several Cashmiris are still, I hear, pointed out, but I can not learn whether these people came from the valley itself or from towns in the Panjab, neither can I ascertain why the trade ceased – I presume however that the purchases came from Cashmir direct and that the troubles which ensued on the death of Tymoor Shah of Cabool put an end to a traffic of comparatively little value.
5. The fact is however of importance for in their own justification, the Sikhs may assert with Mr. Moorcroft (I, 346) that Ladakh is the entrepot between the countries producing and consuming shawl wool. I can not here however learn any thing of the engagements and ancient custom mentioned by Moorcroft and, on the whole, I would say that his information was derived from interested parties, the officer of the Ludakh Government or the Casmiris who threw all the obstacles in his way they

could, and who were no doubt concerned in the wool trade.

6. Shawl wool is generally produced in Ladakh as throughout the valley of the Indus and its tributaries above Leh, but the goats are also bred along the valley of the Sutlej above Tholing and around the Mansarowar Lake, while some few are reared in Spiti. The finest wool however is that of Rudok and our traders either purchase it direct from the goat herds, or from the Government officers, who are said to store up large quantities on their own account in exchange for tea etc. or they resort to the Garoo fair and then proceed to Ram Pore to dispose their investment.
7. In Gartok,[12] goat-herd man or farmer, has occasionally as many as 1200 goats male and female, and to tend them he keeps from 30 to 40 servants. The goats live to the age of 10 years or so, the wool is taken off at any age, but is considered best when the aimals are 4 or 5 years old. It is carefully combed off in the month of June. The goat-herds throughout the Chinese provinces give one animal in twenty, with the wool on, to Government in the way of duty, but no tax is levied on the sale or purchase of the wool itself. The price of the article in Roduk some years ago was eight annas per seer, but the increase of purchasers has latterly almost doubled its value. No wool of the wild

12. Perched at a height of 15,000 feet, Gartok (Garo) was situated in the middle of an extensive plain which was swept by wind from all sides. It served as the administrative headquarter of western Tibet. The administration was carried on by Garpons (Viceroys) appointed by Lhasa. The outlying areas were placed under subordinate officers called Jongpens and Tarjums. Being exceedingly cold in winter, its entire population migrated after a journey of two or three days to Gargunsa, which lay on the main branch of the Indus and had solidly built houses. In the end of August or beginning of September, the great annual fair was attended by traders from Hindustan, Ladakh, Kashmir, Tartary, Yarqand, Lhasa and proper China. The spiritual matters of the province were under a Khanpo (archbishop), who was based in a large monastery at Totling which was home to nearly 300 Lamas. Charles A. Sherring, *Tibet and the Indian Borderland*, pp. 145-149, 153-154, 157.

goat appears to be taken to Ram Pore, though it is known as an article of trade to Cashmir.

8. Sheep wool and woollens are produced generally in Thibet. The wool is purchased by the Kanawaris at about 4½ seers per rupee. The woollens measure from 25 to 40 feet by 1½ feet and sell in Ram Pore for Rs. 3.00 to Rs. 6.00 each piece.
9. Salt is produced in a series of lakes to the north west of Roduk. The people engaged in the trade pay, as duty to Government, a ram loaded with cow dung for every hundred ram loads of salt they may produce. The excellent pasturage near the lakes induces people to send large droves of cattle to their banks to graze, and in these districts cow dung is very useful. The salt is sold on the Kunawar frontier at from 25 to 30 seers per rupee or weight for weight for barley.
10. Borax is also produced in small quantities in the salt lakes of Roduk and is of a good quality. That article however is chiefly brought from the northern part of the district of Rupshoo (in Ladakh) and nine days journey from Shulkur. In some parts it is found nearly pure, as in Rudok, but the mass of that taken to Ram Pore is mixed with earth, nor can the people of the country refine it; a valley near a village named Puga seems the most productive spot, and it there sells for 32 seers per rupee. The trade in this article to Ram Pore is chiefly in the hands of the Khampas, as the itinerant traders of Ram Pore are called.
11. Sulphur is also found in an impure state near the village of Pugha; above Mahir it is partially cleaned and then sells on the spot for about 4 annas per seer; felts, leather etc. from Yarkand, and silk musk from Garoo are other articles of occasional than of regular trade.
12. Tea of three kinds is brought to the Garroo fair, it is made up in packages namely 'bhuddwans' each weighing from 3¼ to 3¾ seers. The packages are of paper and several 'bhuddwans' are packaged into one box or skin. The first sort is termed 'Zungcha' and the second 'Choongcha'; they may be called black teas and sell for about six rupees per chuddum. The third sort is called 'Kopringeh'; it may be considered green tea, and sells for 18 rupees per

'bhuddwan.' The leaves of the first and second sorts are not rolled, those of the third (Kopringeh) are, and it is described as resembling our tea.

13. Of our exports, I may mention, first is the tea of Bassahar, as it attracted the notice of Mr. Moorcroft. The most common kind, and which seems as much green as black is described as the produce of a tree named 'Pungcha,' which attains a height of 20 feet or more and grows on the higher parts of the hills near and above Lippor on the Sutlej. The leaves are gathered in July and after exposure to the sun for two days, they are coloured with a gum named Julto or Chungto, which oozes from a tree named Zrin, when it grows old. The leaves after two days further exposed to the sun are then packed for sale or use. The bark of a tree named 'Sungcha' is used instead of Chunano, the substitute in India for sugar with us. The 'Sungcha' tree is found along the Sutlej south of the snowy range, and the 'Chungto' or gum tree is found below the junction of the Spiti. The tea is only carried to Garoo by petty traders, and is not always saleable, but when there is a scarcity of Chinese tea in the market, some what more than a seer may be sold for a rupee after other kind of tea mentioned by Mr. Moorcroft, I have simply heard that such is produced and it seems but little known as an article of trade or of house consumption.
14. Wooden cups are manufactured. They are used for tea, but also for other articles of food. The trade has declined of late, but about one thousand rupees worth of cups are still exported.
15. The only grains exported are rice and barley – a small quantity of atta is however occasionally taken to Garoo. Madder, though produced in small quantities in these hills, is nevertheless exported to Tibet, as there is of necessity a considerable consumption of it, being used to die the garments of the red borders of Lamas. All the grain exported and most of the dried fruits are the produce of the Hills.
16. As carriage, rams, goats, asses, mules, ponies and zhos (the male by breed of the Tibet yak and hill cow) are used

but men also are employed. The zho is slow and can only perform small journeys, it should moreover rest every four or five days. The following statement shows the average value of each beast and also the load each will carry in the Hills.

Animal	Price	Load
Rams	Rs. 2.5 to 3	8 Seers
He goats	4 to 5	8 Seers
Asses	10 to 16	32 Seers
Mules	50 to 80	64 Seers
Ponies	50 to 60	64 Seers
Zhos	16 to 17	64 Seers

A man will carry 32 seers or half as much as a mule or pony.

17. In Ladakh, under the native Government, the subjects of Bassahar were exempt from all duties, but I have not yet satisfactorily learnt the circumstances connected with this rule – a long standing friendship between the two Rajahs is usually talked of as the cause as a let off, however the Kunawaris say that in Ladakh they are told by Chinese traders that they especially, as British subjects, cannot be allowed to go to Yarkand. In places under the Chinese Government, Kunawaris pay as other people, but duties appear to be taken in Rohtuk only, where one in ten on imports are levied, no duties are demanded at the Garoo fair, nor at the fairs held at Shaktud (a march to the north of Shulkur), where the people of Rudok, Tashigong etc. equally bought salt and other articles to exchange for grain etc. with the Kunawaris. This freedom from duty has reference of course to the state of affairs before the Sikh invasion.

18. All the people of Kunawar appear to be traders,[13] petty

13. Comprising largely the valley of the upper Sutlej, Kinnaur formed the north eastern portion of the state of Bashahr. It was bounded on the north by Spiti, on the east by Chinese territory, on the south by Bashahr proper and Tehri, and on the west by Kochi subdivision of Bashahr. Its estimated area was 1,730 square miles

ones however, for none realizes more than Rs. 300 in a year and of these more respectable ones, I can only hear two who trade with their own means; the others borrow money in Ram Pore at 20 per cent almost entirely for the purchase of wool. I have not yet got any information of much interest about the 'Kampas'. They are Tartars, profess Lamaism and move about the country with their sheep and goats living guided in their movements partly by the seasons and partly by the lines of the periodical fairs. The different camps or sects have however their regular seats, and those of Kunawar do not appear to range beyond Leh, Rohtuk and Garoo.

19. The trade is entirely in the hands of money lenders of Ram Pore, satisfied with great gains in their petty way of the poor people of the hills, rejoiced at the smallest profit. They desire only to subsist. Trade cannot be much extended until a road is carried from the table land of Tibet to the plains of India, and the transport of merchandize is simplified and rendered secure. At present the road or way, specially beyond Kotgarh is barely practicable for four footed beasts, and is enough to appeal any one not in the pursuit of money, or of fame, or desperately resolved on living pleased with the hills at all hazards. Were a road however carried throughout the Himalayas, similar to that which reaches Simla, that is suitable for the easy passage of laden mules, the merchants of Delhi and Amritsar might be induced to come forward with their large means to embark

---

and population in 1901 was 17,741. Possessing a rugged terrain, it was 50 miles in length and 40 miles in breadth. The precipitous banks of the main Sutlej offered little scope for cultivation, but the valleys of its tributaries were assiduously tilled. Upto the middle of the nineteenth century, an ample production of grapes was converted into raisin wine and strong spirit. The population consisted of a mixed Tibetan and Hindu race. A Turanian element preponderated in the north, while the Aryan type inhabited the south. Chini, which was the headquarter of Kinnaur, served as the favourite hill resort of Lord Dalhousie. *Imperial Gazetteer of India* (*Provincial Series*): *Punjab*, Vol. II, pp. 372-373.

in the trade of the Chinese provinces, and to secure among other advantages the continued manufacture of shawls in the plains.

20. The present road which is barely kept passable by the Raja, runs high up the precipitous ravines of the Sutlej and in crossing the petty streams falling into it, frequent sidelong ascents and descents are rendered necessary. Thus going up merely to go down again, and turning to the right merely to make a turn to the left, is most wearisome in every way, and after a laborious journey the traveller may perhaps see the place he left some five miles behind him. The road should I think be found almost in the very bed of the Sutlej, and its irregular course in general carefully followed. In this manner a road moderate undulating and not very winding would be obtained. The principal outlay would be in cutting or blasting where the river runs almost between walls of rocks, but precipices requiring to be treated in a similar manner would be met with on any time that could be chosen anew or for improvement, another expense would be that of bridges across the streams joining the Sutlej and occasionally across that river itself, but such are even more required in most cases, and timber is plentiful until near the junction of the Spiti.

21. As the Raja of Bassahar would most directly benefit by the opening of the new route, I think he might with propriety be required to defray at least half of the original expense of the road, within his own territories and also to keep it in repair out of the duties he levies on goods brought to Ram Pore.

Camp Shalkur
13 November 1841 J.D. Cunningham

FDSC No. 40 of 20 December 1841 Ultimo/Proximo

From J.D. Cunningham To G.R. Clerk
Camp Shalkur
18 November 1841

1. With reference to the 5th para of my letter of the 8th instant, on the subject of the claims of the Bussahar Raja on the purgunna of Pin in Ladakh and on the village of Gheo rightfully subject to China, I beg to inform you that I can get no satisfactory reply to my enquiries from the Sikh authority, Mian Doolo Singh stationed in Spiti. On the 4th instant, I wrote and asked him whether he had himself or whether Zorawar Singh or other had given orders to withhold the Bussahar claims in question, he replied that the 30 pieces of cloth due from Pin, should be sent without further delay, and the people of Gheo said nothing was payable by their village to the Raja of Bussahar.

   As I wished however principally to ascertain whether the Sikhs had given orders to withhold what was due to a British tributary, I wrote to Mian Doolo Singh that as he appeared not to have properly understood my meaning, it would be well if he came in person to speak with me on the subject. To this, he replied that he could not come as he did not see why I wanted him and that moreover he was not allowed to proceed in this direction and was busy making preparations against the expected arrival of Zorawar Singh. I then wrote a third time to him to mean to effect that as he would not explain in person how matters stood, I wished him to say distinctly, whether he or others had given any order regarding the Bussahar claims. To this, today I have received in reply that the case had been referred to Wazir Zorawar Singh. Under these circumstances, I have written to the Wazir himself on the subject and I would have addressed him in the first instance, had he not been a month's journey distant or had it been necessary for his subordinate to have said same i.e. that he or his predecessor had acted under the Wazir's orders.
2. I wrote to Mian Doolo Singh that my meaning might not

be liable to misconstruction, in case of reference, as he has none with him who reads or writes anything but the Tibetan of this quarter, I annexed translations of my parwanas in that language and the answers I have received are in the same dialect. Perhaps my meaning may not have been clear to the Mian or it may have been willfully distorted by the Ladakhi subordinates about him, as they are said to have advised Zorawar Singh to stay further payment to Bussahar, on the part of this Pin pargannah, but upon the whole as I think he is blamable for refusing to answer to this purpose. My enquiries in person or in writing, I annex copies of this correspondence in order that you may if you think proper, notice his behaviour to the Lahore Government.

3. Perhaps Mian Doolo Singh may not have been informed of my deputation to this quarter and may in consequence regard my requests with surprise – and perhaps he may be a rustic unacquainted with the relations of the two Governments and of the mode in which business is carried on between them. The latter suspicion is almost justified by his asking me that he is not afraid to come and I have myself little doubt that he neither knows who I am nor for what purpose I am here.

4. I would not, however, infer from this ignorance of an agent so subordinate that the Lahore Durbar has not given instructions to Zorawar Singh to withdraw or that he is slow in acting on such instructions as may have reached him. Should orders have gone to him from the Maharaja immediately after the receipt of your letter to His Highness of the 28th September, they ought now to be in the Wazir's possession and possibly the rumour afloat of his speedy return to Ladakh, may have referred to these orders. But it is not reported by any that he relinquishes his conquests and I have as frequently heard that he is watching at Darchin, on the western side of the Lakes, the effects on the Lhasa authorities of his recent aggression, and that he is about to return to Leh and moreover should he be about to visit that city, it may be with the view of pushing forward reinforcements or ammunitions or in

communication with the Central Government of Tibet. Should no orders have been sent to him until after the receipt of your letter of the 19th October to the Maharaja's address, the Wazir can not yet know what he is to do.

5. I am confidently assured by the people in this neighbourhood that the road from Garoo to Leh can be traversed in the depth of winter, that there are no passes of any elevation and that as the winter is progressing the road is almost better in the cold than in the warm season. This may not be literally true, but I apprehend that Zorawar Singh will not be able to urge any reasonable pretence for not withdrawing on account of the weather, though he may himself be willing to seek expenses for delay and may have been instructed to avoid the appearance of going at our bidding. I wrote to him on the 14th instant requesting, he would let me know his arrangements for carrying into effect the Maharaja's instructions, for evacuating the Chinese territory and informing him that I proposed to march in the direction of his camp in a few days. To this I may have a reply by the end of the month, if the Wazir is proceeding towards Leh, but if he is still at the Lakes, I can not hear from him until about this time in December.

6. Since I last wrote to you about the Sikh movements (on the 8th instant), I can not hear of any Chinese authority, except those in the hands of the Sikhs, nor about the Sikh force have I learnt anything of moment except that it suffers much from the cold and that many men perish daily. The reinforcements of 350 men or thereabout recently arrived from Cashmere is still described as awaiting orders in Leh. My own means of enquring news have not yet had time to take effect and until my messengers return or until I get near Zorawar Singh's camp, I shall not be able to give much correct information. I move eastward the day after tomorrow, having ascertained that I shall be welcome in the Chinese villages so far as the poor people themselves are concerned.

Camp Shalkur J.D. Cunningham
18 November 1841

P.S. I received last night your demi-official letter of the 8th instant enclosing a copy of the Maharaja's reply to your's of the 25th September and also his kingship's Parwana in original to Zorawar Singh about his withdrawal to Ladakh. Ratnoo, Sikh Agent, through whom I should forward the Parwana to the Wazir, has not yet joined me, nor do I know more of their movements than that they were at Surhan (14 marches from Shalkur) on the 5th instant and talked to Raja Mohinder Singh of setting out to join me in a few days. They may be here immediately, but as they may not reach me for a fortnight, I will consequently send the Parwana to Zorawar Singh through Mian Doolo Singh or as I hear this morning that he has proceeded to meet the Wazir in the direction of Tashigong, I will send it to the Kardar of Chooret, subordinate to Doolo Singh.

If this Parwana is the first which has been addressed to Wazir Zorawar Singh about his withdrawal, his reported going towards Ladakh can not hardly be commenced to the evacuation of the Chinese provinces, nor can the troops south and west of the Lakes be within the Ladakh territory by the 10th proximo.

I hear too from a pretty good authority that a party of 700 men has reached Hanleh,[14] 6 or 7 marches north of Shalkur, on their way to join Wazir Zorawar Singh.

Shalkur J.D. Cunningham
November, 1841

---

14. Situated at an elevation of 14,276 feet, the Hanle village lay on the left bank of the Hanle river. It boasted of a monastery which was built on the summit of a steep hill rising abruptly out of the plain. Most of the wealth comprised of flocks and herds that belonged to the Lamas. The Hanle plain, covering a diameter of 6 or 8 miles, had several tortuous and sluggish streams. All streams converged to a point at the north eastern end of the plain and, uniting into one, continued the course down an open valley in a northerly direction towards the Indus. The road from Hanle to the Indus followed the left bank of the stream, the banks of which were bordered by a belt of green herbage. *Gazetteer of Kashmir and Ladakh*, pp. 354-355.

FDSC No. 37 of 27 December 1841

From J.D. Cunningham To G.R. Clerk
Camp Chooret & Shalkur
23 November 1841

1. I have the honour to inform you that on the 21st instant, I reached Chooret, a village about 15 miles north east of Shalkur in which the Sikhs have erected a small fort 60 or 70 feet square and keep up a party of 25 men, I wished to learn the manner in which I should be viewed by Zorawar Singh's followers and also by the people of the usurped territory, and I may add, to ascertain whether my letters to Zorawar Singh had been sent by trustworthy messengers, for Mian Doolo Singh, then at Dunkur in Spiti, had not informed me of the manner in which he would forward my communications, nor indeed acknowledge that he had received them.
2. I found at my arrival at Chooret that the letter which I had written to Zorawar Singh on the 11th instant requesting to be informed of the manner in which he proposed to carry out the Maharaja's orders for the evacuation of the Garoo provinces had not been taken beyond that place, as the messenger sent along with me by Mian Doolo Singh demurred about proceeding further at this season of the year, and the Sikh civil authority on the spot thought it advisable to detain both men as Mian Doolo Singh himself could take the letter, he having been ordered to join Zorawar Singh with all expedition. I found also that the man whom I had despatched to Mian Doolo Singh with a request that he would forward my letter to the Wazir about the Bassahar claims, had gone to Chooret in the expectation of meeting Mian Doolo Singh there, but as he appeared not yet to have left Dunkur, he brought the letter back to me.
3. As at Chooret, I could not ascertain that Zorawar Singh was really on his way to Ladakh or even about to visit that city or to move westward from the Lakes at all. I requested the Sikh Thanadar to allow two of his sepoys

to proceed with proper guides to the Wazir's camp with the letter above mentioned and also with one enclosing the Maharaja's Parwana to Zorawar Singh received with your demi-official letter of the 8th instant.[15] I sent the Parwana as I received it under cover to Jeewan Singh and Ganesh Dass, who I hear left Rampoor on the 11th instant. As I thought it more proper as well as more prudent to let Zorawar Singh break the seals of a despatch to an agent of his own Government than to do so myself. I explained however to the Wazir that the absence of the Sikh agents was the cause of my sending the Parwanah so enclosed to him. I have endeavoured to quicken the motions of the sepoys by a present donation and by the promise of another if they bring me the reply speedily.

4. Neither the Sikh Thanadar nor the Kardar or civil authority knew about the object of my coming to their country and upon the whole my belief is much strengthened that the Parwana which has first passed through my hands is the first that will reach Zorawar Singh about his retirement to Ladakh. I heard indeed at

---

15. Technicaly speaking, the word *parwana* was a letter of conferment of a piece of land, *milk* or *madad-i-maash* on the destitute from the Wazir, which was drafted in accordance with the imperial *farman*. It differed from the royal order (*farman*) in two respects viz. it did not require the royal seal and it was inscribed in the Tughra character, but without abbreviating the first two lines. The word appears to have some similarity with *parwancha* (*farmancha* or little royal order). During the early Mughal period, it was used in the case of salaries and scholarships, but later on for a large variety of orders that did not require a royal *farman*. In practice, these were issued in due course and almost immediately afterwards to confirm a royal order in accordance with the terms mentioned on the verse of the *farman*. Therefore, their object was to supplement or confirm and verify a royal order. Khwaja Yasin, *Dastur-i-Malguzari*, Persian Text and English Translation, S. Hasan Mahmud, Kitab Bhavan, New Delhi, 2000, p. 142; Momin Muhiuddin, *The Chancellary and Persian Historiography under the Mughals*, Iran Society, Calcutta, 1971, pp. 85-86.

Chooret that two Sikh messengers who preceeded me by a few days on my way through Kunawar had a Parwana from Raja Dhian Singh for the Wazir. That Parwana is perhaps by this time in his possession, but I doubt whether it was written with reference to your letter to the Maharaja's address of the 28th September last or if it were that it contains a positive order to the Wazir to give up his recent acquisitions.

5. During the last four or five days, I have heard more reports of the Chinese having resolved on driving the Sikhs out of the Garoo district. Some represent Chinese agents as being present in Zorawar Singh's camp and urging him to remain where he is until their troops arrive. Other reports speak of the march of these troops and others again describe an engagement between the two parties, but are silent as to the result. On the whole I am inclined to believe that an active correspondence is going forward between Zorawar Singh and the Chinese and, as my information is second hand or third hand, it would considering the season, be considered less credulous.
6. Concerning the trade to our Bassahar Provinces, I was informed by the authorities at Chooret that, when the Sikh force passed on from that place, instructions were left with them not to allow shawl wool or borax to be taken to our provinces and that, about the beginning of October, an order had been received from Zorawar Singh to allow all articles except shawl wool to be exported to Bassahar on the payment of duty and also to levy a duty on all articles brought from Bassahar.
7. I have at present only further to observe that I found the Sikh authorities civil and obliging. "The English," they said, "and Raja Gulab Singh being one," and that I have daily assurance, I shall be welcome in the Chinese villages.

Camp between Chooret and Shalkur — J.D. Cunningham
23 November 1841

FDSC No. 37 of 27 December 1841

From G.R. Clerk To J.D. Cunningham
13 December 1841

1. Received your letter of 23rd ultimo.
2. Enclosed find a letter from the Commissioner of Kumaon from which it appears that the Chinese authorities are already engaged in repelling the encroachments of Zorawar Singh on Lhasa.
3. It was the intention of the Government to have prevented the approximation which was being accomplished of the Jammu Dominion to the Nepal frontier. Consequently in so much as the present active measures of the Chinese authorities may serve to interrupt that junction, the necessity for your pressing forward to that part of frontier is diminished.
4. It is superfluous to recall your attention to my instructions of the 25th September last restraining you from penetrating into the Chinese Tartary without having ascertained that you will be well received, through the beneficial purposes of your mission being rightly understood, and without the attendance upon you of an officer on the part of the authorities there. But a collision between Chinese and Sikh troops having actually occurred, it is still more important than before that you should advance with extreme caution, and that if in advancing there be risk of your position being misconstrued by the Chinese authorities, you should select a station, whence you can observe the progress of the quarrel, and report it to your Government, without any personal danger. I apprehend that Shalkur in Bassahar may thus be the most eligible abode for you.
5. Should these results of Zorawar Singh's indiscreet movements entail any uncertainty on the Bassahar border, you will in communication with Erskine, require Raja Mohinder Singh to protect it.
6. As regards to the awkwardness to which in a late letter you adverted of restoring Garroo, while in another

quarter, your Government is at war with China, it seems probable that the Chinese authorities will now realize it themselves, but should they be inclined to listen to truth, in comprehending the object of your mission, the awkwardness is to be obviated by plainly stating that you came as a peace-maker, and that the British Government had determined to prevent Jammoo encroachments in any quarter, that could prove troublesome to itself, in the same manner as it will prevent any encroachments westwards by the Chinese, that can be felt to be injurious to British interests.

FDSC No. 61 of 4 January 1842

From G.R. Clerk
Agent to the Governor General
11 January 1842

To T.A. Maddock
Secretary to the GOI

1. I am enclosing a copy of letter from J.D. Cunningham dated 17th ultimo together with a copy of my reply to him.
2. Cunningham had not yet received my letter with instructions which enjoined him not to advance further to the south east, while Lhasa authorities are in arms there against Zorawar Singh, but the severity of season has prevented him in prosecuting his intended journey in that direction to Zorawar Singh's camp.
3. After that has been reported by Lushington of the success of the Lhasa troops, I do not consider that even Cunningham's intention of following the route across the Indus, near Chimmeting and so upto Leh, is altogether without risk of his encountering the Lhasa authorities who are in the field. Supposing the season to admit of it, I should not be surprised at their following up their late success and, with the same facility with which they have recovered Garoo and other places, advancing upon several points in Ladakh and recovering the whole of that province, before the Sikhs or the Jammoo Rajas have time to reinforce their few troops now accompanying it.
4. The Maharaja has difficulty in keeping his throne from the Sindhanawalia party,[16] and Raja Dhian Singh requires all

---

16. Being collaterals of Ranjit Singh, the Sandhawalia nobles – Attar Singh, Ajit Singh, Lehna Singh and Kehar Singh – enjoyed vast estates and influence. Following the death of the Maharaja, they played a prominent role in the political developments. During the reign of Kharak Singh, they joined a conspiracy which led to the murder of Chet Singh Bajwa. As ardent supporters of Chand Kaur, they opposed the regime of Sher Singh and Dhian Singh. In consequence, their estates were confiscated. Lehna Singh and Kehar Singh were imprisoned, while Attar Singh and Ajit Singh sought asylum with the British across the Sutlej, where they began to recruit troops for further mischief. The murder of Chand Kaur

his Hill troops in readiness to maintain him in his position at Lahore. Raja Goolab Singh is engaged in the Hazara and Peshawar and it would appear from Lushington's reports that there is little chance of the Raja's any longer having the services of the beleaguered Zorawar Singh, to whom they returned everything relating to the administration and the protection of Ladakh.

5. I presume that, in the case supposed, the British Government would not much care to restrain the Lhasa troops from releasing Ladakh from the Sikhs, but that it would interfere to prevent the extension of Chinese authority west of Ladakh.

---

forced the Sandhawalias to retrace their steps. They were reinstated in their respective positions owing to the intercession of George Russel Clerk. They carefully intrigued to sow the seeds of discord between Sher Singh and Dhian Singh, but ultimately killed (15 September 1843) both of them. This foul deed generated a storm of revulsion against them, so that Hira Singh eventually was able to kill Ajit Singh and Lehna Singh, while the Sandhawalia forts and bungalows were destroyed.

FDSC No. 61 of 24 January 1842

From J.D. Cunningham
Camp Chooret
17 December 1841

To G.R. Clerk

1. Sir, I have with regret to inform you that I have been compelled to abandon my intention of proceeding to the vicinity of Wazir Zorawar Singh's camp, by the way of Tholing, owing to the state of the passes or roads and the setting in of the winter season in all its ferocity. On the 26th ultimo, when at Namgeo, a third of the distance from Chooret, snow began to fall and until the 14th instant, I had but one clear day. As soon as the weather broke up many of my porters or coolies deserted me and it was with difficulty that I got enough to gather to enable me to make a march on the 4th of this month to Shalkur, a village on the Sutlej.
2. As this march which included a pass of 13,500 feet was accomplished with much difficulty, although it did not exceed nine miles and the snow was not more than 15 inches deep and as the weather showed no symptoms of clearing, I did not think it would be prudent to attempt to cross the Sheerong Ghat which still lay between me and Tholing and which has been estimated on good grounds as rising somewhat more than 18,000 feet above the sea. This pass is a march of about 14 miles, and though I might have tramped down a road way by means of the cable of the villages near it, yet this might have been destroyed in a few hours and under any circumstances, I have apprehensions that the extreme cold and the length of the journey would have caused some of my party to have lagged behind, and to have perished in the snow.
3. The only other road from Shalkur to Tholing is up the bed of the Sutlej when frozen but as the foaming stream of that river might not be too great until the middle of January and as by that time Zorawar Singh, if he had any intention of immediately obeying instructions of his Government,

should be well on his way to Ladakh, I did not think it would be advisable to remain shut out from all communications with the Sikhs for five or six weeks and accordingly resolved to proceed to the nearest attainable point on the Indus, so as to be in the way of obtaining tolerably accurate information of their proceedings. I was also very doubtful whether I would ensure the assistance of the people of the Chinese villages, for many of these had not been visited by the Sikhs and neither I nor the Lahore Agent with me had means to force the labour of the inhabitants or the use of their cattle, while at Shipkee too, I had to inform the Wazir of my change of places, but no offer of a fair reward could induce any to be the bearer of my letter until the Sutlej should freeze.

4. I had ascertained that a road from Shalkur to Ladakh is usually open even in the winter season. This road crosses the Indus near Chumurtung more than half the way from Garoo towards Leh. I yesterday reached the Sikh post of Churit. On my way from Shipkee to that place and now endeavouring to make arrangements for reaching it or some road higher up the river, I can not be sure that I will succeed for the cold is increasing and at this place, the elevation of which is about 12,300 feet, the thermometer stood 10 degrees below zero today at sunrise, while to reach the Indus, I must cross a mountain or cover at least three or four thousand feet higher. I would not at present allude to the difficulties which may be thrown in my way by the Sikh authorities, because I hope to overcome any thing may raise, but I need confess that the people on the spot do not seem so ready to aid me as they should and after the trouble I have had with the people of Kunawar beyond their own territory, I do not consider it possible to take them and the requisite quantity of supplies at the present.

5. The Sikhs have not received any instructions about returning within the Ladakh frontier and regarding Wazir Zorawar Singh they heard some time ago that he had come towards Garoo, but now they understand he has again

proceeded to the southward of the Lake Manasarowar.[17] Mian Doolo Singh, regarding whom I have before written, proceeded about a fortnight ago to join the Wazir and Magna Ram who went towards Ladakh from the Lake Manasarowar with his sister, the Wazir's wife, has left her about two-third of the way and is about to join Zorawar Singh. Therefore the Wazir can not have received peremptory orders about withdrawing until he got the Parwana which I forwarded to him from this place on 22nd ultimo. That however should now have been in his possession and I may shortly expect to hear of his intention with regard to the instructions conveyed to him.

6. Since I wrote to you on the 30th ultimo, I have not learnt anything of moment about the rumoured repulse of the Sikh troops by the Chinese, but a report is current here that the Chinese have pushed forward a small force into the Pargannah of Poorung, that they have dispossessed the Sikhs of a post in that tract and stationed two hundred more in the village of Tukhlakot. The Sikhs however are still occupying that post. It is also said here that there are

---

17. Two large lakes Mansarovar and Rakas Tal were situated between two mountain ranges, Kailash and Gurla Mandhata, respectively at 14,850 feet and 14,900 feet. Endowed with a circumference of nearly 45 miles, they were joined by a 100 feet wide stream. On east and west of Mansarovar, there were luxuriant pasture lands stretching for miles, where the tribe of Dokpas tended flocks of sheep and cattle. This area produced wool which was exported to different directions viz. Ladakh, Nepal, Simla and Kumaun. Salt and borax came from mines situated to the north of the Kailash range at the same height as the lakes. There were several monasteries on the lakes that were managed by different ecclesiastical chiefs. The area was held sacred by the Hindus and Tibetan Buddhists. According to the Hindus, Mansarovar was formed by the mental effort of Brahma in response to a request from the Rishis. It constituted the abode of Shiva and contained the golden Shivling. It was believed that one who bathed in it went to heaven, being released from sins of a hundred births. Charles A. Sherring, *Western Tibet and the Indian Borderland*, pp. 32, 36-37, 47-48, 260-268.

Gurkhas on the side of the Sikhs, but whether as mercenaries or as auxiliaries is not known.

7. As the country to the east of the Lakes is inhabited by a pastoral people only and as the Sikhs draw supplies from Ladakh and, I am told, from Cashmere. It is difficult to understand how too considerable bodies of troops can be satisfied for more than a few days in the neighbourhood of the Lakes themselves. I am not, therefore, disposed to think that the Chinese are making any considerable effort at present to revert to their lost provinces, for had a large force advanced from Lhasa, it must either have retired or have been repulsed or have driven the Sikhs before it and have moved towards Ladakh for the lack of provisions, but I do not hear that any one of these three supposed occurrences has precisely taken place, although rumours of the approaching of the Chinese are very prevalent.

Camp Chooret
17 December 1841

FDSC No. 61 of 24 January 1842

From G.R. Clerk To J.D. Cunningham
11 January 1842

Subject: Critical Position of Zorawar Singh in Chinese Tartary

Received your letter of 17th ultimo.

1. I trust, you have received the copies which I have sent to you and several reports from the Commissioner in Almora relating to the success of the Lhasa troops in ejecting the Sikhs from the greater part of Zorawar Singh's late usurpations, their being in considerable force under a leader named Kulsir Kwang, their having besieged Zorawar Singh himself with his small detachment in Anamye and the extremely harassed, broken and starved condition of his few remaining garrisons.
2. You will therefore, as already instructed in a letter which I dispatched to you on the 13th ultimo, consider it your first duty to place yourself only in positions where you are secure from encountering the Lhasa troops and of communicating with the British territories.
3. The means of communicating with some of their authorities will probably present themselves to you, when you will state that certain views of your Government brought you there, which embraced the restoration to them of their own, but as they are now themselves in the way of accomplishing this, you anticipate from the restoration, the advancement of trade in general, and in particular the satisfaction of British subjects and allies, who had since the usurpations of the Jammoo Rajas on Chinese territory been subjected to restrictions and annoyances, which the British Government could not contemplate with indifference.
4. At the same time, your language should not encourage an endeavour to release Ladakh. It need not however be very strong in discountenancing such an intention.
5. But against any design and encroachment by the Chinese

authorities beyond the western limits of the conquests made by the Jammoo Rajas in the name of Ranjit Singh in 1836 and 1837, you should remonstrate and signify the probability of the British Government having an interest in preserving the state of dominion subsisting there previous to that period.

FDSC No. 62 dated 24 January 1842

From T.A. Maddock
Secretary to the GG
24 January 1842

To G.R. Clerk
GG's Agent at the Sikh Darbar

Received your letter concerning the latest correspondence with J.D. Cunningham. In reply I may write that GG-in-Council would not wish to authorize any declaration on the part of your assistance to either the Sikhs or the Chinese of the views of this Government regarding the future disposal of Ladakh or any other matter in dispute between them. It will be much more desirable that Lt. Cunningham should at present be a looker on, and should interfere in no way to influence the conduct of the contending parties as to the manner in which they will settle their differences and the future boundaries of their respective possessions.

FDSC No. 74 of 7 February 1842

Subject: British interference to prevent Chinese from Ladakh

From G.R. Clerk — To T.A. Maddock
Agent to G.G., NWFA — Secretary to the Govt. of India
19 January 1842

1. I am sending three reports from J.D. Cunningham dated 20th, 24th and 27th December 1841 along with a copy of my reply to this date.
2. The rumours alluded to in the first of these letters corroborate the intelligence which was procured last month by the Commissioner in Almora, and by his assistant across the passes at the back of Almora.[18]
3. It seems probable that the beleaguered garrison of Zorawar Singh may have sent to Leh for assistance as Cunningham had reported; but as far as I can learn, they will not obtain much assistance thence until Raja Goolab Singh has had time to reinforce that post.
4. It has now been reported both in Almora and in the quarter where Lt. Cunningham is staying, that some Gorkhas are

18. Almora was the headquarters of Kumaun Division in paragana Barahmandal of Kumaun district. It was 30 miles from Nainital, 46 miles from Kaladhungi and 19 miles from Ranikhet. The town, along with its civil and military station, were built on a bare ridge having an elevation from 5200 to 5500 feet. Towards the west, it was connected with the higher ridges of Simtola and Kalmatiya. On the east and south, it was bounded by the Suwal river and on the west by the Kosi. Important features of the town were a principal street which divided into two bazaars, the Mission School on the site of the residence of former rulers of Kumaun and a charity run asylum for lepers. Suitable as a resort for consumptive patients, the town relied for supply of water on springs and wells. In 1872 its population was 5884. In general appearance, the town was compact and clean, while the conservancy arrangements have been satisfactory. Edwin T. Atkinson, *The Himalayan Gazetteer*, Vol. III, Part I, Cosmo Publications, Delhi, (Reprint), 1973, pp. 5-11.

serving with the Chinese troops acting against Vizeer Zorawar Singh. I too think it likely that such is the case. The Gorkhas are in a manner tributary to China and they are neighbours.

5. The difficulty which Cunningham finds in accounting for the reduced numbers of Zorawar Singh's troops, as at present reported to him, is explained by the intelligence communicated by Lushington that several of Zorawar Singh's garrison and detachment had been put to the sword.
6. It is not a subject of regret, I think that Cunningham can not now proceed, as he is desirous of doing, to confer more nearby with the Chinese authorities. He will subsequently have received my injunctions against his further advance to the eastward. There seems no necessity for it in this altered condition of affairs there, and might be attended with risk of his being made prisoner.
7. I agree with Cunningham's para 5th and 6th of his letter of 27th December that Chinese may advance as specious a plea as the Sikhs to the possession of Ladakh, but it does not seem to me that the interposition of the British Government to restrain the Jammoo Rajas on the Chinese frontier, from usurpations unauthorized by their sovereign, and embarrassing to the interest of the British Government, can give the Sikhs any title to claim our assistance, should the Chinese after themselves recovering those late conquests from the Jammoo Rajas advance to release Ladakh. Should the war with the Chinese Government be protracted, it might be expedient to check them in Ladakh, otherwise I do not see that the Government of India need to concern itself about hostilities between the Chinese and Jammoo Rajas at the back of the Himalayan mountains, further than to deter the Government of Nepal from a closer connection with either side. General Matabar Singh sometimes remarked to me that the advisers of his Raja will now be proposing to themselves to aid China with soldiers in the present expedition from Lhasa against the Sikhs, since nothing satisfactory to the many enemies of the British Government

at his court comes of the endeavours which they have now for so many years, been making to obtain the use of the troops, and the treasures of the Punjab to act against the British.

Sd.
G.R. Clerk

FDSC No. 75 of 7 February 1842

From J.D. Cunningham To G.R. Clerk
Camp Chooret
20 December 1841

1. I yesterday had some talk with a man who had recently left the camp of Zorawar Singh and, as his story is confirmatory of what I related to you regarding the advance of the Chinese in my letter of the 30th ultimo, I think it proper to give you the substance of what I heard. The man belongs to one of our Kumaon villages and, being attached to the monastery of Tashigong on the Indus, it fell to his turn last year to proceed with three other Lamas to Garoo to read on selected days the doctrines of his creed before the Chinese Governors in the chief temple of the place. He fled with the farmers on the approach of Zorawar Singh's troops and was taken to Tashigong from where he escaped. He took service for the sake of a livelihood with some owners of asses and oxen who had been forced to attend on Zorawar Singh's army with their cattle.
2. The Lama says that about the 15th of November 1841 previous rumours of the approach of the Chinese reached the intelligence that they had taken Tuklaghar and killed or made prisoner about 150 of the garrison. Zorawar Singh who was then encamped at Tirthapooree, about three marches from Tuklaghar, not crediting to the full extent the reports which he heard, sent off a party of 200 horse only to aid the troops in the district. This detachment soon gave information that the Chinese force was numerous and Zorawar Singh then added 400 men to their numbers, but speedily hearing that his enemies mustered a power of 5,000 men, he set off himself with his whole force to Tuklaghar. The Lama and his employers took this opportunity of deserting and I am consequently ignorant of the result of the action if any took place.
3. A Ludakhee reached this place the day before yesterday and he appears to have left the Sikh camp a day or two after the Lama. His only additional intelligence in so far as I can learn is that he had heard a Sikh of some rank had

been made prisoner. This man who is described as a sipahee has been kept carefully out of my men by the Sikhs here, but from what I hear, I should infer that he has brought orders to send a party of the people of Spitee to the Vizeer, that the Vizeer has also urgently required reinforcements from Ladakh. I can not fully depend on this statement but it has an air of probability about it.

4. The Chinese troops are said to number about 5,000 men as before stated. Their leaders are named as Zorkung (of the rank of Vizeer) and Denee Pishee, the same names being given in the body of my letter of 30th ultimo. But if the Chinese force is of such amount as to make victory decisive in its favour or its defeat of importance to the Sikhs, I am still at a loss to understand why no action has taken place or, at least, why the report has not reached its neighbourhood.

Sd.
J.D. Cunningham

From J.D. Cunningham To G.R. Clerk
Camp Chooret
24 December 1841

1. On the morning of the day before yesterday the Sipahees of the Fort at this place enjoyed some feast in honour of a victory which they said they had heard had been gained by the Sikhs over the Chinese force, which recently advanced into the Pargannah Poorang. I first supposed that this was done only to deceive me. But the story current among the villages is quite different.
2. The Sikhs give out that an advance party under the Ladakhi chief Nonoo Sunnum was at first overpowered and that a Ladakhee of some rank deserted to the Chinese, but that Zorawar Singh was enabled to retrieve affairs and to gain a victory. They further add that the Chinese leader, who was present at the fight which took place after the capture of Chuprung and Garoo, was slain.

Sd.
J.D. Cunningham

FDSC No. 75 of 7 February 1842

From J.D. Cunningham To G.R. Clerk
Camp Chooret
27 December 1841

1. Yesterday some men whom I had sent to Tholing about the end of last month returned; the news they bring further corroborates previous reports of the advance of the Chinese force towards Garoo. Two of these men were sent with the copy of Raja Dhian Singh's Parwana to Vazeer Zorawar Singh to withdraw to Ludakh, which I received from you on the 28th ultimo (November 1841) and which was dispatched to the Vazeer from Tholing on the 8th or 9th instant by the Jamadars of Sipahees stationed there.
2. My messengers left Tholing on the 9th instant and were informed by the Kimboo or Chief Lama that the Chinese had moved forward a force of about 6,000 men and defeated a body of Sikhs under the Ludakhees Nono Sunnum and Golam Khan (the latter of whom was murdered), that they had occupied every place in the Poorung Purganna south of the Lakes excepting the Fort of Tuklaghar into which Zorawar Singh had thrown himself and the whole of his force not exceeding 1,000 or 1,100 fighting men, that 4,000 Chinese were beleaguering the place, while 2,000 were about to march westward to seize Magna Ram, who may be considered the next in rank to Zorawar Singh. The Kimbo added that 400 Goorkhas were serving with the Chinese, a communication which I also received yesterday from the Lama and astronomer of Rheeo near Tholing mentions generally that the Sikhs were unable to withstand the Chinese, but I am at a loss how to reconcile the present reduced amount of Zorawar Singh's force with his recent numbers of three or four thousand men of Jammoo and the Punjab. They can not desert the explanation that the cold has killed some and that others are absent with Magna Ram and the Vazeer's wife, is scarcely sufficient.
3. The Kimbo, who is the chief Lama and also the temporal manager of Tashigung and Tholing, had been for some time

in attendance on Zorawar Singh, but had obtained leave of absence to return to Tholing, where he arrived about the beginning of this month. My messengers mention the alarm of the Sikhs on the approach of the Chinese and on the interference of the British and states that Sipahees stationed in Chuprung had abandoned their post and come to Tholing partly to consult about what they should do.

4. About my further progress, however, I still await the reply of Magna Ram, who I believe to be in the District of Hanle, and who has the direction of affairs under the Vazeer from Spitee and that place eastward along the Sutlej. Until I hear from him, I refrain from any remarks on the conduct of Zorawar Singh's subordinates.

5. The opinion seems general, but I can not yet trace it to any certain source, that the Chinese will advance on Ludakh, if they succeed in crushing Zorawar Singh. In driving him from the Garoo districts, they will be aided by the season, by the distances of his resources and by the desertion from his stand of nearly all, save the men of the Jammoo hills and the Sikhs themselves, these men form now the majority as well as the strength of Zorawar Singh's small force and he can not look for the immediate aid of the detachment which has reached Leh. (In occupying Ludakh, the Chinese will be aided among the principal people, by the worldly religious feelings of an oppressed population and, as in these barbarous countries, the temporal may not very well be distinguished from the spiritual authority.) The Chinese may advance as specious a claim to the sovereignty of Ludakh on the plea of the supremacy of the Dalai Lamas, their feudatory, as the Sikhs can do on the plea of the triennial presents made through the Governors of Cashmir to the Emperor of Delhi. Nor can the short possession of 8 or 9 years or our tacit acknowledgement of Sikh usurpation add strength to the claims of Lahore or weaken those of China, while the probable free invitation of the present nominal Raja, the grandson of the dispossessed ruler, may place the right entirely on the side of the ruler.

6. But as we have ordered the Sikhs to evacuate their recent acquisitions, it seems to me that they can with some

plausibility, demand our assistance, of what we have acknowledged to be their own, require that we shall prevent the Chinese crossing the Ludakh frontier and mediate between them, on points arising out of the seizure of Garoo. On this subject, I shall be glad to receive your instructions and, in the meantime, if circumstances required me to interfere, I will advise the Chinese not to cross the Ludakh boundary and to endeavour to obtain the redress of their just grievances by peaceful negotiations, but I will also carefully avoid, committing Government to any line of conduct, while I receive distinct instructions, how to act.

Camp Chooret — Sd.
27 December 1841 — J.D. Cunningham

FDSC No. 75 of 7 February 1842

From G.R. Clerk To J.D. Cunningham
14 January 1842

1. Received your two letters dated 20 and 24 December 1841.
2. The reports of operations of the Chinese authorities against Zorawar Singh are generally corroborated in the intelligence received last month from the Commissioner in Almora which was forwarded to you.
3. The questions put in the concluding para of the last of your letters had been anticipated in my instructions to you of the 11th instant (a copy enclosed).
4. That which has occurred to you seems to me to be the proper course for you to pursue namely, if circumstances require you to interfere, you should advise the Chinese, not to cross the Ludakh boundary and you should endeavour to obtain redress of their just grievances by peaceful negotiations at the same time carefully avoiding to commit your Government to any line of conduct.

FDSC No. 76 of 7 February 1842

From T.A. Maddock
Secretary to the GOI
7 February 1842

To G.R. Clerk
Agent to the GG, NWF

That the Governor-General-in-Council will approve of your recalling Cunningham from any places beyond the frontier of Bussahar to which he may have advanced and of directing him to remain within that territory till on the return of summer, it may be easy to communicate with the countries beyond, and to ascertain the position of the contending parties. The Governor General can see no advantage from Cunningham's seeking personal conference with the leader of the Lhasa forces and, on the contrary, of probability of much embarrassment to the Government arising from his intercourse with them, even if he himself is exposed to no personal risk on the occasion.

Sd.

FDSC No. 83 of 21 March 1842

From G.R. Clerk
Agent to the GG, NWF
2 March 1842

To T.A. Maddock
Secretary to the GOI

1. Received your letter of 7 February 1842.
2. The sort of communications which Lt. Cunningham appears to hold with the Chinese frontier authorities, is not likely as far as I am aware to be attended with any inconvenience to lead him to deviate from the instructions of the Government for his guidance dated 24 January 1842.
3. I some time ago directed J.D. Cunningham to abandon the intention of crossing to the Indus or to the vicinty of any tract of country, which is likely to be the scene of hostilities between China and the Jammoo Rajas in the ensuing contest, but to place himself where in security he can best apprise his Government of all that may there transpire.
4. It can scarcely be said that the reinforcements which the Jammoo Rajas are now sending to Ludakh can be regarded as a measure not executed in good faith, as supposed by Cunningham in Para 3 of his letter No. 14. Reverses had overwhelmed the Jammoo troops, which Cunningham was then but imperfectly informed of, and it has in consequence become of vital importance to the present prisoners of Ludakh to reinforce that province in time for its defence against the invasion which it is to be expected the victorious Lhasa toops will be prepared to undertake with ensuing summer.
5. The progress and character of Jammoo aggrandizement have always appeared to me in the light in which they are viewed in the 12th para of Cunningham's letter of 6th ultimo.

G.R. Clerk

FDSC No. 85 of 21 March 1842

From T.A. Maddock
Secretary to GOI
21 March 1842

To G.R. Clerk
Political Agent
North West Frontierc Agency

1. Your letter of the 2nd instant and its enclosures were laid before the Governor General-in-Council and in reply may write that the Governor-General-in-Council is of the same opinion, as when I addressed you on the 7th ultimo, with respect to the risk and probable embarrassment of Lt. Cunningham's present advanced position, and will be happy to hear of his retiring within Bussahar portion or to some other point of security.
2. On the subject of an anticipated renewal of the contest between the forces of the Jammoo Rajas and the Tibetan army now at Garoo, Governor General-in-Council feels that while we are demanding the cooperation of Raja Goolab Singh in the direction of Peshawar, we can not expect his cordial aid, or that of his brother Raja Dhian Singh, if we at the same time offer any obstacle to their maintenance of their authority in the province of Ludakh. That province has been in their unquestioned possession for several years. The claims of the Chinese or Lhasa Government to authority over it, if any such existed, were never urged, as far as this Government is informed against its occupation by the Jammoo Rajas. But the case is entirely different with respect to the territory to the south-east of Ludakh, which was last year overrun by Zorawar Singh. There the supremacy of the Lhasa Government was undisputed. And the invasion of the country and the usurpation of its Government were acts of unwantonable aggression against which the British Government was bound to protect, as its silence on the occasion might have been construed by both the parties and the Chinese Government as an encouragement or approval of the measure and the consequence of the measure were at the same time likely to be prejudicial to the commerce of our own subjects.

3. The defence of Ludakh by the Jammoo Rajahs against any attempt of the Chinese or Tibetan authorities to wrest it from their hands must be regarded by the British Government as a measure in itself perfectly legitimate and one to which this Government would wish every success and the Governor General-in-Council would wish the Jammoo Rajahs to be fully informed of this feeling in their favour.

FDSC No. 84 of 21 March 1842

From J.D. Cunningham
Camp Chooret
5 January 1842

To G.R. Clerk

1. I yesterday received a message from the Choorpun or Commander of ten (of local levies) of the Chinese villages of Shipkee to the effect that on the 28th ultimo a written order had reached him from the Roopum or Superior of the Choorpuns of his district to be ready with his quota of men as the Sikh army had been dispersed and their leader made prisoner, and as it was the intention of the Lhasa authorities to march on Ludakh within the next four months. The Roopum further added that the men must be prepared for a seven years war.
2. The Roopum is residing near Bheoo between Tholing and Shipkee, a tract of country which the Sikhs have not been able to visit owing to pressing affairs near the Lakes, and if he received any orders similar to the above, they probably reached him about the 24th or 25th ultimo. I attach however but little credit to the details of this story, and I have related it chiefly as in a degree confirmatory of the views of the Chinese on Ludakh alluded to in my letter of the 27th ultimo, and I may further add that I have ascertained the Ludakhee of rank stated in my communication of the 24th ultimo to have gone over to the Chinese to be Gunbo (the favourite of the deceased Raja of Ludakh), and whose oppressive rule is said to have induced several of the principal men of the country to form a party in favour of the Sikhs during the period of Zorawar Singh's first incursions. I do not by any means feel assured of this man's escape or desertion from the Sikhs, but if he has left them, he may possess or assume the authority to repeat the offers of allegiance to China said to have been frequently made by the father of the present Raja.
3. I have thought it advisable to write to the leaders of the Chinese force, especially as now I am within Chinese

territory and propose to proceed further within it. I have simply informed them that the British Government disapproved of the occupation of the Garoo districts by the Sikhs and of the stoppage of the trade to our Hill Provinces, that the Maharaja with our advice had ordered his general to withdraw immediately to Ludakh, that I had transmitted the order in question to Zorawar Singh sometime previously and that I had come to these Provinces to see whether he obeyed the order.

4. The Lahore Agent with me has not yet received any reply to either of his applications to Magna Ram relative to the carriage and supplies to enable me to reach the Indus. Repeated falls of snow however during the last five days may have detained his messenger.
5. After I had written to you yesterday, I heard that two men who had been dispatched to Hanleh on some business by the Thanadar of Spittee had returned (in 6 or 7 days) to this place, and though they were immediately sent to their homes, I ascertained through my channels of information, that they had brought intelligence of the advance of Sikh troops from Leh towards Garoo, of Magna Ram having gone to the former place to expedite their march and of the people of Spittee having been called on to send their quota of militia to aid Zorawar Singh, but I heard too that they had brought some message for Jeewan Singh, the Lahore Agent with me.
6. I do not expect that a reply would come from Magna Ram during the next fortnight or three weeks and as snow continues to fall and the disinclination of the people to carry burdens increased as the season advances. I have almost given up all hope of reaching the Indus until the approach of spring. I will not therefore delay any longer some observations on the conduct of the local authorities. Chiefly however as showing the unprincipled nature of the higher functionaries and of the Sikh and Jammoo ambition of which indeed the petty frauds and oppressions of the subordinates are the natural products.
7. When I was here for two days in November last, I had little to ask, so little could be and nothing was refused to

me. The English name and a few rupees procured what I chiefly wanted viz. two stout Sipahees to carry Dhian Singh's Parwana to the Vazeer. When Jeewan Singh, the Lahore or rather Jammoo Agent joined me, he wrote to the Spittee authorities that he wanted some money partly to enable him to present me with a 'Zeeafat' and partly for his own expenses from Mian Doolo Singh and the Jamadar of Sipahees of this place, he received in reply that they were under Magna Ram, that the collections had been sent to him and so on. When I found that I could not reach Tholing, I told the Lahore Agent to make arrangements for my march from Chooret onwards to the Indus, and he wrote two different times about what was requisite. When I reached this place, I learnt that nothing had been done, the Jamadar was absent, Mian Doolo Singh had gone to join the Vazeer (Zorawar Singh) and the Ludakhee Thanadar had not arrived from Spittee. The Thanadar's deputy and the Sipahees of the fort bought grain and wood in insufficient quantities, the former of a bad quality and for each high prices were asked, grass or rather hay was refused and I need only further observe that in the village there was abundance of each article and that the owners would have readily disposed of their property had they dared.

8. The Ludakhee Thanadar arrived in a day or two and the Jamadar of Sipahees came also on being sent for. Dhian Singh's Parwana to all authorities was shown to them by the Lahore Agent, but they said that they were under Magna Ram and that Magna Ram was under the Vazeer and that no order had come from them about me or about Jeewan Singh, the same difficulties continued about supplies and I was plainly told that no arrangements could be made during the present season for carriage and supplies to enable me to get even a part of the way towards the Indus. The Lahore Agent confessed to me that he was nobody and that Dhian Singh's or Gulab Singh's order to be current here must come through the channel of Zorawar Singh and his deputies. In a few days however the local authorities mended the matters

somewhat. Jeewan Singh was supplied with money, grain etc. produced in sufficient quantities if not in abundance, but still no arrangements could be made for my onward march.

9. In the meantime, the Lahore Agent stated to me his belief (confirmed by other reports) that Mian Doolo Singh had been embezzling the revenues of Spittee and that the object of the Jamadar and the Sipahees in going some marches off was to be out of the way of troublesome questions about money, while I should be here. I also ascertained independent of the Lahore Agent that Magna Ram had been sent and that the Jamadar, while no coolies could be provided for me, was beating and confining the neighbouring villagers, because they made objections to furnish men and cattle to aid in the removal of the above mentioned plunder. Magna Ram's desire to get the property to a place of safety was increased by the rumour of the approach of the Chinese and the same circumstances, I have since heard, had induced the Thanadar's Deputy, a dissolute Mohammedan of Leh, to think of absconding with the revenues of three or four villages, now in his hands; and with the amount of sundry taxes levied for imputed crimes. The deputy is getting together coolies, as secretly as he can, the Jamadar of Sipahees attempted to proceed direct to Lerrtee, with some men and cattle, but was foiled by the depth of snow on the Bootpo Ghat and he is now endeavouring to make a circuit to the same place. While Magna Ram's journey to Ludakh may be explained by the apparently prolonged resistance of the Vazeer and by the hopes arising from the arrival of fresh troops. The petty difficulties made about grain, wood etc. I would impute to the wish that I would be induced to renounce and leave them to carry on their designs free from observation. The really capable persons are, I think, the Jamadar of Sipahees and the Deputy Thanadar, who being the creatures of Magna Ram, leave the dull but well intentioned Ludakhee Thanadar completely at their mercy.

10. From what I have above stated, and from all that I have seen and heard since I crossed the Himalayas, I would infer that the new rule in these provinces is extremely grinding and oppressive, that in all details, the subordinate agents are very independent of their superiors, that responsibility is not or can not be rigorously exacted upon these superiors by Zorawar Singh and that he again is not very strictly brought to account by his master Goolab Singh, and this comparison I would leave to be understood with reference to the usual loose Government of Eastern Countries. I am not aware that a confident Agent on the part either of Ranjeet Singh or of the Jammoo family ever visited Ludakh to learn and report on its resources, nor has Zorawar Singh been to the Panjab during the last three years to give any account of his proceedings, he would seem to have done and to still do much as he pleased, careful however to satisfy upon the whole expectations of his employers. Some degree of discipline among his men and superior weapons have enabled him to trample on a poor and most unwarlike people, but as his only responsibility has been small, and as the country is extensive, the oppressions of his subordinates have been as unrestrained in the degree as his own. All too appear to have acted in ignorance, rather than in disregard, of the responsibility due to us by the Jammoo Rajahs either directly or otherwise and indeed the subordinates do not seem to know Goolab Singh in his capacity of a Lahore feudatory.
11. Zorawar Singh's invasion and entry into Ludakh were without Goolab Singh's direct knowledge and that without referring to his superiors, he took Chutterghar on the Chenab; a dependency of Chamba (since its capture called Goolab Garh), merely because it was on the best road from Ludakh to Jammo. He appears indeed to have a general liberty of occupying such places as he can, and I can suppose that Dhian Singh and his brother did not well know whether Garoo was to be brought under subjugation or not until perhaps the Vazeer told

him, that he was about to march against the place and that it was not a plan matured at Jammoo is, I think, evident from the circumstances that a Sikh collector of taxes crossed our boundary and that otherwise our rights and those of our subjects have been interfered within a manner little in accordance with the good sense of the Rajahs. Neither do I think that any particular view of connecting the Sikh and Nepal dominions to our eventual detriment suggested the expedition. The chief men in either country have of late been too much occupied in maintaining their influence at home to give their time or inclination for combining to deprive us of any of our provinces, though vague schemes of future aggrandizement may amuse their fancy.[19] I would say that objects of more immediate interest require and obtain their attention.

12. I do not intend what I have above said as any palliation of the conduct or views of the Jammoo Rajahs. On the contrary it appears to me that, while they may wish to avoid giving umbrage to us, they grasp territory on all

19. The British success in the Anglo-Nepalese War of 1814-16 had important implications. The British, by occupying Kumaun, Garhwal and adjacent hill states, had created a wedge of territory between Lahore and Kathmandu, thus precluding the possibility of a direct contact between the two states. Ranjit Singh noted with regret the expulsion of Gurkhas from the Punjab hills. Since he could not rely entirely on the British, he could win over the Gurkhas by offering the fort of Kangra to them. Nevertheless, from 1834 onwards, there was frequent exchange of diplomatic missions between Lahore and Kathmandu. In 1838 the Gurkha general Matabar Singh entered Punjab and, having received a high command in service, facilitated the recruitment of Gurkhas by the Sikh kingdom. After the demise of Ranjit Singh, Naunihal Singh (the de facto ruler during the reign of Kharak Singh) and Dogra brothers became very keen to forge an anti-British league with the Gurkhas, 'which was intended to serve as the keystone of the projected coalition of the Indian powers against the English.' C.L. Datta, *Ladakh and Western Himalayan Politics*, Munshiram Manoharlal, New Delhi, 1973, pp. 169-170.

sides and endeavour to lay now a claim of some kind or the other to provinces or cities, trusting to chance for the consolidation of their acquisitions under our vigorous rule.

Sd.
J.D. Cunningham

FDSC No. 14 of 6 January 1842

From J.D. Cunningham To G.R. Clerk
Camp Chooret
7 January 1842

1. I sent for Jeewan Singh in the evening and he then told me that the Jamadar of Sipahees in Hanle had written to him that his two letters for Magna Ram had been received and had been forwarded with reference to the expected arrival of a body of men from Jammoo under Commandant Deewan Singh and accompanied by Mian Surat Singh, the immediate agent of the Raja (Gulab Singh), that his (Deewan Singh's) messengers had been detained until the replies should be received from Magna Ram who indeed was himself expected to vacate Hanle within seven days. This letter according to Jeewan Singh contained no mention of the movement of troops from Leh towards Garoo, but he said the men who brought it had heard, that a detachment had either commenced its march or would immediately do so.
2. Though Zorawar Singh may have called for reinforcements in ignorance that he was himself to retire immediately to Ludakh, yet an order for troops to forward from Jammoo or Kishtwar to that place must I should say have been given or their march might easily have been countermanded subsequent to the arrangement made with the Maharaja of evacuation of the Chinese provinces and as already a body of about 700 men had recently been sent to Ludakh, and as Zorawar Singh should himself shortly be present in the same quarters with his whole force, it does not seem that the further dispatch of troops was in any way necessary for the tranquility of the Provinces and I would consequently infer that the Jammoo Rajas are prepared to retain if possible some of their recent acquisitions from the Chinese or it may be to extend their possessions to the eastward of Iskardo or to take advantage of a favourable opportunity for interfering in any direction.

Dhian Singh may possibly be able to give a satisfactory explanation of this strengthening of the Ladakh force, but to me the proceedings hardly seem in good faith.

3. No mention is made of the strength of this new reinforcement beyond the vague term of a Regiment, but as a 'pulton' is usually applied to the regulars of the Lahore and Jammu army, it may be presumed that they have been drilled and that they are armed with muskets and consequently that they are not intended to act as a mere police. The body which reached Leh some months ago is I hear about 700 strong and is composed of the part of retainers of the late Udham Singh, the eldest son of Raja Gulab Singh. They are also described as regulars. Wazir Lakhpat, who accompanied these men, appeared to have been the Wazir of Kishtwar Raja before it was occupied by the Jammu family and also to have been long in the confidence of Gulab Singh and, if credit may be given to the probable opinion of the Sikh Agent with me, he was sent to Ladakh as much to check and report on Zorawar Singh's financial administration as to be a suitable representative of the Raja in that city during the Wazir's absence.
4. The man whom I dispatched to Zorawar Singh from the place on the 23rd November with Raja Dhian Singh's Parwana has not yet returned. There are many possibilities of this – fall of snow, Zorawar Singh hemmed in, closure of Passes etc.

FDSC No. 84 of 21 March 1842

From J.D. Cunningham To G.R. Clerk
Camp Chooret
9 January 1842

1. On the 7th January I received your letter of 6th and 13th ultimo, and with reference to the most important points mentioned in them viz. my journey to the neighbourhood of the Sikh and Chinese Camps, I need only here observe, in addition to what I have said in previous communications and especially in my letter of the 6th instant that the inclemency of the season and the interested views of the Sikh authorities on the spot are likely to detain me in the neighbourhood of Shalkur for some time, although were I able to proceed eastward, I have no doubt from what I have seen and heard that I should be welcomed by the local Chinese functionaries, possibly however the leaders of the force from Lhasa may know the relations of England with China, and be informed officially with the usual dislike of us, while among the people we are only known as the mild and equitable rulers of India. As I find I am better situated at this place (Chooret or Shaktud) for obtaining information than at Shalkur, I propose to remain sometime longer, but in order that I may not press heavily upon villages belonging neither to ourselves, nor to the Sikhs, I will draw good amount of my supplies from Kunawar district.
2. In the first para of my letter of the 18th November, I mentioned that as I could obtain no satisfactory reply from the Sikh authorities in Spittee about the withholding of the Bissahir claims on that District, I had referred the case to Vazeer Zorawar Singh and indeed Mian Doolo Singh appears also to have done the same thing. There the matter now rests so far as redress is concerned, for no reply to my letter has so far reached me from the Vazeer. But I may take this opportunity of informing you of what I heard further on the subject. Jeewan Singh, the Sikh Agent with me, says he can not suppose that Zorawar Singh would

ever give any orders at variance with our rights and that he had heard instructions to withhold the 30 pieces of woollen cloth had been received from the Ludakhee subordinates of the Vazeer in Leh, but this opinion and this report are not entitled to any weight or credit and the Thanadar or Naib Thanadar of Spittee (both Ludakhees) assured me that when they were at Leh, on Zorawar Singh's return from Iskardo, he directed them to withhold what was due from Spittee to the Chinese and Koolloo Governments, and also for the present what was due to Bissahir, as when an agent of Bissahir Raja would come to him, he would settle what was to be done.

3. Mian Doolo Singh was now I understand sent to Spittee on a special business and his replies forwarded with my letter of the 18th November can not perhaps be considered as those of a proper authority and as conclusive, that no redress is to be obtained on the spot. He however has now left the district, and the Ludakhee Thanadar and his Deputy assure me they can do nothing without orders from Zorawar Singh or their immediate superior, Magna Ram. It is but justice to these men to say, that I think that they have been tutored not to confess that the order to withhold the 30 pieces of cloth originated with Zorawar Singh, though out of hearing of others, they have confessed to me what is perhaps the truth or at any rate what if known would tend to their disadvantage.
4. With regard to the Bissahir claims on the Chinese village of Gheo, I find on further enquiry that though the Rs. 7.50 had never been paid, they had never been demanded and that so far as I have yet ascertained no order has ever been given about the same due by Zorawar Singh or his subordinates. The headman of the village confesses the claim to be just, but as the Sikhs have exacted much from them, they hope the Raja of Bussahir may remit the amount this season. The above was the reply brought by the person usually sent to collect the money and who was deputed by my direction to the village. About a month ago, simply to ask the headmen whether they were ready to pay the sum as usual, and further one of the two headmen who

came to my camp, admitted to me in person that the claim was a just one, and that no orders had been received to withhold it.

5. The above is somewhat at variance with what I have written on the subject of the claims on Gheo, in the 5th para of my letter of the 8th November, and since I dispatched my letter of the 6th instant, I learn that Mian Doolo Singh has rather been guilty of unusual extortion than of embezzlement. I am sorry that I should have to modify any of my statements, but this is not the last occasion on which I may have to do so, for it is extremely difficult to get the truth and above all the whole truth out of a rude people who have little occasion to methodize their thoughts or to convey information in clear language and proper sequence.

Camp Chooret
9 January 1842

Sd.
J.D. Cunningham

FDSC No. 84 of 21 March 1842

Extract of a demi-official letter from Lt. Cunningham to G.R. Clerk, Chooret, 10 January 1842

No papers which I have given contain any account of Zorawar Singh's correspondence with or unacknowledged proposals to the Nepalese. I can only make out that some Goorkhas brought a letter to the Vazeer, and took back a reply, yet I would infer that he had some designs of wintering in Nepal; perhaps at your convenience you will let me have copies or abstracts of such papers, as may have bearing on the subject. For though I do not suppose Zorawar Singh's chief or even secondary object in taking Garoo was to propose to the Pandeys to drive us into the sea,[20] yet the correspondence will be curious.

Sd.
J.D. Cunningham

20. The Dogra invasion of Western Tibet provided an opportunity to Nepal to compensate itself for its losses in the Anglo-Gurkha War. King Rajendra sent his envoys to a large number of Indian states to create a grand anti-British coalition. He refused (March 1841) to make any commitment to a Ladakhi delegation regarding military aid against the Dogras. Instead he formulated a plan to make a simultaneous attack on Tibet and occupying a gold mine. His plans being thwarted by his advisers, he cultivated friendship with Zorawar Singh through the Gurkha governor of Jumla. In consequence, several missions were exchanged between this governor and Zorawar Singh. The Dogra-Gurkha alliance could not be consolidated due to differences over trade and the defeat of Zorawar Singh in the winter of 1841. Therefore, Nepal was constrained to explore other options to realize its ambitions. C.L. Datta, *Ladakh and Western Himalayan Politics*, pp. 172-176.

FDSC No. 100 of 20 March 1842

From	To
Agent to the GG	Secretary to the GOI
North West Frontier	Fort Williams
Camp Lahore	
15 March 1842	

I have long been apprehensive that the position which Lt. Cunningham had reached in progress to the eastward of Ludakh might under the suddenly altered state of affairs, these involve him in some embarrassing discussions.

It would perhaps be advisable in anticipation of coming struggle in Ludakh to make some little demonstration of our vigilance in the Hills.

The severity of the season has been the cause that my directions to him to withdraw to a less prominent position than that he had advanced to, have been so long in reaching. But it is satisfactory to find that at the date of his last letter he had nevertheless returned to Chango.

FDSC No. 101 of 30 March 1842

From J.D. Cunningham
Camp Chooret
2 February 1842

To Poiltical Agent
North West Frontier
Ludhiana

1. On the night of the 28th ultimo a man, whom I had dispatched to Hanle on the 18th December, returned to this place. He accompanied one sent by Jeewan Singh, the Lahore Agent, with a letter for Magna Ram about carriage and supplies for my journey towards the Indus and which I informed you in my communication of the 16th ultimo had been forwarded on to Ludakh by the Jamadar of Sipahees in Hanle. The reply was received at that place about the 16th ultimo and the Sipahees who brought it set for Chooret along with a cooly carrying his treasures and with my own and Jeewan Singh's messages on the road perished.
2. On the following night or that of the 29th ultimo, one of the two men, whom I had sent with a letter for the leaders of the Chinese army, returned from Tasheegong accompanied by a man of that place bringing letters for the heads of villagers in the neighbourhood. This man had also a letter for the Bassahir Agent with me from one of the authorities of Tasheegong to the effect that my letter for the Chinese leaders had been forwarded on to them by my other messenger along with a man of his own.
3. From the stories of these men I gather that Zorawar Singh committed the fatal error of moving from his camp near Mienser or Missur to relieve his outposts in the Poorungh district, that a battle took place between the Sikhs and the Chinese at Kurdar immediately to the south of the Lakes (the Gurdon or Garendha of our maps), about the end of December or the beginning of January, when Zorawar Singh was killed by a ball through the head when hastening in person to support his main body, which apparently was either disordered by the Chinese or could make no impression on them and that the Sikhs

fled as soon as their leader fell and suffered severely from the pursuing Chinese.[21] I learn also that detachment of troops in Garoo, Tasheegong and other places fled towards Ludakh and that many of these men, as well as of the fugitives from the field of battle, were set upon at night and killed by the people of the country. It appears that verbal orders from the principal Chinese head or Kalon, Zoorkung, had been received at that place to put to death the Sipahees who might be there. Similar orders by message have been issued for the Tasheegong authorities to the heads of the villages in their neighbourhood, with regard to the post of Chooret, while in writing they have been told by the same authorities to follow their example and repair immediately to the Chinese headquarters.

4. I further gather from the messenger that Nono Sonam, the brother of the first Raja set up in Ludakh by the Sikhs, as well as Gumbo, the favourite of the dispossessed ruler, had joined the Chinese, that Ahmad Shah of Iskardo was killed at the same time as Zorawar Singh. That Gulam Khan had been made a prisoner. But that other Ludakhees of some rank had as yet escaped by flight. The Chinese army is now described as amounting to 2,000 men and

---

21. Modern writers have identified factors for the defeat of Zorawar Singh. The Dogra general wrongly judged that conditions would be similar to Ladakh which was peopled by unwarlike peasants. The invading army had advanced too far in an inhospitable and barren land, while the supply lines had not been put in place and no assistance could arrive from Ladakh or Kishtwar. The invading army was a motley assemblage of Dogras, Ladakhis and Baltis, who showed lack of common interest. The troops were ill equipped to deal with the intense cold at an altitude of over 15,000 feet. On the other hand, the Tibetans not only enjoyed the support and protection of the Chinese, but also had the advantage of fighting on home ground as well as superiority in numbers. Janet Rizvi, *Ladakh: Crossroads of High Asia*, Oxford University Press, Delhi, 1983, p. 65; C.L. Datta, *General Zorawar Singh: His Life and Achievements in Ladakh, Baltistan and Tibet*, Deep & Deep Publications, New Delhi, 1984, pp. 77-78.

one hundred tents of the Goorkhas are said to be present with it. From what I hear, I infer that all the troops are provincials and that Vazeer Zoorkung is himself a native of Lhasa, one indeed of the four deputies of the two Rokong villages.

5. The general rumour still is that the Chinese will advance on Ludakh and, from what I hear, I doubt not they will be welcomed by the people of the country. In other month, they may be on their way to that city and I am therefore very desirous of receiving some instructions with regard to this probable movement. In your letter indeed of the 15th December, you say that we will prevent any encroachments of the Chinese which may be injurious to ourselves, but this scarcely meets the case in point as Chinese rule in Ludakh would perhaps be less disadvantageous to our interests than Sikh rule has been.
6. My Hanle messenger states that when these orders were received from Ludakh to have supplies in readiness on the main road for a body of 400 Putans [Pathans] about to march towards the Lakes and that he heard of the arrival of this detachment near about a third of this way towards Gartok. At the same time, however, that is about the middle of January reports became numerous regarding the death of Zorawar Singh and two days after he left Hanle, he says, he heard of the retreat of the force towards Leh. This man also met at Hanle one of the two Sipahees whom I dispatched from this place in November last with Dhian Singh's Parwana for the Wazeer (Zorawar Singh). The soldier simply said that he was on his way to Ludakh, but that the Parwana had been taken on by his companion and by my own two messengers of Kunawar. He also gave the man a letter from Meean Doolo Singh there in Sirahee (between Shalkur and Tasheegong) to the Sipahees of this place, which concluded by saying that a battle had taken place between the Sikhs and Chinese in which a few of the former and many of the latter were killed. Sirahee however is off the road and Meean Doolo Singh was not likely to learn the truth at an early date.

7. I do not think that any reasonable doubt can now be entertained of the death of Zorawar Singh and of the dispersion of the Sikh army – both events are implicitly believed by the people of this neighbourhood, and the heads of the villages were, and still are, ready to act on the verbal message of the Tasheegong authorities, and put to death the Sikhs near them. On 29 January 1842, I heard from my Hanle messenger that such an order would be given to the heads of villages. I let these men understand that I was aware of the directions they would receive and that I hoped no violence would be done, as such seemed unnecessary. The order was delivered by the Tasheegong messenger that evening and only the next morning people were dispatched to collect the peasantry of the other places. I then sent to the headmen and recommended them to consider what they were about to do – that it would not be well if they killed anyone in my presence, as it were, as if I had come here to do them good in a peaceful way and that probably the Sikhs would now go of themselves, especially as they knew they were to vacate the Chinese provinces. They replied that out of deference to me, they would not kill the men, but that it was absolutely necessary they made them prisoners.
8. Next morning i.e. on 31 January 1842, the heads of villages wrote to the Bassahar Agent with me that they had received the orders of Chinese superior at Tasheegong to put the Sikhs at this place to death, that in accordance with my wish they would only secure their persons at present, that they were ready to secure them, and that if I would not assist them in making the men prisoners, they wished me to give them permission to set about doing so in their own way. I told the headmen to come to me in the evening, when I would speak to them on the subject. I soon perceived that – the hope of recovering some of their property now in the fort and the expectation that, if they got rid of the Sikhs, they would be spared the distinctive presence of their own troops – were their own chief motives for desiring to put the men here to death and, as they admitted that the Chinese leaders had not sent them

any orders direct, nor denied the Tasheegong authorities to give them any about cutting off the detachment, they soon agreed that the soldiers should have the option of going away quietly with their arms in their hands, but towards the Deputy Thanadar, the active instrument of oppressing them, their animosity was such that they would only consent to spare his life until they should receive orders from their superiors about him. Before coming to any final resolution however, they said, they would like to speak with the headman of a neighbouring village, who was expected the following day.

9. Yesterday i.e. 1 February 1842 I told the Bassahar Agent to talk with the headmen about their intentions and to endeavour to show them that if they now seized the Deputy Thanadar or adopted any other violent measures, the Sipahees would probably from their villages destroy their cattle and retreat to Spittee, that they should well consider what means they had of resistance than 18 men here stationed and that although they might seize 3 or 4 wandering about, 14 or 15 well armed soldiers would remain to revenge the death of their comrades. The headmen confessed they had very few matchlocks indeed and said they would not do anything just now. They wished one however to tell the Sipahees to go away and I agreed to explain to the men how matters stood with regard to the Wazir and their main army and different detachments.

10. This morning I sent for Jeewan Singh, the Lahore Agent, and I told him what I knew of the fate of Zorawar Singh and added that, to my knowledge, the people of the country believed the reports and considered that the best way of avoiding the punishment they knew they deserved for submitting quietly to Zorawar Singh would be by killing all the Sikhs they could lay hands on; that apparently no one of the army remained to give orders to the post here or at least cared about doing so that the Jamadar of the detachment as he knew had absconded, that perhaps two months must elapse before instructions could come from Ludakh, that in the meantime one

detachment might be cut off and the men thus fall on useless sacrifice to a point of honour among themselves or to the culpable negligence of superior officers, that he (Jeewan Singh) was aware of the orders of his Government to evacuate the Chinese province that I thought he could under the circumstances take before himself to give what directives were best and that if he believed in Zorawar Singh's death, the men should retire. Jeewan Singh is now counseling with the men as to what they should do, but I do not suppose they will come to any resolution for a day or two.

11. I had little hesitation in giving the above advice first because I believed that all the Sikhs in the country were now intent only on their own safety. Secondly, because in the absence of all authorities the men might well act on the orders of Dhian Singh and, thirdly, because I know the neighbouring villages were bent on putting the men to death. I had little hesitation either in trying to dissuade the headmen of the villages from their purpose, as from the first I expected the motives of an unmanly people and soon learnt that the harshest crime of self interest chiefly moved them to strive unfancied severity, but in the business generally my difficulty has been to prevent a cruel effusion of blood without giving orders to Chinese subjects and the difficulty is the greater as in the servile minds of Asiatics, the hopes or wishes of a person in authority are readily confounded with a command and as the people here would gladly exchange the Lhasa rule for our own at my bidding, the headmen of villages would lay aside their remission against the Sikhs, but they would do so in the belief that Garoo was to become an English province. Similarly I have found the native authorities of Ludakh more desirous of meeting my wishes than of obeying the orders of Jeewan Singh, the Lahore Agent.

12. As I experienced more difficulty than expected in drawing supplies from Spittee and Kunawar and saw that I was pressing hard on the people here especially for firewood, I had made up my mind a week ago to return to Shalkur or rather to Chango which is near it,

where wood is less scarce than here about. The recent turn of affairs has made it the more advisable that I should be encamped where either my own orders or those of the Sikh Agent are current, and I only await the arrival of coolies to set out from this place.

13. As Vazeer Lakhpat, who arrived from Jammoo during the summer, is now the principal Sikh authority in Ludakh, I have written to him to know what orders he has received regarding the Chinese provinces.
14. It is difficult to say in what light the Chinese authorities will view our interference between them and the Sikhs, neither do I know to what extent the Government may consider it expedient to take part in the affairs of Ludakh, but I may here remark that if active measures are resolved on we must depend on our own provinces, or upon Cashmere for grain of all kinds, that the cavalry soldiers of the plains will be useless in Tibet, a few company soldiers and that some ponies of the country would do good service and that some pieces of artillery, mortars, howitzers or guns, would be of great use, provided they could be taken to pieces and carried sometimes for several marches on man's shoulders. The most serviceable men in these countries would evidently be our Hill Battalions and Light Infantry regiments and the quantum of baggage should be the smallest possible, compatible with continued efficiency in a cold but variable climate.

Postscript:

Last night two men, whom I had sent on 8 January 1842 via Hanle with a letter to Zorawar Singh, expressing my surprise that I had received no reply to my first communication, returned to Chooret. They left Hanle on 22nd January bringing back my letter, as they were assured of Zorawar Singh's death. The Sikh soldiers stationed there had fled, though it is a part of Ludakh proper – an advance party of Chinese had, it was said, occupied Garoo and a detachment of 300 men was on its way to Rudhok by the north bank of the Indus. Meean Doolo Singh whose report of the battle in Poorung, I have quoted in this letter, had fled to Ludakh.

FDSC No. 102 of 30 March 1842

From J.D. Cunningham To G.R. Clerk
Camp Chango
22 February 1842

1. The information which I have received from my messengers now confirm the account of affairs which I gave in my letter dated 2 February 1842 to you, but there are some variations as to the particulars. I am now disposed to believe that Zorawar Singh was killed so long ago as 12 December 1841, though the fact was not known at Tasheegong until early in January, as a Ghat or Pass near Gangree remained closed for some time after the action. The account now I have is as follows:
2. Zorawar Singh heard of the near approach of the Chinese about the 7 November 1841 and immediately sent the Ludakhee (Nonoo Sannum) with 300 men to oppose them. This detachment was nearly all cut up by the Lhasa troops, then encamped at Kurdun, to the south of the Lakes. Nonoo Sannum however escaped and on 19th November he was again sent with another Ludakhee Golam Khan and 600 men to drive back the Chinese. The party was cut up and the two leaders made prisoners. Zorawar Singh then moved from his camp at Tirtha Pooree with his whole available force amounting to 3,000 men and he seems to have maintained a desultory kind of battle for the Chinese for three days (10th, 11th and 12th December 1841).[22] On the third day, he was hit by a ball

22. Tirthapuri was situated on the western edge of the holy country comprising the two great lakes and Mount Kailash. It was three days march from Darchen on the river Sutlej. The locality has acquired a peculiar interest for devotees and pilgrims, owing to a combination of sulphur springs and ancient traditions. This was believed to be the spot where Parvati manoeuvered the destruction of a demon who dared to misuse the powers secured from Shiva. The local monastery was found in a picturesque site at the junction of three valleys, with the river Sutlej winding through large tracts

in the shoulder and falling from his horse, was immediately surrounded and slain, his main army fled in all the directions and 600 men, who he had with him (as a reserve) were made prisoners. 6000 fighting men and followers are said to have perished during the three days battle and in petty actions before and afterwards with scattered detachments. Those however of these men appear to have been killed by exposure to the weather than by the hands of the enemy, and as the Chinese are said to have numbered 10,000 men, I can not but think the Vazeer acted most imprudently in abandoning a good position at such a season especially as the road to Garoo seems to be liable to be closed by snow.

3. Ahmad Shah of Iskardo was taken prisoner and not killed as I before mentioned. A Ludakhee by name Nasko (Bazgo) Kalon was also made prisoner. This man and Nonoo Sannum have been sent to Lhasa (along with 600 soldiers, Zorawar Singh's reserve) because they had been instrumental in bringing the Sikhs into Ludakh. Golam Khan had the flesh torn from his limbs and was thrown out to die, as he had been active in plundering temples. Ahmad Shah and his son are apparently treated well, and Gumbo the favourite of the late king of Ludakh is in high favour. Some Ludakhee and Balti men are all said to have gone off under a promise to assassinate Magna Ram, Zorawar Singh's brother-in-law and also some others. The detachment at Rudock is said to have been cut up.[23]

---

of green grass. A sacred circuit has been marked by funeral memorials (chortens) and piles of stones. Hindus and Buddhists went across the holy way amidst some of the most beautiful surroundings in western Tibet. Charles A. Sherring, *Western Tibet and the Indian Borderland*, pp. 284-286.

23. The Tibetans appear to have subjected Zorawar Singh's mortal remains to cruelty. As soon as the Dogra general had fallen, according to a popular story, the Tibetans rushed upon him and pulled out his hair, which was like eagle's feathers all over his body, as they wished to keep it for the future good fortune. His flesh was cut up into small portions and every family in the district

4. There are two Kahlons or Vazeers present with the Chinese army as deputies of the Peking Viceroy. My messenger found out one in Garoo with 1,000 Lhasa soldiers, the other was expected in a few days with a like number of men of the same country. A considerable detachment of Lhasa men also had returned to that place, escorting prisoners, but the greater part of the Chinese force seems to have been composed of the population of districts immediately to the north and east of the Lakes and the soldiers have been sent to their homes owing to the scarcity of supplies.

---

carried away a piece, suspending it from the roof of their house. According to popular belief, the mere presence of the flesh of such a great man must necessarily confered a brave heart on the possessor. A rumour claimed that these pieces sweated for many a long day, a sign regarded by the most sceptical as indicative of the dead general's bravery. Interestingly, a large funerary memorial (chorten) has been erected over the bones of the deceased at Toyo (two miles from Taklakot), the place being regarded with veneration. Charles A. Sherring, *Western Tibet and Indian Borderland*, pp. 197-198.

FDSC No. 102 of 30 March 1842

From J.D. Cunningham To G.R. Clerk
Camp Chango
22 February

1. In my communication of the 22nd instant, I mentioned that the letter which I had written to the Chinese Sardar had been forwarded on from Tasheegong by a man of that place and by one of my own messengers. On the 8th instant, the latter returned from Garoo (which he left on the 26th ultimo) accompanied by one of the sons of the Tasheegong authorities, who was ordered by the Chinese Wazir (Zoorkang) to be the bearer of his reply to me. Unfortunately these men were attacked near Hanleh (in Ludakh) by some fugitive Sikh Sipahees formerly on duty with Meean Doolo Singh in Spittee and they, to save their lives, abandoned their baggage in which were the Chinese Wazir's letter and some pieces of cloth intended as a present. I am thus perhaps ignorant of the light in which my mission is viewed by the Chinese. But from the manner in which my messenger has talked to and from the statements of the young man who has accompanied him, I have many reasons to suppose that the reply to my letter was friendly. Still the Chinese appear to have some suspicions with regard to our interference, as the young man above mentioned was desired to hint to the Bassahar Agent with me that there would be some difficulty in supplying me with provisions, if I now marched towards Garoo owing to the exactions of the Sikhs and that it would be much better that I went back. By the Chinese messenger I have sent a second letter to this effect that I was now in our own territory and that my present intention was to remain where I was until I received instructions from my superiors. I have also to say that when the Sikhs should have withdrawn or been expelled from Garoo, I had looked forward to a period of peace and to the renewal of trade, but I have heard that he was about to carry the war into Ludakh instead

of seeking redress from the Sikhs by negotiation; however, I conclude that common report might be wrong in this case as in many others.

2. A deputation from Nepal waited upon the Chinese leaders to proffer assistance, but it was told that the Goorkhas would not be required at present.
3. Concerning the march of troops from Lhasa and the deputation of men of high rank, I presume the court of Nepal has accurate information and that it is not concealed from our Resident. I presume also that Hodgson will be informed by the Durbar, if a requisition is made by the Chinese for Goorkha aid to drive the Sikhs out of Ludakh.
4. The Chinese leaders are now making enquiries about the Sikh force in Ludakh and their talk is that if necessary both of them will go, but they suppose the presence of one with a portion of their force will be sufficient. In their opinion, they may be right if they reach Ludakh by the beginning of March (for the whole country is in their favour and the Sikh troops there can not much exceed a thousand men), but it seems plain that they can not retain Ludakh for a month with such troops as they have against the force which Goolab Singh may pour into the country by the end of April. Thus if the Lhasa authorities are bent on retaining Ludakh, it is not likely, the war will soon end.
5. I do not at present see any reason to suppose that we shall be confounded with the Sikhs or that our dependencies will be invaded, but even if we remain entirely neutral, Goolab Singh will most likely make as free use of our friendship in his talk and in his communications as to cause us to be suspected, it may therefore be prudent to show ourselves ready for action and to prevent any violation of our frontier by keeping a small force during the summer months close upon the boundary line.
6. The post of Chooret has been relinquished or abandoned by the Sikh detachment, but I regret to say not without bloodshed. When the Sipahees were told about Zorawar

Singh's death and dispersal of his army and of the order to put them to the sword, they seemed willing to retire on the terms I mentioned in my letter of the 20th (February 1842) instant viz. with arms in their hands. After however recovering from the first surprise, they affected to disbelieve the Vazeer's (Zorawar Singh's) death, nor was the Lahore Agent disposed to put entire confidence in my assurances, but as I considered it an object to get the men away without any collision, I put on paper my belief and my opinion that he, the Agent should take upon himself to give orders to the men to do what he thought best. The document would I consider remove all responsibility from him, but still he will not give the necessary order, though their Jamadar (or immediate superior) had deserted them some weeks previous and they were thus without a proper head.

7. In the meantime, the forcible seizure of the Deputy Thanadar somewhat enraged the soldiers and on the 4th instant I arranged with him and the Headman that they should vacate the fort the next morning carrying away with them their arms and all their personal property, except what they had taken from the neighbouring villages, but leaving the stores etc. in the fort untouched. They were also to be accompanied to the boundary line by men on my part and on the part of the Heads of the villages and one of the latter agreed to remain with me as a kind of hostage until the men should get beyond the frontier. As the Sipahees however appear to have domineered without mercy over the Bhotee population in Ludakh and elsewhere and as they had somewhat recovered from their alarm, their pride and overweening presumption got the upper hand and when the time came for them to depart they told my messenger that they must have three years pay before they went and also have their expenses provided to Lahore, I assured them I would advance money to the Maharaja's Agent for the latter purpose, but with regard to their pay I could do nothing. The Sipahees then said that they would not go at all and told my people to make a particular sign when they went

to get water as they intended to fire on all others who came near the fort. On hearing this determination, I asked the Headmen not to adopt any violent means while I should be in Chooret to which they at once agreed. I also asked the Sipahees to keep quiet during my further stay of a few days to which they at the time accepted.

8. On the 6th (February 1842) instant the Sipahees seized two men of another village on their way to Chooret. They beat one and confined the other. They also seized some sheep grazing near the fort but, on my representation that this was not according to their promise, they released both the men and the animals. On the 7th instant their courage or confidence abated and I arranged in writing with them and the Headmen that they should go away the next morning with all they chose to take of their own, and be accompanied to the frontier as before stated, but that the stores etc. must be left in good order. The next day the villagers were ready to act upon the agreement but the Sipahees, when I sent for them, said that it was a holiday and they would not go then, while going about another time, they said that they would consider. I then told both the parties, they must hereafter make their own arrangements as all my endeavours were vain.

9. On the afternoon of the 8th (February 1842), the messengers alluded to in the beginning of this letter arrived and, on the part of the Chinese leaders, brought direct orders to cut off the detachment. The Heads of villages again came to me and said that they were still willing to let the Sipahees go on the terms last agreed on. I sent for Jeewan Singh, the Lahore Agent, and reassured him of the death of Zorawar Singh etc. and put on paper my opinion that he ought to order the men to go on the terms last came to. This Parwana was circulated to remove all responsibility from him, even should his master be inclined to blame him. He however gave them no distinct order, but sent them a copy of my Parwana with an addition of his own that, if they did not go, they would have themselves to blame for the consequences.

Their reply was that they would consider about going, but this I did not learn till the following day.

10. Before daybreak the next morning, the men without informing anyone decamped taking with them all they could carry and, after rendering the spare arms on the fort temporarily useless and destroying the ammunition and better kind of stores; at half past seven, the Heads of villages asked me if the Sipahees had gone in that fashion by my direction. I replied that most likely they had gone in consequence of what I had written to Jeewan Singh, but that they had not kept faith in any way and that I would not hold myself responsible for the mode of their going. At 9 O'clock they repeated the same question and added that if I had not told the Sipahees to go in that manner, they would fall on them. I replied that I could give them an order or advice, but to take care not to cross the British boundary if they went in pursuit of them. The villagers set off and overtook the Sipahees struggling in twos or threes, they killed ten and took two wounded men prisoners. Two others concealed themselves and the remainder four crossed the boundary somewhere before the villagers could come up with them. I have got one of those wounded out of their hands and I think they will be persuaded to send the others to me.
11. The Sipahees on getting a paper from the Lahore Agent, seemed to have argued with themselves that it would bear them out in leaving the fort and that under its cover they could do some mischief with impunity. I believe the villagers would not have followed them had I desired them not to do so, but in that case the Chinese leader would assuredly have been told that I had authorized the Sikhs to destroy the property in the fort and had advised them in so doing and so the Sipahees did not care to risk a misrepresentation prejudicial to the Government, nor did I think that humanity required more of me than I had already done. The Sipahees put themselves out of my protection and chose to risk a pursuit by their faithless and wanton conduct and the villagers chose to risk themselves to gratify their revenge.

12. In the 7th Para, I mention that the Deputy Thanadar, a Mohammedan of Leh, had fallen into the hands of the Chinese villagers. They got possession of him however by no means in the way I could have wished. About 10 O'clock on the night of the 2nd instant, people were heard moving about in different directions when suddenly Meerchoong, the Deputy Thanadar, rushed into my servant's room (within a few yards of my tent) closely followed by 30 or 40 villagers armed with sticks. The Headmen were not among them, but they came on being sent for and said they had watched marching and finding him about to escape, they had followed him. The man appeared really to have tried to escape and he had with him 1,000 rupees in cash. As all parties however were a good deal excited, I thought his life might possibly be taken and accordingly said I would retain charge of him until the morning when I would do with him as seemed to be the best. On this assurance, the people after a time quietly dispersed.
13. To deliver up a person who has sought our protection does some violence to the generous feelings of our nature and in almost any circumstances, in the present case however I had but little right to be on Chinese ground, nor could that nor my good intention entitle me to invest any two or three tents etc. and Havildars guard with the privilege of our own territory or of British Camp and, if I had assured my little encampment to be inviolable, I might soon had more refugees to protect than men to defend them with, for the soldiers in the neighbouring fort might have sought the same asylum as the runaway Thanadar.
14. I was satisfied that I had no right to continue my protection to the fugitive, but I was in some little doubt as to whom I should give him for the Sikhs, more still the de facto though not rightful ancestors of the place and I was there as much in virtue of their strength as of Chinese goodwill. My doubt however was soon at an end. In the morning I asked the Sipahees if they wished to give protection to the Deputy Thanadar. They said they did

not, that when they first heard of Zorawar Singh's death, they had told him to remain with them in the fort so that what happened to one might happen to all, that he without letting them had quitted the fort on the preceding morning and that as he had voluntarily left their protection they would not now increase their own difficulties by again taking charge of him. Such being then the determination, I had not thought any pretext save personal feeling for keeping the man out of the hands of the Chinese and the Heads of villagers accordingly took possession of him.

15. I stayed in Chooret so many weeks as I did because I was more in the way of getting information there than at Shalkur. But though that end has been ensured and served, I have been forced by circumstances to become a party in some unpleasant and awkward affairs. I hope, however, that neither Government nor yourself will see cause to disprove of my conduct. I was careful to avoid assuming any authority and giving orders to foreign subjects – Sikhs or Chinese – but I used the influence of our name to spare if possible a needless effusion of blood.
16. From the foregoing narrative, you will perceive that the Sikh Agent with me does not consider himself invested with any authority even over a common soldier with regard to the affairs of Tibet, while his timidity or indifference prevented him taking on himself any responsibility. His instructions appear only to reach to supplying me with provisions, but if Government proposed to take any part in the probable contest for Ludakh between the Sikhs and Chinese, the Lahore Agent with me should I think be informed of the views of his own Government and be vested with some discretionary power.

Camp Chango J.D. Cunningham

FDSC No. 10 of 31 August 1842

From J.D. Cunningham
Shalkur
4 March 1842

To G.R. Clerk

Subject: Intelligence about the Affairs of Ludakh

1. A man who left Leh about the beginning of February 1842 reached me today. He says that the Sikh troops have betaken themselves to the two forts in the neighbourhood of that town, one of which is a new one, built by Zorawar Singh, soon after he got possession of this place. The man adds that the nominal king is at large which does not seem likely, and the Ludakhees had written to the Chinese leaders, that they could not do as desired viz. assassinate Magna Ram and others owing to the amount of the Sikh force stationed near the city. The accounts given by this man all go to show that the Sikhs have now no authority in Ludakh except in the immediate vicinity of their troops.
2. One of the two men whom I dispatched in January by the road of Tholing with a duplicate of my letter to the Chinese Vizeer returned some days ago. This man says that two only of the Sikh detachments in Tholing had escaped towards Ludakh, and has brought me an original order from the Zeang Pene or Commandant of Chuprung to the heads of villages and to the Koopun or Chief of Commanders of ten of the local levies east and west of Chuprung,[24] to the effect that Zorawar Singh had been killed on the 12th or 13th December last, and that they were to hold themselves in readiness to proceed to Garoo when called on.

---

24. The village of Chaprang was situated below the plateau of Gyanema and in the valley of the Sutlej. Standing at an altitude of 12,400 feet, it served as the summer residence of Jongpen, an executive officer who was subordinate to the Garpon stationed at Gartok and superior to the Tarjum. The Mana Pass in Garhwal led from the area near the temple of Kedarnath to Chaprang. Traders from Bashahr and Tehri Garhwal visited Chaprang. Charles A. Sherring, *Western Tibet and the Indian Borderland*, pp. 326, 338, 340.

FDSC No. 11 of 31 August 1842

From J.D. Cunningham To G.R. Clerk
Camp Nako, Near Shalkur
13 March 1842

Subject: Report of Intelligence about Ludakh

1. With reference to Para 1 of my letter of 12th ultimo, mentioning that messengers conveying to me a letter and some pieces of silk on the part of the Chinese leaders, had been plundered of these articles by a party of fugitive Sikh soldiers. I have to inform you that yesterday pieces of silk were brought to me by a servant of Gumbo, the favourite of late Raja of Ludakh, together with a piece of cloth on the part of that person himself. The man says that his master being on his way to Ludakh, fell in with the Sipahees above alluded to and having heard of the loss of the letter and silks, he demanded both from them The Sipahees gave him the silks, but said that they had destroyed the letter. Gumbo has not sent me any written communication.
2. In my letter of 2nd ultimo, I stated that Gumbo had deserted to the Chinese, but from the statement of his servant, it appears he was made prisoner, a not willing one perhaps. The man's story is as follows:

   When the Lhasa army approached the Mansarovar Lake, the Chinese leaders wrote to Zorawar Singh that it would be well if he would settle the affairs of Ludakh and Garoo with them in a peaceful way. Zorawar Singh would not listen to this proposal, but immediately dispatched a small force under Nonoo Sunnum and Goolam Khan to drive back the Chinese. This force was defeated. Zorawar Singh then sent Gumbo and Goolam Khan to treat with the Chinese leaders, but immediately set out himself with his whole army towards the Chinese camp. The Chinese leaders on hearing this said, Zorawar Singh was trifling with them and made Gumbo and Goolam Khan prisoners; soon after this the battle so fatal to the Sikhs took place.

3. With regard to Gumbo's proceeding to Ludakh, his servant simply says, he was told to go there, and that the Chinese will follow him. The man also says the Chinese wish rather to arrange with the holders of Ludakh for the regular transmission of the usual presents to the Grand Lama and for the Viceroys in Lhasa, than to enter into a contest with the Sikhs for the possession of the country itself. They may of course give their designs this colour if they see the Rajas are quick in pouring a large force into Ludakh.

FDSC No. 89 of 30 March 1842

From G.R. Clerk To T.A. Maddock
Agent to the GG, NWFA
Secretary to the GG-in-C
7 March 1842

I am sending an extract of a demi-official letter from Lt. Cunningham dated 29th January last.

Though it would appear from his letter that the designs of the Chinese against Ludakh, which I some time ago anticipated, will soon in all probability be undertaken. I shall continue to require Lt. Cunningham to conform to the instructions of Government of dates of the 24th January and 7th ultimo (February) which were intended for his guidance in such a case.

FDSC No. 89 of 30 March 1842

Subject: Chinese Designs on Ludakh

Extract from a demi official Report from J.D. Cunningham to G.R. Clerk from Camp Chooret dated 29 January 1842

My messenger relates very circumstantially the death of Vizeer Zorawar Singh and the consequent desperation of the Sikh army. Perhaps about the 20th December the Vizeer was shot through the head in an action with the Chinese and his troops took to flight as soon as the leader fell. The Chinese have seized all the Sikh posts by force or they have secretly assassinated the Sipahees composing the weak detachments guarding them. Two of the principal of Ludakhees viz. Gumbo and Nonoo Sunnum had gone over to the Chinese, others had fled, while some had been made prisoners. Ahmed Shah of Iskardu had been killed in action.

My messenger further says that the Chinese force has been considerably increased since it reached the Lakes, and that every one believes it will march on Ludakh in a very short time.

FDSC No. 146 of 29 June 1842

Subject: Intelligence about Tibetan Movements

From J.D. Cunningham To G.R. Clerk
Camp Leo on the Spittee River
1 April 1842

1. Last night two men, whom I had sent towards the Indus by the Ludakh road returned to my camp. They say that a detachment of two Chinese was on its way to Leh. When hearing that the small pox had broken out in that city, the party had halted at Aimamen about 8 marches east of Leh. They were also told that most of the people of Leh had betaken themselves to the forts in its neighbourhood along with the Sikhs, by which perhaps may be understood that the Sikhs had forced the principal people to leave their homes and remain with them as hostages.
2. With regard to the march of a detachment from Garoo to occupy Spittee, of which I had heard, these two men say, it is understood that if the Spittee authorities do not tender their submission, a small force will proceed to occupy the valley as soon the road is open. So far as my messengers learnt, the Spittee people had not been called upon to join the Chinese and, from the Thanadar of Spittee himself, I hear that he had as yet only received a message from the manager of Tasheegong to give up the horse and other property with him of Magna Ram, the brother-in-law of Zorawar Singh; a requisition he had for the present evaded on the plea I presume that the roads were not passable.
3. My messengers were told that a party of Bultee men would march from Iskardo to cooperate with the Chinese.

FDSC No. 24 of 22 June 1842

Subject: Cunningham's Intelligence about Ludakh

From G.R. Clerk — T.H. Maddock
Agent to the GG, NWFA — Secretary to GOI
1 May 1842

1. I am sending a letter from J.D. Cunningham on affairs on the Thibetan frontier.
2. Governor-General may perhaps see no impropriety in constituting Lt. Cunningham a mediator between the Lhasa and Ludakh authorities, should they incline to listen to advice from the British Government, and should their differences assume a form seeming to render them susceptible of living by such means adjusted.
3. Raja Goolab Singh having now proceeded by Dak to Drassel, on the east of Cashmere, it will be found that his energetic command will soon turn the tide of success in favour of his mountaineers again. He and his brother would be very averse to desist from this conflict without establishing their frontier towards Thibet on such a footing, as to place the wool and tea, trade of Cashmere, beyond all risk of deterioration, of opium, the property of Sikh merchants, simultaneously with that destroyed at Canton, belonging to British merchants. It would be scarcely reasonable to expect some day to see Cashmere in the heart of an empire of their own.[25]

---

25. Owing to the nature of his dealings with the neighbouring chiefs, Lahore Darbar after Ranjit Singh's demise and the British, Gulab Singh emerged as a controversial figure. It was true that he created a large independent kingdom, enforced rigorous measures for maintaining law and order, outlawed Sati and female infanticide, and guarded Kashmir's monopoly of Pashmina trade from the British onslaught. On the negative side, his land revenue system was oppressive, his administration denied any significant role to the Muslims and his army suffered from neglect in training and equipment. A shrewd diplomat, he was skilled in the art of

management of men and affairs. Single minded in the pursuit of his personal ambition, he was seen as a rank opportunity, a ruthless tyrant and an unprincipled liar. Parshotam Mehra, *A Dictionary of Modern Indian History 1707-1947*, Oxford University Press, Delhi, 1985, p. 276.

FDSC No. 25 of 22 June 1842

From J.D. Cunningham To G.R. Clerk
Camp Nako on the River Spittee
28 April 1842

1. Although from Secretary Maddock's letters of the 7th March and 21st March to your address, Government appears desirous of avoiding all participation in the disputes between the Sikhs and the Chinese authorities in Thibet, I nevertheless think it proper to draw your attention to some of the more prominent points of discussion, which are likely to arise between the two parties, especially as both the Jammoo Rajas and the Lhasa Vizeer may become anxious for our mediation.
2. From the letters of the Lhasa Vizeer Zoorkung, to my address which I forwarded to you on the 9th instant (April 1842), you will perceive that he attaches considerable importance to the periodical deputations from Ludakh to Lhasa. The Vizeer says, these deputations went to do obeisance, but I believe they merely conveyed presents from the Raja to the Chief Lama, who occasionally sent presents in return. My information however on this point is not satisfactory, but whether the presents were merely sent as a mark of religious respect, as I think they were, or in the way of ordinary friendship between two princes; the Chinese will no doubt arrogate to themselves a superiority of long standing and urge the continuance of the presents as essential to a good understanding between the two Governments. On the other hand, Raja Goolab Singh will be most unwilling to consider himself a feudatory of Lhasa, but as he appears to have adopted a double form of Government in Ludakh and to have kept up titular Raja, he may not object to allow him to send devotional offerings to the head of his religion; perhaps also the Chinese may not object to such an arrangement, as to themselves, they can put upon it what construction they please.

3. The Lhasa Vizeer has sent as prisoners to that capital the following persons of some rank besides a considerable party of Sikh troops. Rae Singh, the second-in- command, when Zorawar Singh was killed, Nonoo Sunnum, the brother of the person, first made titular Raja of Ludakh by the Sikhs and also Basko Kahlon, another Ludakhee of some consideration. The Lhasa Vizeer likewise holds Ahmad Shah, the deposed Raja of Iskardo in a kind of honourable durance. The Sikhs may demand the release of all the prisoners, and though the Chinese may not object to give up Ahmad Shah, who is near Garoo, the restoration of those now in Lhasa may be less easily agreed to.
4. During the occupation of the Garoo district by the Sikhs, they appear to have plundered several temples, and also to have carried off a good deal of private property. The Chinese may justly claim the value of all this property and some compensation for the injury generally inflicted on the country, as the price of immediate peace. With regard to plundering temples, the Sikhs may however say, that was the act of one Goolam Khan more immediately than of others, and that the Chinese having taken retribution in their own hands by putting him to death after he was made prisoner, they can not well now demand the value of the property he carried away.
5. The Chinese may threaten to stop all trade to Ludakh unless their demands are agreed to, and as the prosperity of Cashmere depends on its manufacture of shawls, and as there is also a considerable trade in tea to that country, the threat may have much weight with the Jammoo Rajas. Nearly all the shawl wool is produced in the districts of Garoo and Rohtuk, and the sale would not be greatly diminished, were it disposed off at our town of Ram Pore on the Sutlej instead of at Leh. Much of the wool indeed sold at the former place, is taken as far as Noor Poor, which is about midway between Cashmere and Simla and probably the price in Cashmere itself would not be enhanced to 10 percent by the more circuitous route. All the tea sold in Cashmere and Ludakh comes either

through Lhasa or Yarkand, and the trade in it could therefore be put an end to without difficulty.

6. On the whole it appears that the Sikhs may lose more than they can gain, if they show any pertinacity in their discussions with China, for I presume we will not allow them to carry points by threatening to reoccupy the Garoo and adjoining districts or at least by actually proceeding to reoccupy them, as we have already in a manner pledged ourselves not to permit them to be aggressors on that quarter.
7. My messengers report the march from Lhasa,[26] of a body of soldiers of Chinese proper. The reinforcement however is perhaps not a large one, as I have generally understood, that 1,000 genuine Chinese troops only are maintained in Lhasa district. The Chinese leaders were still respectively in Garoo and in Poorungtz to the south of the Lakes.

---

26. Lhasa (Place of Gods), the largest town in Tibet, served as the capital of this kingdom. Founded in 400 AD, it was situated on the Ky, a tributary of the Brahmputra. Potala Palace, the most imposing edifice in Tibet, was situated on a low hill. The eleven storeyed central pile was surrounded by monasteries, offices, stores and quarters for palace staff. The main palace, which served as the residence of the Dalai Lama, comprised innumerable audience halls, throne rooms and apartnments for sacred effigies. Apart from a private monastery, there was a college for the training of monk officials. The rich Jokang Temple, which was built in 652 AD, was the principle object of interest. The main square of the town, which served as a market place, was surrounded by government offices, shops and inns. An important feature of the town was the four royal monasteries (Tengyeling, Chomonling, Kundeling and Tsecholing) that provided candidates for the office of Regent. This early twentieth century account has been provided by the British Trade Agent who served in Tibet for fifteen years. David Macdonald, *Cultural Heritage of Tibet*, Light and Life Publishers, New Delhi, n.d., pp. 248-255.

FDSC No. 40 of 6 July 1842

From Agent to the GG	To Secretary to GOI
North West Frontier	With the GG
17 May 1842	HQS, Allahabad

1. I am sending herewith two letters received from Lt. J.D. Cunningham.
2. Whatever measures it may now or hereafter be thought proper for the British Government to take in consequence of the war, which is likely soon to prevail between independent states on its northern frontier, or whatever advice, it may be deemed expedient to offer to the belligerents, the presence of the Sirmooree or the Mussouree Battalions upon that frontier would I think be useful. It would there be in a position to act promptly for protection or for interference or it would give weight to advice.

FDSC No. 43 of 6 July 1842

From R.A. Maddock	To G.R. Clerk
Secretary to GOI	Agent to the GG
Allahabad	NWFA

1. I am directed to inform you in reply that the Governor General can not sanction any movement of troops, having for its object the giving of weight to any advice the British Government might think to offer to the Sikhs or to their opponents beyond the Himalayas.
2. The Governor General does not contemplate any armed interference in disputes beyond the mountains, believing such armed interference to be altogether inconsistent with British interests.
3. If the British frontier should be threatened, then Commander-in-Chief will take such measures as he may think proper.

FDSC No. 41 of 6 July 1842

Subject: Chinese Movements towards Ludakh

From J.D. Cunningham — To G.R. Clerk
Camp Chango on the Spittee River
2 May 1842

1. Yesterday two men, whom I had sent to Namamut on the Indus, returned to my camp. They say that the Chinese detachment (250 men) which had halted there on hearing of the prevalence of the small pox in Ludakh, had proceeded onward about the 9th April, although the disease had not altogether disappeared. A Chinese by name Singheb who had recently brought 700 men from Lhasa was hurried on to take command of this detachment, probably because he had previously visited Ludakh, as chief of annual convoy of merchandise from Lhasa.
2. My messengers also met in Namamut two Kunnawaree traders, who had just come from Ludakh. These traders said, and this news is perhaps of the 8th or 10th April, that the young Raja of Ludakh was not with the Sikh garrison, but at large and indeed exercising the authority of sovereign under the guidance of Gumbo, the favourite of his grandfather, and who fell into the hands of the Chinese on Zorawar Singh's death, but was afterwards released by them. The Sikhs were confined to the old and new forts of Leh and were enduring a kind of blockade by irregular levies of Ludakhees and Baltee men, the latter under a son or nephew of Ahmad Shah, their dethroned Raja. About 50 Sikhs, who had left the forts at different times for purposes not known, had been killed. The report previously current that Zorawar Singh's widow had fallen into the hands of the Ludakhees is now confirmed. At the time, two traders left Leh, there was no report of the near approach of Sikh reinforcements, though the party sent from Cashmeer should not have been distant, had it ventured to proceed.
3. Two men, whom I sent to Garoo some time ago also returned yesterday. They left that place on the 10th or 11th

April. They say, there are only about 180 men with Kalon (Vazeer) Zoorkung. That 700 men recently brought by Deva Singheb (referred to in Para No. 1) are quartered near Darchin, (north of the Lakes), and that the other Lhasa Vazeer has about 2,000 men with him in Poorung (south of the Lakes). These messengers also say that 18 persons of respectability had arrived from Lhasa and gone by way of Rudhok towards Yarkand to lay in supplies, and make other preparations for the march of a body of genuine Chinese troops from the last named place, and I further learn that six Ambons of China proper would soon reach Garoo – to assume, I suppose the general charge of affairs – Ambon[27] – being the term applied to the Pekin Deputies in Yarkand and Lhasa.

4. On the 6th ultimo (6 April 1842) the manager of this Purgunnah on the part of the Bashahir Raja informed me that during the current month, he usually sent for the 30 pieces of woollen cloth, one from the Spiti district to the Raja, and which had been withheld last year by order of

27. According to an account of the early 1880s, The Chinese resident (Amban) stood at the head of the Tibetan army. His Chinese staff consisted of an Assistant Amban, two Laoyeh and a paymaster. There was a Tibetan general (Magpon), six divisional commanders (Dahpons), six regiment commanders (Rupons) and several subordinate officers. Amban was the medium of communication between the Tibetan government and China. He settled differences between Lhasa and various Tibetan states. He conferred titles and honours on native military officials. Theoretically, he had no authority in internal administration of the country. Residing ordinarily at Lhasa, he undertook an annual inspection of Nepalese frontier as far as Tingri. In military matters, the Amban exercised authority over the local prefect (Djongpon), checking the yearly account of the military stores of the prefectural town (Djong) and assessing the local contingents with reference to their proficiency in schooling, riding and athletics at the annual inspection. He conferred blue or crystal buttons on the soldiers to be worn on their official hats. Sarat Chandra Das, *Journey to Lhasa and Central Tibet*, Manjusri Publishing House, New Delhi, 1970, pp. 176-178.

the Sikhs, as you are already aware. The manager asked me, whether he should now send for the 30 pieces, which had again become due, and whether he should make any demand for those previously refused. I told him to apply for those now in the manner he had always applied, and to say with respect to those refused last year, that the Spiti authorities could, appeared to them good – for probably I thought same order may have been conveyed to them. With regard to the Bashahir claims, a few days ago the man sent to Spiti returned bringing with him the 30 pieces formerly withheld and bearing a verbal message with respect to the latter, that they were now sent, although Zorawar Singh had once directed them not to be given. I have not thought it worthwhile to object to receive these pieces of cloth, as neither the conduct of the Sikh leader nor our sense of complaint against his master, appear to be affected by sending on this subject my letter No. 15 of the 9th January last, may be referred to.

Camp Chango on the Spiti River J.D. Cunningham
2 May 1842

FDSC No. 42 of 6 July 1842

From J.D. Cunningham
Chargoon, Spiti
3 May 1842

To G.R. Clerk

1. Last night I received a letter from Gumbo, the personal favourite and treasurer of ex-king of Ludakh, which I annex herewith. Gumbo fell into the hands of the Chinese about the time of Zorawar Singh's death and was shortly afterwards released, being considered inimical to the Sikhs, and sent to Leh in the expectation that he would be able to raise the country and expel the Sikh troops from the capital, without any direct assistance from the Lhasa force. Gumbo, as I have reason to believe, is not much better disposed towards the Chinese, than he is towards the Sikhs, and some vague hopes may have excited in him, by my presence on the frontier. I am not therefore surprised at the tenor of his letter, nor at a more plain verbal message of the same kind, he has sent me by his servant.
2. As desired by you in your letter No. 123 of the 8th (April 1842) that I will make known the good wishes of the British Government towards the Jammoo Raja in their contest for Ludakh with the Chinese. Gumbo at present is the virtual ruler of the country, so far as he is independent of the Lhasa Vizeer and as knowledge of our sentiments may induce him to cooperate heartily with the Sikhs, as soon as they arrive in force in the country. I have accordingly replied to his letter, but in very general terms, and I annex a copy and original of the Persian letter. To Gumbo himself, I have written in Persian and Tibetan.
3. The bearer of the letter from Gumbo tells me that the Chinese Vizeer compelled Ahmad Shah and Gumbo to admit the supremacy of Lhasa over Bultee and Ludakh respectively, but without requiring anything from the latter, beyond the presents formally sent, and we may suppose a similar mark of allegiance from Iskardo. He also says, the original proposals made by the Chinese to Zorawar Singh were, that he should evacuate Garoo, Ludakh etc., that what

was due from Ludakh to Cashmere from of old, should be regularly sent, and that no compensation should be asked for the expenses incurred in fighting the Lhasa force or for the general injury done to these countries. It would further appear from this man's story that the Chinese are resolutely bent on driving the Sikhs to the south of the Himalayas, and that a large body of genuine Chinese troops has been collected in the Yarkand district, but that its march has been stayed for the present at the intercession of Gumbo, who says the country can not maintain so many troops, and that perhaps their presence will not be required. Gumbo may have said this partly to spare his country, but chiefly in the hope, that we would interfere. The whole party left Leh on the 19th April, and they have also brought with them a letter from Kunawari traders, who reached the place a few weeks before they quitted.

4. Along with the bearer of Gumbo's letter, two sets of messengers, whom I had dispatched so far back as the 3rd of February 1842, with a letter for the Sikh Vizeer Lakhpat, as mentioned in my dispatch of the 2nd February, also returned. This letter was taken from the messengers at a place three marches east of Leh by a body of Ludakhees and Bultee troops, ostensibly on the orders of Gumbo.
5. The state of affairs as given by the people is as follows. The account may of course be fully depended upon. Magna Ram Thanadar occupies the new fort with 40 or 50 men and a body of 300 or 400 Putans (Pathans) have converted some enclosed ranges of stables near the fort into a defensive post; besides these men there are no other Sikh troops about Leh, though they still possess some places towards Cashmere. Of Vizeer Lakhpat, I can learn nothing. The Sikhs made an early attempt to seize the person of the young Raja after they heard of Zorawar Singh's death, but were not successful, and since that time, they have been three times attacked by the assembled Bultee and Ludakhee troops. There are 900 or 1,000 Ludakhee soldiers and the same number of Bultee men, but they have no guns, while the Sikhs have. The Sikhs have also an abundance of provisions and ammunition; but a few days before my

messenger left Leh, the Chinese detachment of 250 men with two guns had arrived, and the two parties became thus more upon an equality. There was no certain intelligence of the approach of the Sikh reinforcements and I suspect that oriental dilatoriness and want of preparation, rather than snow, must detain them. The Sikh garrison of Iskardo has fled.

6. The young Raja of Ludakh occupies the fortified palace, which previously had been mentioned to me as the old fort of Leh. Gumbo is his Vizeer and his Durbar is attended by the sons of some of the chief functionaries, now dead, of his grandfather, or of Chowang Dendoop Vizeer and of Banka Bah, master of the horse mentioned by Moorcroft in his travels.The Bultee men appear to be under the command of Husein, the Vizeer of Iskardo, and none of Ahmad Shah's sons are present. With respect to Zorawar Singh's widow, my present information leads me to think that she may have reached Kishtwar in safety.[28] Notwithstanding the reports that she had fallen into the hands of the Ludakhees, the men who have just arrived know nothing about her. The trader above mentioned, and to whom I had given a certificate that he was a trader and nothing more, was sent

28. The Ladakhis sang a song of Zorawar Singh's wife, whom they believed to have accompanied her husband to Ladakh, and who had to return alone across the Zoji Pass. In this song Urdu words are mixed in a quaint way with the Tibetan: I do not wish to eat bread received from the sinful northerners / I do not wish to drink water received from the sinful northerners / Amidst the inhabitants of this land I have no friends and relations / In the northern plain I have no brothers and friends / In the place of friends and relations I had only Zorawar / In the place of brothers and friends I had only Zorawar / And it was only Zorawar who made me a despised widow / And it was only Zorawar who made his queen a despised widow / When arriving on the Zoji Pass, my fatherland can be seen / When arriving on the Zoji Pass, Lahore and the Panjab can be seen / Although I can see my fatherland, I shall not arrive there / Although I can see my fatherland, Zorawar's queen will not arrive there. A.H. Francke, *A History of Ladakh*, Sterling Publishers, New Delhi, 1977, p. 162.

by the Ludakhees to the Sikhs to propose they should go quitting away to their own country, they replied they would give up their posts to Raja Goolab Singh or to myself, but no one else.

7. I am still uncertain of the real meaning of the presents annually sent from Ludakh to Lhasa and the united kingly and priestly character of the Grand Lama equally enables the Chinese to assert their supremacy, and the Ludakhee ruler to ascribe them to his devotion. Presents are sent at the same time to the Raja (Gelpo) of Lhasa, but the functionary may be considered so far as I can understand as the Grand Lama minister for temporal affairs and not as a separate authority.

3 May 1842 Sd.

J.D. Cunningham

Translation of a letter from Gumbo, the Treasurer of Ludakh, to Lt. J.D. Cunningham, Leh dated 18 April 1842

The letter and presents which the Lhasa Vizeer sent to you were plundered on the road. I recovered the presents and forwarded them to you. But the letter could not be found. The letter was to the effect that the Sikhs have seized the forts and holy places of this country and exercised great oppression on the people.

Now the troops of the Lords of Lhasa have come to Ludakh. If the arms of two powerful Governments fight in this small country, we shall be reduced to great extremities. The English showed much kindness to the son of the late Raja. To settle affairs and to restrain these Governments, do not consider it a trouble, but come here quickly. I beseech you to come.

Reply of J.D. Cunningham to Gumbo Chango on Spiti River dated 3 May 1842

Your communication of the 18th ultimo has been received and its contents understood. If the country of Ludakh became a battle field between the Sikhs and the Chinese, I shall be sorry, for the people must suffer greatly. The English wish that there should every where be peace and particularly in the countries bordering on India.

At present, with regard to Ludakh, it is known that it has been in the possession of the Sikhs for some years. It is also known that there has been a friendship of longstanding between the English and the Sikhs.

Last year, it is true the English were displeased that the leader of the Sikhs Zorawar Singh stopped the trade in shawl wool through Kunawar, and also that he did other things, but as the Sikhs made reparations, the English are now their well wishers. If the subjects of the English trading to Ludakh or other places are treated wrongfully by the Sikhs or the Chinese, or by any one, that which is good will be done.

More than the above, I can not at present say.

FDSC No. 50 of 14 September 1842

From J.D. Cunningham To G.R. Clerk
Shalkur
19 May 1842

1. Two men whom I sent to Garoo some time ago, returned today. They left Garoo on the 30th ultimo. The Chinese Vizeer Zoorkung is still in that place with a small party of men. The other Vizeer is also still in the Poorungtz district (south of the Lakes), but it is reported that he will soon go to Rohtuk (Rudok), while in Garoo the men heard that three Ambans (Deputies of the Supreme Government of China)[29] and 3,000 Chinese soldiers had reached Meusir or Missur (north of the Lakes) on their way from Lhasa. They also heard a general report of Chinese soldiers being on their way from Yarkand.
2. As the men went to Garoo, they saw in Damchuk on the Indus (three or four marches west of Garoo) on the 22nd April a detachment of 100 men under a Chinese of rank named Peshee on its way to Leh and, on their return, they saw in Hanleh on the 9th instant a man who had

---

29. According to a first hand account, the Ambans were a terror for the Tibetans who hated them from the depth of their hearts. Whenever the Ambans left Lhasa for excursion or inspections, they forcibly extracted all forms of labour and provisions from poor villagers. The latter were deprived of their ponies and yaks who, owing to ill treatment of Chinese retainers, died in large numbers on the roads. Sheeps and tsamba were also carried away. There was neither any compensation for the losses, nor admission of any complaints. In cases of revolt by the people against the oppression of retainers, the district officers (Djongpons), being creatures of the Ambans, settled the matter in unjust manner. Moreover, the Ambans were authorized to issue passports to those who travelled from Tibet to China. Armed with this permit, the travellers freely used the whip when villagers delayed in meeting their demands. Sarat Chandra Das, *Journey to Lhasa and Central Tibet*, pp. 178-179.

accompanied the Peshee to Leh, and who had told them that a vigorous but unsuccessful attack had been made by the Ludakhees and Bultee men on the fort held by the Sikh troops. It appears the Lhasa detachment which recently reached Leh has not yet been actively engaged as the Chinese authorities wish that the Ludakhees should themselves drive the Sikhs out of their country.

3. On the 17th instant the Thanadar of Spittee sent to inform me, that two men whom I had dispatched to Leh, had returned, and reported that the fort had fallen, and then he himself had been ordered to repair to Leh forthwith. Four days however beyond this, I heard that these men simply reported that a breach had been made in one of the towers, and I was therefore suspicious about the capture of the fort, the story now told by my own messengers also leads me to think it untrue, though it is probable, the Ludakhees have by this time (19 May 1842) got possession of the place. The Thanadar of Spittee knowing that a Sikh Agent was with me would naturally wish to advance good reasons for his going to Leh and he may accordingly have given out as accomplished what he considered must soon happen.
4. Concerning the march of troops from Lhasa and the deputation of men of high rank, I presume the court of Nepal has accurate information and that it is not concealed from our Resident. I presume also that Mr. Hodgson will be informed by the Durbar if a requisition is made by the Chinese for Goorkha aid to drive the Sikhs out of Ludakh.[30]

---

30. In the wake of British defeat in Afghanistan and Anglo-Chinese dispute at Canton, Nepal sent a letter to the Chinese Emperor offering to attack the British in India. The Amban refused to transmit the letter to Peking and advised Nepal to live in harmony with its neighbours. But encouraged by the Chinese reverse in the Opium War, King Rajendra sent an envoy to China (July 1842) seeking troops or financial assistance, so that the British threat to Tibet could be met. The proposal was backed by territorial concessions. Since the Opium War had ended, China rejected the idea of sending troops to protect countries of foreign barbarians like Nepal. Thus Nepal failed to rouse Chinese anxieties over

possible British trans-Himalayan expansion. Since Chinese attention was focused on defending its heartland from encroachments of Westerners and it had suffered a humiliating defeat in the Opium War, it could not spare its resources to meet a fresh challenge on its outer periphery. Leo E. Rose, *Nepal: Strategy for Survival*, Oxford University Press, Bombay, 1971, pp. 100-102.

FDSC No. 51 of 14 September 1842

From J.D. Cunningham
Shalkur on the River Spittee
20 May 1842

To G.R. Clerk

Subject: Intelligence of Political Events in Ludakh

1. Two men today have arrived from Garoo to whom I sent with a letter to Zoorkung of 21 December with a reply from him. Lhasa Vizeer has sent a reply dated 6th instant, but as it more plainly shows the resolution of the Chinese Government to expel the Sikhs from Ludakh and Bultee, I annex a translation of it.
2. My messengers say that during the 4th, 5th and 6th instant, 8,000 troops in all reached Garoo viz. 6,000 horse and 2,000 foot under a third Vizeer from Lhasa named Doorrup. In a few days, the second Kalon or Vizeer Rukurshukpa would reach Garoo with 2,000 men and some guns were being brought from Meusur (north of the Lakes), but whether they had accompanied the force from Lhasa, or had originally belonged to the Sikhs, I do not know. Most likely they were taken from Zorawar Singh. These messengers say that the three Ambans (Deputies from China proper) mentioned in my letter of yesterday had only reached Poorung (south of the Lakes) and that they were accompanied by no more than five hundred genuine Chinese soldiers.
3. In Garoo, it was generally reported that a large force (10,000 men) had marched from districts beyond that is perhaps north of Tisho Lamho and Lhasa and arrived within 12 or 14 days of march from Rudok.[31] This force

31. According to an acute observation pertaining to 1880, the regular army of Tibet consisted of 6,000 men, half of whom were under arms and the other half at home on half pay. Those in active service served for three years at a monthly pay of two ounces of silver. After this, they returned home and entered the territorial army (yulmag) from where they could be recalled any moment for active service. Usually without uniforms, some wore a black Chinese

did not proceed by the Mansarovar Lake. Covering reinforcements from Yarkand, my men simply heard that if they were wanted, they would be sent for.

4. One of the present Garpuns or Governors of Garoo, told my messengers that the Nepalese had sent five different times offering their acceptance to the Vizeer Zoorkung, but that the Vizeer, after consulting with him, had simply replied, that the Goorkhas would not be required and that if the present force was not sufficient for the purposes intended, troops would be brought from China proper.[32] The Garpun also told my men that the Chinese and English were as one people, and that the Kunawarees therefore should come as usual to trade and fear nothing, though a large force was present. This Governor was formerly, I understand, Thanadar of Poorung distict adjoining Kumaon and his observations, whether or not true and sincere, may show that he knows something of our relations

---

jacket. They were armed with matclocks, bows and arrows, spears and slings. Besides this regular army, the government could summon all forces of the country in time of need. On such occasions, each family had to supply one man fully equipped and provisioned. Every landholder sent one man for every unit of land (kang) and a follower to carry his provisions. The chief men – Kalons, Jongpons and Dahpons – furnished quotas of cavalry (tamag), so that all having ponies were incorporated. In addition to the expenditure on maintaining this army, each Chinese private was paid Rs. 14 a month and 30 surs of Tsamba, while every Tibetan was given Rs. 2.25 a month. Sarat Chandra Das, *Journey to Lhasa and Central Tibet*, p. 180.

32. In the wake of Dogra invasion of Western Tibet, Nepal developed contacts with Dogras, Ladakhis and Chinese. Having failed to form alliance with any of these powers, Nepal made several offers to provide assistance to Tibet in expelling the Dogra invaders from its lands in the west. Since the Tibetans were aware of the opportunistic tactics of the Nepalese king, they refused to accept these latest overtures. Thus Nepal failed to make any gain from the recent conflagration in Western Himalayas, primarily on account of the disastrous defeat of the Dogras. C.L. Datta, *Ladakh and Western Himalayan Politics*, pp. 176-178.

with Nepal and of our desire for the prosperity of trade, as well as a wish to magnify his own importance and to have the fair of Garoo as well attended as usual.

5. On the 6th instant, a horseman arrived at Garoo with the intelligence that the fort of Leh had fallen and with the suggestion that perhaps it would not be necessary to send more Chinese troops. On the following day, three horsemen arrived with the memo that a Sikh army of 13,000 men was within a few days march of Leh. When my men left Garoo, they had not learnt the intentions of the Chinese authorities and perhaps they will not come to any resolution without consulting the three Ambans mentioned in para 2nd. The Thanadar of Leh, Magna Ram, and a Rana (name unknown) together with some others of inferior rank were prisoners in the hands of the Ludakhees and all the common soldiers had either been killed in the assault or put to death afterwards. Between Leh and Garoo a horse post had been temporarily established and I therefore place faith in this report, although the memo has not reached me by any other road.
6. My letter of 28th ultimo will have given you some notice of the point of discussion likely to arise between the Sikhs and the Chinese. The Chinese seem resolved to keep the Sikhs to the south of the Himalayas, while the Sikhs, we may suppose, are fully resolved to maintain themselves in Ludakh. If the Sikhs are well led, they will I think have the superiority in the field and they may reoccupy Garoo and Rohtuk in order to carry their points with the Lhasa Government. Should the Sikhs thus again pass their own boundary, I shall be glad to learn whether I am to interfere or to remain neutral.

Endorsement No. 1

Translation of a Letter from the Lhasa Vizeer Zoorkung to Lt. J.D. Cunningham of 6 May 1842 from Garo

1. On the 2nd May, I received your letter dispatched on the 3rd July last. It is of the same tenor as your former letter, and

as I send you a reply to that, I would here repeat what I said before.

2. Now you and I, like wide spreading trees, should cast our protecting shadows over petty princes and rulers, we should have a regard for their welfare. Such is the way of great kings, I do not know what were the views of Zorawar Singh, when mad man like he seized Ludakh and Baltee, and plundered and slew the people and put an end to the trade carried on by the subjects of petty Rajas and other inferior rulers.
3. If in these countries affairs are again placed as they were before Zorawar Singh came to Ludakh, it will be good for all. I have impressed this on the minds of the people of Ludakh and Baltee. The duty of the powerful is to keep all people on their rightful places.

FDSC No. 36 of 22 June 1842

Subject: Details regarding Thibetan trade of British Hill States

From J.D. Cunningham To G.R. Clerk
Shalkur
27 May 1842

1. I am enclosing a statement exhibiting the export trade of Tibet to Ram Poor for the last five years (1837 to 1841, both years inclusive). The statement is as detailed as seems useful and it is as accurate as I can make it.
2. In the statement which accompanied my letter No. 8 of 14 December 1841, a quantity of Yarkand shawl wool is separately specified. The article so entered however really means Churrus of Yarkand. In the list, which the Raja of Bussaher furnished to me, this article followed immediately after Pushum or shawl wool with the heading 'Yarkund,' the name commonly given to this Churrus in the bazaars of upper India, I mistook it for Pushum of Yarkand which is very inferior to that of Garoo. At the time too I was not aware of the great extent of the trade in this drug, while the name 'Uttur,' which it bears in this quarter helped to deceive me.
3. The injurious effects of the late Zorawar Singh's invasion of the Chinese provinces adjoining Ludakh can be seen at a glance and require no comment.

Tabular Statement of the Export Trade of Tibet to Ram Pur (Bashahr) during the years 1837-1841, both inclusive

	Pushum or Shawl Wool								
	White			Black			Wool		
Year	*Quantity Cutcha 40 seer or 16 seer pukka*	*Rate*	*Value in Rs.*	*Quantity Cutcha 40 seer or 16 seer pukka*	*Rate*	*Value in Rs.*	*Quantity Cutcha 40 seer or 16 seer pukka*	*Rate*	*Value in Rs.*
1837	1185	3½ Rs. per vattee or 2 seer pukka	33,180	175	1/12 Re. per vattee or 2 seer pukka	2,457	1092	8 seer cutcha per Re.	5,460
1838	1481	4/-	47,392	190	2/-	3,040	784	8 seer	3,920
1839	1463	6/-	70,224	119	3/-	2,856	787	8 seer	3,935
1840	1400	8/-	89,600	157	4/-	4,332	1570	7 seer	8,971
1841	200	10 ½-	16,800	23	5¼-	966	58	6 seer	387

	Borax			**Churrus**			**Miscellaneous**	**Total**
Year	*Quantity Cutcha 40 seer or 16 seer pukka*	*Rate*	*Value in Rs.*	*Quantity Cutcha 40 seer or 16 seer pukka*	*Rate*	*Value in Rs.*	*Estimated value in Rs.*	*Rupees*
1837	394	3¼ Rs. seer cutcha per Re.	1,189	215	6¼ Rs. per vattee or 2 seer pukka	10,750	2,500	55,529
1838	566	16 seer	1,415	236	4½ Rs.	8,496	2,500	66,763
1839	678	15 seer	918	241	5¼ Rs.	10,122	2,500	94,445
1840	505	13 seer	10	57	5¼ Rs.	2,394	2,500	109,804
1841	22	13 seer	-	16	7½ Rs.	960	500	19,679

FDSC No. 20 of 24 January 1842

Subject: J.D. Cunningham's Report on the Trade of Thibet

From J.D. Cunningham — To G.R. Clerk
Camp Chango in Kunawar
14 December 1841

1. I am sending a statement exhibiting the quantity of shawl wool and some other articles exported from Thibet for sale at the Ram Pore fair, during the years 1837 to 1841, both inclusive. I procured the statement from the Raja of Bussahir in order that some idea might be formed of the falling off in the trade by the Sutlej, consequent on the occupation by the Sikhs of the Chinese provinces along the Indus. The Raja has not specified the description of maunds in his statement, but I have no doubt the cutcha maund which is equal to 16 seers only is meant, as in these parts business is usually carried on in that weight.
2. I will take this opportunity of correcting a statement made in the 17th para of my letter of the 13 November 1841, regarding the trade of our Kunawaree subjects to Yarkand, as since writing it I have learned from what I consider good authority, that the Sikhs, and not the Chinese, prevent our people from going to that city.
3. Since the Sikhs took Ludakh, they also have levied a duty from our subjects of Kumaon,[33] who previously traded free to that city. The duty is only half of what is taken from other people and perhaps the Rajas of Jummoo thought that this tax might pass unheeded equally with other regulations affecting the trade of our dependencies.

---

33. The kingdoms of Kumaun and Garhwal witnessed protracted military conflict during the pre-British period. In 1791 the Gurkhas extended their sway westward across the Kali and occupied many parts of Kumaun, including its capital Almora. Following their defeat in the Anglo-Gurkha War, the Gurkhas were forced (Treaty of Sagauli 1816) to cede Kumaun to the British. The Kumaun region was merged with eastern half of the Garhwal region, so as to

Statement Exhibiting the Principal Imports from Thibet to Ram Pore Fair during the years 1837 to 1841 inclusive, furnished by the Raja of Bussahir

	Shawl wool								
Year	*White*	*Black*	*Yarkand*	*Sheep wool*	*Borax*	*Salt*	*Sheep & Goat*	*Churrus*	*Tea*
1837	905	175	75	710	350	10,000	400	11	7½
1838	1000	190	80	510	450	12,000	500	26	6
1839	894	119	94	450	560	11,500	450	30	10
1840	1540	48	1,500	450	15,000	200	18	10	
1841	169	9	40	15	500	80	"	"	

constitute the Kumaun Province which was governed as a chief commissionership. According to the official record, it formed the northern division of the United Provinces and, being situated entirely in the Himalayas, extended from the borders of Tibet to the submontane tract of Tarai. It comprised the districts of Nainital, Almora and Garhwal. Sparsely inhabited with a density of 88 persons per square mile, it had a population of 9,28,823 in 1872. *The Imperial Gazetteer of India,* Vol. XVI, The Claredon Press, 1908, p. 18.

FDSC No. 40 of 22 June 1842

Subject: Movements of Sikhs towards Leh

From J.D. Cunningham To G.R. Clerk
Shalkur
28 May 1842

1. My messengers who were sent to collect intelligence from Leh, met Soba or Local Manager of the Rhoopshoo district of Ludakh, who has written to the Bussahir agent with me. My messengers did not go beyond the neighbourhood of Choomoorti, about seven days' journey from Shalkur towards Leh.
2. The Soba's letter is nine days old and he says that a large Sikh force had reached Leh; that the young Raja of Ludakh with his Vizeer Gumbo had fled to a place of safety, and that the Chinese commander Deva Singheh had hastened to Garoo for reinforcements. My messengers add that they heard that the Ludakhees had battered down a tower of the fort of Leh, but not that they had captured it. They also say, they heard that the Bultee levies in Leh had declared for the Sikhs.

FDSC No. 157 of 29 June 1842

Subject: Intelligence of Chinese advance towards Leh

From G.R. Clerk To T.H. Maddock
22 April 1842

1. I am enclosing a letter dated 6th instant from Cunningham to my address.
2. It does not strike me that the British Government is at all mixed up in any new form in the existing differences between China and Lahore or that any inconvenience will arise from suppositions in this respect on the part of the Lhasa authorities, which are unreasonable.
3. To a certain extent, the interests of the British Government are involved in the differences regarding trade which prevail upon the Ludakhee border, and hence the propriety of its closely watching the progress of the events there.
4. Lt. Cunningham is now fully apprised of the instructions of Government for his abstaining from interference.
5. Raja Soochet Singh is a brave soldier, but not being in confidence of either of his brothers, Dhian Singh and Goolab Singh, there is no probability of his being sent to Ludakh.

FDSC No. 158 of 29 June 1842

Extract of a Letter from Lt. Cunningham to G.R. Clerk dated Leo, on the Spittee, 3 April 1842

A respectable man, the treasurer or cash keeper of Tasheegung Lama (the chief ecclesiastical authority in these parts) has reached near my post, and he has unofficially written to the Bussahir Agent with me, asking that he had heard the Sikhs are on their way to Ludakh and now I come to these parts to drive out the Sikhs. The argument of course is inapplicable, but it shows how we are mixed up in the affairs of these parts in the minds of Lhasa people. And if they get into difficulties, they may possibly appeal to me in some point or another. I shall therefore look daily for your reply to my question of the 15th March, as to what I am to do, if so appealed to by either Sikhs or Chinese or both.

Extract of a letter from J.D. Cunningham to G.R. Clerk dated Leo, on the Spittee, 6 April 1842

This morning the two Kunawarees whom I sent from Chooret in November last, along with two Sipahees with Dhian Singh's parwana for Zorawar Singh, returned. They got a march or two beyond Missur (north west of the Lakes), but they were stopped by snow. The Sipahees and my men and also some messengers from Ludakh, with letters for the Vazeer, returned to Daba on the Sutlej. There my men were told to be off, as the road would not be open for some months and they could not support themselves for that time. Later on they were caught by the Chinese and then let off.

FDSC No. 70 of 20 July 1842

Subject: Chinese movements towards Leh

From J.D. Cunningham To G.R. Clerk
Shalkur
I June 1842

The head man of Chinese village of Chooret (two marches from here) returned from Garoo a few days ago. He had been ordered to repair to the place along with other heads of villages, and he appears to have left it about the middle of last month.

He writes to the Bussahir Agent with me that while in Garoo the news arrived of the capture of the defensive post in Leh held by Puthans in the service of Raja Goolab Singh, but that the fort itself has not yet been taken, when the approach of a considerable Sikh army induced the Ludakh Vazeer and the Chinese detachment to retreat. They moved up the Indus one march only, and they appear still to be there, as they learnt the Sikh reinforcement amounted to no more than 350 men and was in fact the party, which had escorted the family of late Zorawar Singh across the Himalayas. The headman also writes that he saw about 1500 Lhasa soldiers march for Leh in three detachments, and that the talk in Garoo is of large bodies of men being ready in Yarkand and Lhasa to march towards Ludakh if necessary.

FDSC No. 29 of 3 August 1842

Subject: Ludakh Raja's letter to J.D. Cunningham regarding British interference in Ludakh

From J.D. Cunningham To G.R. Clerk
Camp Shalkur on the Pittee River
13 June 1842

1. I yesterday received a letter from the young Raja of Ludakh (in the name of himself and the people) of which I annex a copy and translation. I also enclose a copy and translation of an open petition from the young Raja to Maharaja Sher Singh, which you will observe, I have been requested to forward (I have refused to be a transmitter of the same, as Lahore being a separate State).
2. The messenger or agent who has brought this letter is a Cashmeerian Mohammedan by descent and a man of sense. After Zorawar Singh's death he has himself attached to the Ludakh Raja and to his present masters the Chinese. He avers that the letters or petitions of the young Raja were written with the concurrence of the Chinese representative in Ludakh, of whom I have before had occasion to speak under the designation of Dewa Pishee, but whose proper name appears to be Joop Chood, Pishee being that of his tribe or race.
3. With reference to the request of the young Raja that I would forward this petition to Maharaja Sher Singh,[34] I told his

34. Sher Singh, who was claimed by Ranjit Singh's wife Mehtab Kaur as her son, had been treated by the Maharaja as his progeny. After the deaths of Kharak Singh and Naunihal Singh, Sher Singh overcame the opposition of Rani Chand Kaur (Naunihal Singh's mother who shared power in a short lived regency) and ascended the throne with the support of Dhian Singh and some other nobles. During his short reign (20 January 1841- 15 September 1843) he was faced with serious challenges. His position was not accepted by the Sandhawalia chiefs, who were partisans of Rani Chand Kaur and in league with the British. His armed contingents were

Agent that Lahore was an independent sovereignty and that we exercised no interference between the Maharaja and his Chiefs so long as their acts did not affect ourselves directly or through our allies. I would not, therefore, I said in this case be the transmitter of a complaint against the Rajas of Jammu and the paper has been returned accordingly. The design of rousing the suspicion of Sher Singh is not amiss and such course might probably have averted a double exaction from the Ladakhis in the more vigorous days of Maharaja Ranjit Singh, but at present, the appeal virtually lies to one brother of Jammu against the other and were a knowledge of it to get abroad, the affairs of the young Raja might be rendered more hopeless than they are.

4. The agent freely of himself does not conceal an undefined hope of the people that the English may yet think it advisable to occupy Ludakh themselves, but at present his object is to express the wish of the Raja, and of the men of consideration about him, and also he declares of the Chinese Deputy with the Raja that we should interfere and constrain the Sikhs to withdraw from Thibet and thus render active measures unnecessary on the part of the Chinese who, he says, are resolved on keeping the former people to the south of the Himalayas. He further says that every faith is put in the assertion of the Chinese that they only wish to place things as they were before the Jammoo usurpation, but neither the Ludakhees, nor the Lhasa authorities can have any confidence whatever in the Sikhs. I thought, I should not be premature in remarking that we

---

in a state of mutiny at Multan, Derajat, Peshawar, Kashmir, Mandi and Kullu. He was constrained to assist the British in the wake of their disaster in Afghanistan, but could do nothing about the mobilization of the British army on his southern border. He was a silent spectator to the Dogra expansion in Ladakh, Baltistan and Tibet. His weak and tumultuous rule terminated when he was murdered along with Dhian Singh by the Sandhawalias. For details, see Barkat Rai Chopra, *Kingdom of the Punjab 1839-45*, Vishveshvaranand Institute, Hoshiarpur, 1969, pp. 93-247.

were not unwilling to be peace makers, but had no wish to guarantee any arrangement that might be come to.

5. In the present temper of the two parties, I do not think that terms will be easily agreed upon – but when they have tried one another's strength in the field, and the Sikhs see that for the sake of a barren country, they are materially injuring Cashmeer, they may no longer hesitate to leave Thibet – while the unprofitable kind of warfare and the knowledge obtained of their respective power and resources may render each party to be satisfied with the assurances of the other without any guarantee from us.
6. The object of the native Ludakh authorities appears to have been (according to the statements of the young Raja's Agent) to get possession of the fort of Leh before reinforcements could arrive in the expectation that the Sikhs would not under such circumstances attempt to repossess themselves of the country, and in the better founded belief that they would thus also avoid the destructive presence of the Chinese army to coerce the Sikhs. They appear to have underrated to the Lhasa leaders the resources of the Sikhs and, while they could make no impression either on the fort or on the defensive post in Leh, to have concealed from the Chinese even such knowledge as they had of the advance of Sikh reinforcement. Their conduct has dissatisfied the Chinese and caused them to accuse the Ludakhees of deceit. The defensive post, which I previously reported had fallen, appears to have resisted the only one serious attack made upon it.
7. The Raja of Ludakh is now at Ligcheh about 25 miles east of Leh along with the Chinese Joop Chood (or Pishee) and 300 Lhasa soldiers. The Lhasa Vizeer Zoorkung left Garoo several days ago and it was understood, he would have about 5,500 men before Leh by this date, when the Agent started on his journey to my camp (27th or 28th May) The Sikhs had about 2,000 men only in Leh under Vizeer Rutnoo and Deewan Hurree Chand, nor had the near approach of further reinforcements been ascertained. It was understood, the Ludakhees had begun to destroy most of the bridges across the Indus, which in the present swollen state of the

river will render its passage both tedious and dangerous. The chief of Kartaksha[35] had joined the Sikhs, but no other people of rank, whether subordinate to Leh or Iskardo, had done so. The Chinese appear to be ready to call the Kalmac Tartars and to require the aid of the Nepalese if necessary.

8. I understand that no Ambans or Pittee deputies have come towards Garoo, but that they have dispatched confidential agent to observe and report upon what is going on.

Sd.
J.D. Cunningham

Translation of a Persian letter from the Raja, local authorities and people of Ludakh to Lt. J.D. Cunningham dated 16 Rulh 1258 (27 May 1842) from Ligcheh (25 miles east of Leh)

I am enclosing a Persian letter, please send it to Sher Singh, the Maharaja of Punjab. The sirdars of the Chinese Emperor are speakers of truth, and are men of honest intentions, but the Sirdars of Rajas of Jummoo are deceivers and cause of quarrels in order that they may seize what belongs to the king.

We have given our country to the Chinese Emperor and we are now within his possessions seeking a place in which we may dwell. We had no other remedy, what could we do.?

Sayad Mohamud Deen Shah, my agent, can explain to you my wishes. Kindly listen to him.

35. Ali Sher Khan, the chief of Khartaksho or Kharmang, had previously also helped the Dogras in their conquest of Baltistan. For details, see C.L. Datta, *General Zorawar Singh: His Life and Achievements in Ladakh, Baltistan and West Tibet*, pp. 52-53.

FDSC No. 29 of 3 August 1842

Translation of a petition from the Raja of Ludakh to the Maharaja of Lahore, dated 27 May 1842, from Ligcheh near Leh

The affairs of Ludakh are in this state. From of old we have owed allegiance to Chinese through Lhasa. Some years ago Zorawar Singh came to Ludakh, broke this tie, entered the Chinese territories with an army and committed many evils. We of Ludakh urged him not to seize the Chinese possessions, but he in anger threatened to put our chief men to death.

After this an order came from the Emperor of China and the Vizeer was killed, our wish was still for peace with the Rajas of Jummoo, but Magna Ram (Thanadar of Leh) continued to oppress the people and was intent upon seizing my person. On hearing this, the people of the country collected and fought with the Jummoo troops. We then asked the Chinese leaders to come and make peace between us. One Sirdar came with his followers, but since his arrival Dewan Hurree Chand has reached Leh and there is no peace. The Dewan even says that if I don't join the Sikhs, he will follow me wherever I may go. His letter is written in an imperious tone and the Chinese have become incensed and have entered Ludakh with their troops. Troops also are being collected in Yarkand and the country will thus be ruined – on this point we spoke to the Chinese leaders – they said that we must go as usual to Lhasa to do obeisance (burrai salam) and that if we did so, no tribute shall be levied from us.

1. That the Sikhs must retain no places in Ludakh or Little Tibet or levy any tribute from these countries.
2. That the Rajas both of Ludakh and Little Tibet must own as before the supremacy of China.

If these terms are agreed to, the Chinese leaders said, there should be peace.

The Jummoo Sirdars are now arbitrarily levying money and forcibly seizing property throughout the country and thus seem incapable of governing it in a proper manner.

We sent petition to you sometime ago but Dewan Hureee Chand on his way hither seized the messengers. We therefore believe you are ignorant of the real state of affairs in the country. Ghulam Muhiuddin, however, the Governor of Cashmeer, is well acquainted with them.

The Rajas of Ludakh are tributaries two fold – to the ruler of Lahore, they send tea and shawl wool through Cashmeer. My hope therefore is that you will direct the Rajas of Jummoo to withdraw their troops from Ludakh and Baltee. If you thus enable humble people to dwell in our places, we can perform the usual services to you through Cashmeer.

You can learn more of our wishes from the Governor of Cashmeer and whether our representations are true or false. The Rajas of Jammoo have used deceit and raised quarrels between two kings. The Chinese Sirdars desire that old customs should continue. They are speakers of truth and abide by their words. If you do not direct the Jammoo Rajas to evacuate the country, the Chinese army will act, and we shall be destroyed between the two parties.

We have used no deceit towards you, for access to you has been prevented, and being without other remedy, we have asked the Chinese Sirdars to place their troops here. In this case, give me such advice, as a father gives to his son, and send me the Purwana to the Jammoo Rajas I desire.

13 June 1842

Translation of a letter from J.D. Cunningham to the Raja of Ludakh

Shalkur on the Spittee River
13 June 1842

Should Ludakh be distracted by continued dispute between the Sikhs and Chinese, the British Government will regret the misfortune of your house and of the cultivators and traders of the country. The wish of the English is that there should be peace in all countries and that the Governors of each should be able to devote the whole of their time to the welfare of the people committed to their care. The English also wish that the trade of their subjects with Garoo, Leh and other places should suffer no interruption. Trade makes different people as one, it is a bond of friendship.

I have read the other letter brought by your messenger, and have told him what I think about it.

Without the orders of my Government, I can say no more than I have said above. My Government knows what is going on in Thibet and never sees so people distressed without regret.

FDSC No. 59 of 30 July 1842

From G.R. Clerk
14 June 1842

Secretary to the
Government of India

1. I am submitting a copy of memo from J.D. Cunningham.
2. Adverting to the instructions conveyed in your letter of the 25th instant, which have been communicated to Lt. Cunningham, there may seem to be no occasion for forwarding this Memorandum. Nevertheless the document may as well be in the Government office, as it may be useful, should there at any future time be a necessity for making a demonstration by moving a corps into Kumaon.

FDSC No. 60 of 20 July 1842

Memorandum 20 June 1842

1. The best place of encampment is Chango about two miles below Shalkur. Water is abundant, place open and the ground tolerably level.
2. All supplies must be drawn from Hindostan and a sufficiency should be laid in before hand at Chango itself and at each stage. At Chango any number of water mills can be erected, but the mill stones are not well cut and a stone mason might therefore be brought from Hindostan.
3. Wood is very scarce and a quantity should be levied in before the regiment arrives. A commissariat gumashta should proceed ahead to superintend the collection of this article by the villages.
4. The Regiment should not march by not more than two companies at a time after reaching Ram Pore, partly on account of the difficulty of the road and partly on account of the small number of coolies procurable and partly to avoid destroying nearly all the scanty cultivation of villages by encamping on it. Coolies should be collected from all our hill dependencies hired for the march. Kunawar cannot furnish enough.
5. Tents, grain and articles generally that will not be injured by a fall may be carried on cattle, ponies, mules or asses – all other things by men.
6. Officers should not bring tents larger than the hill tents. Stout ponies are the most serviceable animals.
7. It is thought probable that the Regiment may have to remain in this quarter throughout the winter – ample supplies of grain and wood be sent from the plains so as to reach Chango by the middle of November. The road is not properly open again until May and full six months supplies should be sent.

As Sikh and Chinese armies may be on the frontier for some years to come – and as Kunawar offers the simplest or easiest road into India from Tibet, it may be worthy of consideration whether a small mud fort might not be built at Chango with advantage and kept garrisoned by one or two companies of men with a detail of artillery to work some small field pieces and mortars. This fort could be built by the Sappers Corps at no great expense. Both the Sikhs and Chinese have such frontier posts (one at Dunkur in Spiti; the other at Choorut or Shaktud on the Para river and our Shalkur fort is such only in name).

FDSC No. 56 of 31 August 1842

Subject: Intelligence about Chinese movements towards Leh

From J.D. Cunningham To G.R. Clerk
Shalkur
29 June 1842

1. Messengers dispatched to Garoo and Leh for intelligence returned yesterday. Those sent to Garoo left that place on the 17th instant, and their intelligence is as follows:
2. Nearly all the Lhasa troops eastward of the Mansarovar Lake had been sent towards Leh. In Garoo itself there are about a hundred men only, in Tasheegong there is a similar number. Two men of China proper, emissary from Lhasa had reached Garoo; they are not of very high rank, but were revered with marks of respect by every one. These men brought into Garoo two traders of Bussahir, suspecting them to be Sikh spies, but on ascertaining the friendly relations which subsisted between Bussahir and Garoo, they released them. Grain and ammunition continue to arrive from the eastward, and but little demand seems to be made by the Chinese on the people of the country, neither for supplies nor for men to carry burdens. The Vizeer Zoorkung was in Tasheegong. Ahmad Shah, the dispossessed Raja of Iskardo, was also there.
3. The men sent to Leh stopped a few miles short of that place, being afraid of being seized by the Sikh soldiers. A detachment had encamped at a short distance from the city, but the Sikh authorities seem quite inactive. They are probably awaiting further reinforcements, for the troops sent from Cashmeer seem to be the only ones which have entered the Ludakh territory. Uptill at least the middle of this month (June 1842) Leh was almost entirely deserted on the approach of the Sikhs, but a few people are beginning to return. The Lamas or priests however did not quit the place, and I hear, they have been armed and converted into soldiers of the Sikhs.
4. From different accounts I judge that about 3,000 or 3,500 Chinese may now be with the young Raja of Ludakh. The small pox however had broken out among them and the

force had been removed into the higher hills, perhaps 30 miles east of Leh and north of the Indus. No action appears to have taken place between them and the Sikhs, since the latter were reinforced from Cashmeer. The Sikhs had been joined by one person only of consideration in Bultee and Ludakh viz. the Raja of Kurtakshah, a feudatory of the former principality.

5. In the Spitte Valley two agents, one of Gumbo Ludakhee and the other of the Chinese Commander Joop Chood, are endeavouring to levy various exactions. The people are willing to give some thing, but not all demanded, and they appear to have deserted their villages, to have removed their cattle and grain and to have destroyed the rope bridges over the rivers. The men however who brought the letter of the young Raja of Ludakh to me on the 12th instant (June 1842) had reached Dunkur, the chief place in the valley,[36] and he appears to have discontinued the proceedings of the other servants of his present masters, and where my last messengers left, the people were beginning to return to their houses. The Sikhs have not yet appeared in the Spittee valley, nor do they even appear to be in any force in Sooltan Pur (Kooloo).

36. Lying 13,000 feet above sea level, Dankar (pronounced as Trankar by Tibetans) was the principal village in the Piti valley. Situated 1,000 feet above the river, it occupied both sides of a steep ridge. It was built on arid and barren soil, though cultivation stretched from the village level to the river. A narrow road ascended the crumbling mountain to a fortress. Inaccessible on the west, the path was exposed on south east and a pasture was found above the mountain slope. On this rock was located a pond from the bottom of which two rills furnished water for irrigation. The hither one, though lying at a depth, supplied water to the fort. The fort was an irregular narrow figure, differing little from a common house. Some of the defences were whimsically placed. The rest of the houses, built on lower eminence, were constructed of stone and large unburnt bricks. William Moorcroft & George Trebeck, *Travels in the Himalayan Provinces of Hindustan and Punjab*, Vol. II, Sagar Publications, New Delhi, Reprint, 1971, pp. 58-59; Thomas Thomson, *West Himalayas and Tibet: A Narrative on Ladakh and Mountains of Northern India*, Cosmo Publications, New Delhi, Reprint, 1978, pp. 125-126.

FDSC No. 65 of 31 August 1842

Subject: Chinese movements towards Leh

From J.D. Cunningham
Shalkur on the Spittee river
9 July 1842

To G.R. Clerk

1. My messengers who have returned from Tasheegong and Leh have brought the following intelligence:
2. On the 21st and 22nd June, it appears that the emissaries from Lhasa, men of China proper alluded to in my letter No. 32 dated 29th ultimo, reached Tasheegong and though their rank is not thought to be considerable, the Vizeer Zoorkung went out some distance to meet them and accompany them into the place. They only stayed one day and then went back to Garoo, and the common report was that the Vizeer Zoorkung had assured them, he could himself speedily bring the dispute with the Sikhs to an end.
3. My messengers from the Mansarovar Lake could not hear of the near approach of further reinforcements from Lhasa, but he says that the mules loaded with supplies arrive daily from the eastward; and from other sources I learn that a great portion of this grain is afterwards floated down the Indus on rafts to within a few marches of Leh for the use of the Chinese troops.
4. In Leh the Sikhs mustered between 3,000 and 4,000 men including a detachment of 500 strong, which reached that place under a Vizeer named Lakhput on the 8th or 10th June 1842. Of the whole number 1,000 appear to be mounted, and they have 7 small guns in all with them. On the 3rd or 4th June, it would appear that a party of Ludakhees, including some Bultee and Lhasa soldiers, and amounting in all to 500 men, occupied a monastery about a march east of Leh. The Sikh leader proceeded to dislodge them, but could not carry the place. The party however was obliged to surrender in a few days being without supplies. The Sikhs have placed 100 men over one of the Indus bridges in the neighbourhood of the monastery and this appears

to be their most advanced position.

5. The Sikhs are said to have plundered temples in and about Leh and to have forced the Lamas or priests to work as porters or coolies. The report mentioned in my letter No. 32 of the 29th ultimo that they had been turned into soldiers is not correct, and has no doubt been spread by the Chinese and Ludakhees to influence the minds of the people against the Sikhs. The actual proceedings however of the present Sikh authorities seem sufficient to do that, for besides plundering temples etc., it would appear that a considerable part of the city (Leh) had been destroyed and three-fourths of the inhabitants had left the place. A large proportion of those who remain are traders, but on the 7th June they were assembled and ordered to pay two lacs of rupees; under the pretence of that the young Raja of Ludakh and his principal officers had lodged their valuables with them. There was no rumour of Gulab Singh's approach nor any of the departure of the Sikhs from Leh to attack the Chinese. No Sikh troops have yet entered the Pittee valley.
6. The Chinese are said to amount to 7,000 men and the report is they would speedily proceed against Leh. They are at present encamped about four marches east of that place towards the Rohtuk Lakes, and with a high range of hills between them and the Sikhs. They are said to be but little troubled with the small pox at present. In the districts north of Leh, it is said that about 4,000 Ludakhees and Bultee men are assembled in arms.
7. Of late my messengers have met with some difficulties in proceeding through the Chinese districts, chiefly at the hands of the soldiery. They are occasionally robbed off their little property, and are occasionally detained until they pay to be let go. The petty authorities are also suspicious of all strangers, and require proof of their being traders, and not Sikh spies, as they affect to suppose them. This not unreasonable apprehension of Sikh emissaries has caused the Lhasa Vizeer to issue orders for the attention of every stranger, 'excepting the usual strangers' who may cross the boundary. I have seen one of these written orders and have no cause to doubt its genuineness.

8. Some days back Rs. 3/8/- were realized from two Bussahir traders by a Tibetan official as tax, but after protests, the same were remitted. In this regard, I have written a letter to the Chinese authorities (copy enclosed).
9. As we have no reason to suppose that petty Lhasa authorities are less groping, or that Lhasa soldiers are better disciplined than others of native powers in Asia, the interests of our subjects require protection and as we have no troops near the frontier to signify by their presence how watchful we are of these interests, I have thought that my letter may not be without some advantage.

FDSC No. 23 of 7 September 1842

Subject: Intelligence about Ludakh

From J.D. Cunningham To G.R. Clerk
Shalkur on the Pittee River
26 July 1842

1. I beg to enclose a copy and translation (Enclosure No. 1 & 2) of a letter which I have this day addressed to the Chinese Vizeer Zoorkung regarding a Ludakhee who has fled into this territory and whom I have been required to give up. The letter sufficiently explains the circumstances of the case and I need not therefore repeat them here. One of my reasons for writing to the Lhasa Vizeer is, that he should know certainly what our customs are with regard to refugees, instead of being left to form his own opinion from probable misrepresentation of my proceedings in the individual case.

Translation of a letter from Lt. J.D. Cunningham to the Lhasa Vizeer Zoorkung dated Shalkur on the Pittee river, 26 July 1842

A few days ago a Ludakhee with his wife fled across our joint boundary into the Bussahir territory. He was followed by some men of Chooret, who in the name of Oomzud of Tasheegong, lately arrived from your camp, demanded that the Ludakhee should be given up to them.

The Ludakhee says that he was in the employ of his Raja, that he had committed no fault but that seeing the present distracted state of the country, he thought it would be well if he joined the father and mother of his wife, who are of the wandering tribe of the Khampas, but who have been residing for a short time in Nako, a village of Bussahir. I have asked the Oomzud his reasons for wishing to get possession of the Ludakhee and he says that the man was one of the 'Shangeers' (a collector of the tail of sheep and goats) of the Raja and that he had showed allegiance to the Chinese when their troops reached

Leh, that he himself (the Oomzud) had been stationed in Chooret by you to stop all runaways and that he hoped I would send back the man and his wife and also her father and mother, and people had come to conduct them to your presence.

I think it advisable to explain this matter to you, so that you may fully understand our custom in such cases, which is that all refugees can remain in safety in our territories so long as they behave themselves in every respect as one of our own subjects. This custom is not a new one and is well known to all people who have dealings with the English. You will therefore see that the above Ludakhee can not be sent back as requested by your officer.

2. My last information extends to the 10th instant (July 1842) and it is about the neighbourhood of Leh and of the Chinese camp.

The Sikhs are still in the capital, busy in improving the fort or citadel, and the Chinese are still encamped three or four marches to the eastward. Some communication appears however to have taken place between the two, and one of my messengers says that a Sikh Agent with a considerable escort was within a few miles of the Chinese headquarters, when he came away. The messenger who went into the Chinese camp as an itinerant trader says, he does not think there are above 2,000 Lhasa soldiers in all and says, "They have but one gun with them. There appears however to be considerable bodies of armed Ludakhees and Baltee men collected in other parts of the country and I do not hear any one of note has gone to the Sikhs."

Enclosure No. 1 to FDSC No. 65 of 31 August 1842

Translation of a letter from J.D. Cunningham to the Lhasa Vizeer Zoorkung dated Shalkur on the Pittee river, 6 July 1842

1. Lately near this place, one of the petty authorities of your Government levied from two traders of the Bussahir principality a duty on the transport of shawl wool from Garoo into the Bussahir, and though the person, who did this has since said that he took the money, not being sure that the traders were of Bussahir, and has refunded it. I nevertheless think it advisable to ask you to be so good as to caution all the petty authorities not to do anything that may alter the friendly relations which have long subsisted between the Raja of Bussahir and Lhasa through the Governors in Garoo.[37]
2. This is the season of trade and all the subjects of the English from the Sutlej to the Kalee river near the Mansarovar Lake are busy buying and selling shawl wool with the subjects

---

37. Here our attention is drawn to changes in the pattern of trade. In the thirties of the nineteenth century, disturbed conditions in Ladakh and Baltistan led to an enormous increase in the trade of Western Tibet with Bashahr and other British protected hill states. The quantity of shawl wool imported from Western Tibet to Bashahr, which stood at 1080 maunds in 1837, rose to 1,548 maunds in 1840. The total trade of Bashahr was valued at Rs. 55,529 in 1837, whereas it increased to Rs. 109,807 in 1840, marking a steep rise of nearly 200 per cent in just four years. However, the arrival of the Dogra army in Western Tibet led to a dramatic decline in the flow of goods to Bashahr. In 1841 the quantity of shawl wool imported fell to 169 maunds and the total trade valued at Rs. 19,679. Not only this, The Dogras levied a duty on goods that entered Western Tibet from Bashahr. The Dogra general issued an order prohibiting the export of shawl wool and borax from Western Tibet to Bashahr. Five Bashahr traders who defied this order were put to death, while many others were robbed of their property and imprisoned. C.L. Datta, *Ladakh and Western Himalayan Politics*, pp. 156-157.

of Lhasa. At present also there are many troops in Tibet and traders are more likely to meet with the difficulties than at other time. You will therefore, I hope, fully understand why I wrote to you.

3. I have been pleased to learn that some traders of Bussahir who had been robbed got the promise of immediate redresss, when they complained to you; this will make friendly relations more lasting.

FDSC No. 73 of 5 October 1842

Agent to the GG
North West Frontier with the GG
Camp Ambala
14 August 1842

To Secretary to the GOI

1. I am to transmit to you a copy of letter from J.D. Cunningham dated 30 July 1842 accompanying a correspondence of his with the Lhasa Vizeer relating to the protection of traders.
2. I think it is possible that the Sikhs and the Chinese may soon be willing to adjust their existing differences on terms based upon a monopoly of the foreign shawl wool trade in favour of Cashmeer via Ludakh. It is not only that, as observed by Cunningham, the self interest of the Ludakhees and Cashmeeris and the Chinese love of the commercial monopolies, which would result in it, but the Jammoo Rajas see in it their very advantageous aim, because since their conquest of Ludakh for Ranjit Singh in 1836, they have enjoyed the sole management and appropriation of its revenues within their own Hill States and Punjab farms are situated so that their customs benefit by the passage to Amritsar, Noor Poor and other manufactories on the plains of India with the shawl wool re-exported from Cashmeer, and they look hereafter to possess Cashmeer, the value of which essentially depends on its being abundantly supplied with the wool for want of which the condition of Cashmeer is now becoming exceedingly deteriorated.
3. The question therefore arises whether the British Government will regard with indifference the sacrifice of a rising trade and manufacture which first famine and oppression in Cashmeer and later by the war on the eastern frontier of Ludakh have created in the territories of the Government of India and which a source of supply of the shawl wool by the direct route of Bussahir to these plains would greatly extend.

FDSC No. 74 of 5 October 1842

Subject: Chinese Proceedings against the Sikhs

From J.D. Cunningham To G.R. Clerk
Camp Shalkur
30 July 1842

1. Yesterday I received a reply from Zoorkung, the Lhasa Vizeer, to the letter which I wrote to him on the 6th instant about the protection of traders, and of which I sent you a copy and a translation of the reply is enclosed herewith (No.1).
2. My messenger found that Vizeer Zoorkung had gone from Tasheegong, where he had been encamped for some time towards Leh, and only overtook him at Chooshul, a short distance southeast of the city. The Vizeer had about 300 men with him. It was understood that he would immediately join the main body of his troops still encamped at Tanktse, a few marches east of Leh, between whom and the Sikhs, who are still in Leh, no action appears to have taken place beyond the petty one in which the Sikhs surprised a mixed body of Lhasa soldiers and armed peasantry of Ludakh and Baltee, as already reported to you. My messenger did not hear that Goolab Singh had reached Leh and they left the neighbourhood of that place so late as the 21st instant.
3. The assurance of the Lhasa Vizeer about continued protection to trade seems satisfactory, and reiterated his determination to abide by his orders and to place things in Ludakh as they were before the Sikh occupation of the country, may show some fixedness of purpose in himself and his Government, but his application of those orders to the trade in shawl wool carried on by the British subjects may occasion some discussion between the Lhasa authorities and ourselves owing to the perversion of the truth by all those interested in confining its transit to Ludakh. As it is notorious that the people of Bussahir have traded in the shawl wool for more than twenty years, I have at once replied to the Vizeer's letter, but as he says that he does not know

when the trade began, I merely inform him of a fact and do not express my anxiety on the subject. A translation of my copy is enclosed.

4. It is generally said that one of the objects of the late Zorawar Singh's invasion of Garoo was to confine the trade in shawl wool to Ludakh, but I scarcely supposed the present views of the Lhasa Vizeer have been brought about by any recent negotiations between himself and the Sikhs about a settlement of the affairs of the country; I am rather of opinion that the Ludakhee authorities, all of whom are traders from the King downwards, disappointed in direct aid from us and desirous of regaining their old monopoly, have prompted the Lhasa Vizeer to consider his orders applicable to trade and have further assured him that the people of Bussahir took advantage of the disturbed state of the country to share in the traffic in shawl wool. Hereafter indeed, should the Lhasa Vizeer find himself unable to settle the country without coming to terms with the Rajas of Jammoo, it may be well to guard similar suggestions on the part of the Sikhs.
5. That the Ludakhee and Cashmiree merchants will endeavour to monopolize the shawl wool trade, we have already proof before us. Mr. Moorcroft in his journey to the Mansarovar Lake in 1812 was informed at Daba that the article was saleable only to Cashmirees or their agents without special permission to sell to others (*Asiatic Researches*, Vol. XII, p. 430), but this statement is afterwards virtually contradicted (p. 451).[38] At other places, he was distinctly informed that shawl wool could be disposed of to Ludakhees only (*Asiatic Researches*, Vol. XII, 1820-22, pp. 447, 451-470). Again in his *Travels*, he says, the export from Ludakh was exclusively

38. William Moorcroft, a veterinary surgeon in the Bengal Army, was deputed by the British to Turkistan in order to procure horses for improving the breeds in British provinces, to explore possibilities of British trade with trans-Himalayan regions and probably to gather intelligence about the Russian interest in the area. He was granted a two years leave, certificates of introduction and presents for local chiefs. Accompanied by a surveyor George Trebeck and agent Mir Izzatullah Khan, he travelled in a caravan comprising sixty mules and other beasts of burden. After passing through

confined to Cashmeer by ancient customs and agreements (Vol. I, p. 347), that it was considered illegal in Rudokh and Chanthan to allow a trade in shawl wool except through Ludakh (Vol. I, p. 347 & 364) and that the trade in shawl wool through Kooloo was illegal (Vol. I, p. 456 & Vol. II, p. 63). That such was the custom twenty or thirty years ago, we may believe as very little shawl wool was consumed out of Cashmeer and Ludakh was from its position the best entrepot for the whole of the trade, but had there been any agreements between the Lhasa and Ludakhee Governments on the subject, we may suppose that the Vizeer Zoorkung would have quoted them in the present case as conclusive. If such agreements existed, the Kunawaris were smugglers.

6. Since the Sikh occupation of Cashmeer and the occurrence shortly afterwards of a severe famine in the valley, many shawl weavers have emigrated to the plains of India and the hills adjoining Amritsar, Ludhiana and Noor Pur manufacture large quantities of shawls, scarfs etc., and if these places, specially Amritsar and Ludhiana, can only get shawl wool by the circuitous route of Ludakh and Cashmeer, their manufactures will naturally be affected. This custom, therefore of 1812 and 1820 is not applicable to altered circumstances and with respect to the trade in shawl wool being carried on by others than Ludakhees, and by other routes than that of Leh, I may mention that until within the last 50 or 60 years Cashmeeris annually travelled through Kunawar to Garoo to purchase wool. In several villages the traces of those Mohammadens may still be seen. In one of my previous letters, I supposed that Cashmeeri traders purchased the wool from the people of Kunawar, but subsequent information leads me to believe they merely

---

the hills of Kumaun and Nahan, he advanced across Mandi, Kullu, Lahaul and Kangra. Entering the plains of Punjab, he visited Hoshiarpur and Amritsar on his way to Lahore, where he had an audience with Ranjit Singh. He stayed for two years in Ladakh (September 1820 to September 1822), leaving behind an accurate description of the kingdom and signing a commercial treaty on behalf of the British. Subsequently, he marched through Kashmir, Peshawar, Kabul and Kunduz, ending his journey in Bukhara.

passed through this territory on their way to shawl wool districts.

7. Small quantities only of shawl wool appear to be imported into Kumaon (statement dated 7 October 1841 of Senior Assistant Commissioner of Kumaon) and I am not aware for what length of time the trade has been carried on. Shawl wool however is mentioned as an import (*Asiatic Researches*, Vol. XVII, 1833). The trade had thus at any rate commenced before Zorawar Singh's occupation of Ludakh, his first expedition into that country having taken place in 1834.
8. Of the importance of the trade in shawl wool carried on by the people of Bussahir, I need not here say much as the necessary information is given in my letter No. 28 dated 27 May 1942. In 1840 the quantity sold in Ram Poor was 1,400 maunds of 16 seers each and the value of the article amounted to Rupees 89,600.
9. I do not know for what length of time exactly the Kunawarees have traded in shawl wool. The Government establishment for its purchase at Kotgarh was set on foot upwards of twenty years ago and there are still alive several traders of Kumaon who have imported the article for about that period. Kennedy (Ex Agent of Soobathoo) does not, I believe, mention shawl wool in his report on Bussahir dated 6 July 1824, but bearing other things in mind, the only inference from his silence is that at that time the trade had not attracted his attention.
10. Please advise which way I am to adopt, should any attempt be made to exclude our subjects from a participation in the trade in shawl wool. We have to guard against Ludakhee and Cashmeeree misrepresentation prompted by self interest and by the Chinese love of commercial monopolies as simplifying their relations with foreigners. It may also be well to remember that in 1821 (Moorcroft's *Travels*, Vol. I, p. 420) Runjeet Singh demanded the 'lotak' or presents sent through Cashmeer for the Emperor of Delhi, and that although the Chinese authorities now talk of the period of Zorawar Singh's invasion (1834) as bearing on the question of our trade, they may hereafter be induced to reform every thing to the state of affairs previous to the first interference of the Sikhs with Ludakh.

FDSC No. 75 of 5 October 1842

Letter from the Lhasa Vizeer Zoorkung to Lt. J.D. Cunningham dated Chooshool (near Leh) 20 July 1842

Your letter of the 6th July was received on the 18th at Chooshool and gave me much pleasure.

You write that you hope the traders of Bussahir will not experience trouble in any way and that because up to this time they had met with no difficulties, you were pleased. Affairs are thus: A portion of my army has arrived for the relief of Ludakh, other bodies of men are coming from the north and the south and my belief is that for a year or two, there will be constant marching of troops to and fro. For this reason, some boundary regulation is necessary about people going and coming, but as yet the arrangement made by Raja Gaddon Chue (of Lhasa) and Raja Keher Singh of Bussahir has not been infringed, their agreement is still held firm.

Remembering this any Bussahir trader entering this territory met with no impediment, but are provided with certificates for the road, but now that the troops are coming from the north and the south and the men, being strangers, cannot distinguish between the Sikhs and the people of Bussahir, perhaps some of them may do what is wrong. The subject therefore has my constant attention. Do you however impress upon the traders of Bussahir the necessity of being circumspect.

From of old a trade in wool ('bul' i.e. sheep wool) and salt has been carried on with Bussahir and for the future, it is not forbidden, but the orders of my master to me will be placed over all things. In these countries, as they were before the coming of Zorawar Singh to Ludakh and, according to my orders, I must act at my peril, no matter what amount of Sikh troops may arrive and no matter what number of months and years may be occupied, my whole attention is therefore given to the fulfillment of these orders. If before the coming of Zorawar Singh to Ludakh the people of Bussahir traded in shawl wool, and if the people of Bussahir can prove this in the presence of men of Ludakh, no more need be said, but if it is otherwise and the people of Bussahir took advantage of the disturbances consequent on Zorawar Singh's arrival to trade in shawl wool, they can not be allowed to continue this trade according to the present orders of the Lhasa rulers to me. This is a thing of some moment, and although the two governments are one, I can not disobey the orders of my masters.

FDSC No. 76 of 5 October 1842

From J.D. Cunningham
Shalkur on the Pittee river
30 July 1842

To Lhasa Vizeer Zoorkung

I have received your friendly letter of the 20th instant and am pleased that you assure me of your continued protection to traders and that the marching to and from of troops makes you only the more anxious that they should meet with as few difficulties as possible.

In your letter, you write that you have received orders which must be obeyed from the rulers of Lhasa, to place all things in these countries as they were before the coming of the Sikhs into Ludakh, and if the trade in shawl wool carried on by the people of Bussahir arose after that event, it can not be permitted any longer, agreeably to the orders you have received. The trade in shawl wool through Bussahir is now of considerable value, and it is also of importance both to your people and to mine. The people of Garoo and Rudok have now indeed more profit upon shawl wool than they formerly had, and therefore I should not think that the wise rulers of Lhasa would wish to do anything to the injury of their subjects, even if the trade had been carried on by the people of Bussahir for two or three years only, but it is well known that the people of Bussahir have traded in shawl wool for more than twenty years i.e. for many years before Zorawar Singh came to Ludakh. This fact, I doubt not, you have already ascertained. I hope to hear from you that no further enquiry about the trade is necessary.

The English hope that in a short time the affairs of Ludakh will be in good order and that hereafter there may be long peace in all these countries.

FDSC No. 28 of 7 September 1842

From J.D. Cunningham
Shalkur on the Pittee River
3 August 1842

To G.R. Clerk

Subject: Modification of British Relations with Hill States

1. I yesterday received a letter from the Raja of Bussahir to the effect that the time had now come for him to send his usual triennial presents to the Lhasa Governor of Garoo – that in the matter however he should do as I should tell him, but that in his opinion if the presents were not sent, his trading subjects would suffer from the resentment of the Chinese. In the 7th paragraph of my letter No. 25 of 8 May 1842, I brought the subject of these presents to your notice, but I have not heard of the views of Government regarding them. I have accordingly said to the Raja of Bussahir in reply that until Government declares its pleasure, he should send the presents as usual, but as I am at a distance, [he is] to be guided by the instructions of the Political Agent at Subathoo.
2. The relations of our Hill States with the bordering districts under Chinese or other rule require I think some remodelling. Thus the Raja of Bussahir claims an annual payment of thirty pieces of woollens from the Ludakh district of Pittee which may again revert to a native Government or continue under that of Lahore or pass under that of China – and which has in former times been under that of China and which has in former times been under the authority of the Hill State of Koolloo. The payment of these woollens was prohibited by the Sikhs, I have already reported to you. See particularly my letter of 9 January 1842, para 2, and of 2nd May, para 4. Bussahir further claims the annual payment of seven rupees and eight annas (Rs.7/8-) from the village of Gheo in this neighbourhood which belongs to China, and the Bussahir Raja also sends presents to the Governor of Garoo on a footing, I think scarcely of equality, for the Raja is an absolute prince in his territories paying a tribute and his allegiance to us and the Governor

of Garoo is a deputy at least three times removed from the original source of authority, and so far as I can learn derives no rank of nobility so to speak from his station. I have already written about the relations of Bussahir with Lahore in the 6th para of my letter dated 8 May 1842. The Raja should I think refer all external matters to us, instead of endeavouring to settle them independently.

3. Moorcroft in his *Travels* (Vol. I, p. 16) says that the Raja of Garhwal claimed tribute from the Tibetan state of Hinnudes and received it up to the period of the Gorkha conquest of his country. The Raja further told Moorcroft (1819) that since his reinstatement by us, he had demanded the tribute and had been informed the matter would be referred to Peekin. The country called Hinnudes or Snowland includes the districts now under the management of Garoo, but which was formerly under Hindoo princes whose residence was at Chuprung on the Sutlej. The tract came into the possession of the Chinese or at least Lhasa about the year 1710, but while under its native rulers, it may occasionally have been forced to admit the authority of the Raja of Garhwal, or its ruler may have paid tribute to the Raja for small districts.
4. Lushington, the Commissioner of Kumaon, in the 4th para of his report to Government (North Western Province) dated 9 October 1841, states that a Chinese functionary came annually into our Purgunnah of Beans to collect from our subjects their trade [tax] to the Chinese Provinces. Lushinton adds that our subjects also paid other sums at the Chinese village Tukla Kot in the way of customs.
5. Raja of Sikkim is in reality a feudatory of ours although, he does not I believe pay tribute. He also appears to send presents to the Grand Lama. There are several sects of Lamas, and the Raja is not of the Chinese or yellow sect, but I apprehend that all the Grand Lamas or incarnations admit the supremacy of Lhasa in temporal affairs, and these presents of the Sikkim Raja may be equally liable to misconstruction with others.
6. Of the relation of Bootan, I have but little information and can not shorten your own labour in obtaining it by specific

references. The Teshoo Lama or indeed the Grand Lama of the Yellow Sect says in his letter of 1774 to the Governor General that the Bootan Raja, who is of different sect, was a dependent of Teshoo Lama i.e. now of Lhasa or of the Chinese.

7. A multiplicity of relations and a division of allegiance naturally arise during contests of barbarous people and of short lived dynasties, and such a state of uncertainty is always agreeable to the wishes of the able and aspiring rulers who occasionally appear. But the consolidated Empires of England and China have met one another along the Himalayan mountains and it is time that doubt should be at an end. It is not for us to share with others the allegiance of petty princes, nor should we desire that our dependents should have claims upon the territories of foreign states. Our feudatories should have no political connections with strangers although we may allow them to interchange friendly letters and even visits with their neighbours under the rule of others. The presence of a Chinese collector in our territory alluded to in para 4 is I think extremely objectionable and our traders should only pay the usual custom duties at the usual places of collection beyond our own boundary.

Sd.
J.D. Cunningham

FDSC No. 29 of 7 September 1842

From J.D. Cunningham
Camp Shalkur
5 August 1842

To G.R. Clerk

Subject: Sikh Expeditionary Force

Two men have this afternoon arrived from Leh which place they left on 19 July 1842.

1. The Sikhs have in the immediate vicinity of the town about 1,000 men and are leisurely engaged in the erection of a fair sized fort. The main body of the Sikhs is encamped a good day's journey to the eastward of Leh and is said by common report to amount to 6,000 men. A few days before my messengers left, it was rumoured that some Sikhs had been captured by the Chinese or insurgent Ludakhees in Noomra [Nubra] (a district north of Leh) and a party of 500 soldiers was detached to recover them. The Sikhs appear to have sent two or three deputations to the Chinese force, perhaps as much for the purpose of getting intelligence as anything else, but it was commonly reported that the invariable answer they got was, "The Sikhs must evacuate Ludakh."
2. The town of Leh was almost entirely deserted. Some Cashmirees and other traders alone remained and, it was said, they also would soon quit the place. Of Raja Goolab Singh's intention of proceeding to Leh, my messenger heard nothing.
3. I yesterday heard that a considerable body of Sikhs had crossed from Koolloo into Pittee. They have been long expected, but as Pittee is an isolated spot of little importance and not occupied by the Chinese, the men might have been employed to more advantages elsewhere.
4. I think it is probable that the Chinese may avoid an engagement with the Sikhs during the mild weather. From the talk of the common soldiers of Lhasa, as it is reported to me, I should say that they feel themselves inferior in

military spirit, in discipline and in weapons to the Sikhs and from the letter of the Vizeer Zoorkang which I sent to you on 30 July 1842 it would appear, he is prepared for a prolonged war.

5. From the talk of the Sikh soldiery as it is reported, I should say, they have considerable apprehensions of the extreme cold and want of fuel which proved fatal to their army last winter. The Lhasa troops are all inured to snow and their leaders may think they will have the Sikhs at their mercy during December and January.
6. Should the Sikhs not be able to bring the Chinese to action and in a battle at this season, I think they would be victorious. The embarrasment of the Lahore Government will be increased by the falling off in trade to Cashmeer. Should the Sikhs now succeed in defeating the Lhasa troops, they may next year have to withstand hordes of Kalmaks, who though at present Chinese subjects, are doubtless as ready for a plundering expedition as they were when they seized both Lhasa and Ludakh on their own account.
7. I mention these circumstances or showing the probability of the Sikhs remaining in force in Ludakh for some time longer and that there is but a small chance of an immediate settlement of affairs. We are ignorant how far the supreme Government of China may be intent on driving the Sikhs out of Ludakh, but if the local authorities have received instructions to that effect from Peekin, Raja Goolab Singh considering his uncertain power and position, may find himself unequal to maintain a contest with an established empire.

FDSC No. 90 of 26 October 1842

From J.D. Cunningham To G.R. Clerk
Shalkur on the Pittee river
18 August 1842

Subject: Chinese proceedings against the Sikhs

1. I have today heard from the local authorities in the neighbouring Chinese post of Chooret that Raja Goolab Singh had reached Leh and has sent Vakeels to the Lhasa Vizeer Zoorkang. This may not really be the case, but it is probably the truth and I do not wait for a confirmation of the report as I have at present much difficulty in procuring intelligence from that quarter. No one is allowed to pass unless his object is manifest and I have to trust in a great measure to the chance return of traders for the news I receive.
2. In my letter No. 37 of the 5th instant I mentioned the arrival of a Sikh force in the adjoining district of Pittee. The force numbers upwards of 2,000 men and it is accompanied by one gun. On the 15th instant the Lahore Agent with me received letters from the Commander of these troops to the effect that he intended to cross into the Chinese territory in a few days – in short that he was about to avenge the death of Zorawar Singh and the destruction of his army. The officer in question sent also for the perusal of the agent a letter he had received from the Commander of the Sikh troops in Leh, the tenor of which is that he himself was carrying on negotiations with the Chinese leaders.
3. With reference to the Sikhs crossing the Chinese boundary for the purpose of plundering or temporarily occupying the Garoo district. I have told the Lahore Agent that, in my opinion, his troops ought to keep within Ludakh until it is known that the arrangement can be come to with the Chinese about that country itself and that active hostilities had accordingly been commenced against the Chinese. I added however that if the commander of the force in Pittee had the strict orders of his superior officers to occupy any

portion, then he may do, as in that the blame if any, would then attach to these superior officers.

I have also told the Lahore Agent that I considered the question now at issue between the Sikhs and the Chinese related simply to Ludakh and that the Rajas of Jummoo and Maharaja Sher Singh had in October last naturally agreed not to reoccupy the Garoo district, that is permanently, for if the Chinese will not come to any terms about Ludakh itself, it may be advisable in a military point of view to move a Sikh force across the boundary in order to expel the Lhasa troops, the more effectually from Ludakh. Or a temporary occupation of Garoo may be expedient in bringing about the same end.

The above I told the Agent were simply my own opinions as I have not received any instructions from Government on the subject since the state of affairs had been modified by the Chinese views with regard to Ludakh.

Sd.
J.D. Cunningham

FDSC No. 91 of 26 October 1842

From J.D. Cunningham — To G.R. Clerk
Shalkur on the Pittee river
20 August 1842

1. I have today received a reply to the letter which I wrote on 26 July 1842 (see my despatch No. 34 of that date) to the Lhasa Vizeer Zoorkang about a Ludakhee, who had sought refuge in this territory, and who had been demanded by the local Chinese authorities of the neighbouring post of Chooret, and I beg to enclose a translation of the Vizeer's answer for your information and the consideration of Government.
2. The Lhasa Vizeer Zoorkang says, I should reflect whether the withholding of this Ludakhee and his wife after affairs in this quarter have been settled will or will not be a cause of differences between China and England. Such an answer may only betray the Vizeer's ignorance of the customs of independent states or it may be boasting on the part of a man, who feels who has no right on his side to conceal some degree of anger and mortification. Or it also may be another evidence of the ordinary domineering tone of the Chinese Government. I think the answer therefore affords an additional reason for modifying the relationship of our subordinate principalities with Lhasa and for coming to an explicit understanding with Peekin Commissioner about these relations and about some of the more obvious points of international law.

   The Chinese dominion seems as well established in South Eastern Tartary as ours is in India. We may be glad to bound with a consolidated empire and a Government of some system and vigour, and troublesome disputes between the feudatories of the two monarchies can be best avoided by a direct arrangement between the supreme authorities.
3. The bearer of my letter found the Lhasa Vizeer encamped to the north of the Indus and about seven marches east of Leh, with a division of his army amounting, perhaps to

4,000 men. Another division, of perhaps similar strength, is encamped at and about Dangtcheh three marches near Leh. The men reached the camp on the 8th instant (August 1842) and they heard that about the beginning of the month a Sikh detachment had approached the neighbourhood of Dangtcheh and was met by a portion of the Chinese force. Two actions took place between the parties, and the Chinese admit a loss of 400 men , one amongst the killed being the leader of a larger band of mounted plunderers called Jukhpas, who are occasionally taken into the pay of the Chinese Government.

4. My messengers also heard that a few days before their arrival some Cashmeerees had come as Vakeels on the part of the Sikhs to the Vizeer Zoorkang and that they were told no terms could be entered into with their employees, until the Sikhs have withdrawn from Ludakh. The Vakeels were also, it is said, told that the Chinese were prepared for a seven years war, an assertion which has been in the mouth of the Chinese generally ever since the arrival of the Lhasa force in November last and which may mean that they will not easily forego their objects.

   On the 14th instant, my messenger fell in with at Kakgaong on the Indus, a party of 500 Lhasa troops proceeding towards the north western entrance into Pittee, and they heard in Vizeer Zoorkang's camp that another force would enter that valley from the eastwards to aid in the expulsion of the Sikhs.

5. From various accounts given to me, I infer that the Vizeer Zoorkang has taken some active measures to prevent the people of the Hill States dependent on Lahore trading to the Chinese districts or to those portions of Ludakh in their possession and I hear today that of a large part of Kooloo traders having accordingly been detained about half a way between this and the Indus.

No. 1 of No. 139

Translation of a Letter from the Lhasa Vizeer Zoorkang to Lt. J.D. Cunningham dated 10 August 1842

Your letter to the effect that a Ludakhee and his wife, whose father and mother are of the tribe of Kampas, had come to the Bussahir territory and that the Oomzud of Tasheegong had asked you to surrender them as Chinese subjects. Also that you had said you could not give them up.

Perhaps the Oomzud made the request, thinking that the going and coming of such people might give rise to discussions.

If you will not now deliver up the above Ludakhee, you can keep him so long as the disturbances in this country continue. The Oomzud of Tasheegong has been so informed. But if, the affairs of this country are settled, you refuse to give up the Ludakhee and his wife, consider whether or not there will be a cause for difference between the two governments.

FDSC No. 84 of 12 October 1842

From J.D. Cunningham To G.R. Clerk
Shalkur on Pittee river via Simla
28 August 1842

Subject: Chinese proceedings against the Sikhs and Trade of British subjects with the Chinese

1. Yesterday I received a letter from the Lhasa Vizeer Zoorkang regarding the trade in shawl wool carried over by British subjects with the Chinese districts. A translation of the letter is enclosed.
2. The reply of the Vizeer is not conclusive in any way and to place the trade of our subjects on a proper footing, it may be advisable that Government declares its resolution on the subject both to the Chinese and Sikhs and even perhaps that a commercial treaty be entered into with the former. As our people suffer no resolution at present in making their purchases of shawl wool, I do not think it necessary to write to the Lhasa Vizeer about the trade until I hear from you or am in possession of the views of Government.
3. With reference to the request of the young Raja that I would forward his petition to Maharaja Sher Singh, I told his Agent that Lahore was an independent sovereignty and that we exercised no interference between the Maharaja and his chiefs so long as their acts did not affect ourselves directly or through our allies. I would not therefore, I said in this case be the transmitter of a complainst against the Raja of Jammoo and the paper has been returned accordingly. The design of rousing the suspicions of Sher Singh is not amiss, and such course might probably have averted a double exaction from the Ludakhees in the more vigorous days of Ranjit Singh – but at present the appeal virtually lies to one brother of Jammoo against the other and, were a knowledge of it to get abroad, the affairs of the young Raja might be rendred more hopeless than they are.
4. My information from Leh is up to the 10th instant (August 1842). The whole of the Sikh force, amounting to about 3,000

men, had quitted the place about a fortnight previously and encamped near to the Chinese army, which is now described to me as amounting to 9,000 in all. Some attempts at negotiation had been made and a respectable servant of the Bussahir Raja whom I had sent towards Leh ostensibly to make certain purchases, but really to get information appears to have been latterly employed by the Chinese and the Sikhs as a mutual Agent. I last heard of him in the Sikh Camp, and he was then about to be sent to make overtures to the Chinese – who up to that time had insisted on the immediate withdrawl of the Sikhs from Ludakh and on the repayment of all the money, which they levied in it as tribute. The common people of Leh were beginning to return to the city – Raja Goolab Singh was shortly expected, but he had been daily looked for during the last two months.

5. A Sikh force has crossed from Kishtwar into the Ludakh district of Zanskar, the Raja of which place has fled to the Chinese camp. The Commander of the force in the valley of Pittee (which perhaps does not exceed 7,000 men, though given out as numbering 3,000) has not yet moved into the Chinese territory, agreeably to the intention mentioned in my letter of 18 August 1842 and he has informed the Lahore Agent with me that he had written for specific instructions on the subject. The armed populaion of the neighbouring Chinese districts is slowly assembling at Chooret with a view of opposing the Sikhs.
6. The young Raja of Ludakh, his brother and his mother have been removed by the Chinese to Tasheegong on the Indus, the last two were seen there a few days ago by some of our traders. All the reports I have led me to believe that there will be no fair at Garoo this year and that scarecely any shawl wool will reach Cashmere excepting through our provinces.

FDSC No. 85 of 12 October 1842

From the Lhasa Vazeer Zoorkang To J.D. Cunningham
16 August 1842

Your letter of 30 July 1842 reached me on the 16 August 1842 and has given me much pleasure.

The long standing freiendship between Lhasa and Bussahir remains firm as ever – and the traders of Bussahir, both of old and at present time are treated so that they are satisfied and have confidence. On account of the present little differences between the Sikhs and Chinese, some troops have come from Lhasa and others are on the way, and I am careful that traders suffer no injury at the hands of these strangers. Do you however desire your traders to keep at a distance from the newcomers.

You write that now people of Rohduk and Garoo have more profit than formerly upon trade and that you do not think the rulers of Lhasa will do anything to the prejudices of their subjects. Friend although throughout Bhot there is profit on the trade in shawl wool, yet it is not the practice of the Rajas of that country to interfere with any old custom. On this subject, we servants here have much anxiety lest we should incur the displeasure of the rulers of Lhasa. Before this I also asked you to caution the traders of Bussahir to do nothing which would bring trouble on our heads.

Concerning the dispute between the Sikhs and people of Bhot, whatever the orders of the chiefs rulers may be, they must be attended to. No matter how many months and years are consumed in the affair, these orders must be exactly fulfilled. This I mention in the way of friendship.

When the orders of the chief rulers have been carried out, then ourselves and great petty princes will have peace and quietness.

FDSC No. 86 of 12 October 1842

From J.D. Cunningham
Shalkur on the Pittee river
31 August 1842

To G.R. Clerk

1. A man whom I sent for intelligence returned today. He left the camp of the Lhasa force on 16th instant. He was however for several days among the Sikhs and had also been appointed for carrying letters backwards and forwards between the two parties.
2. The Sikhs are now encamped within one march of the Chinese and endeavouring to come to terms with them. This messenger thinks that the Sikhs do not exceed 1,500 fighting men and the Chinese amount to perhaps to 6,000. Another account however received today keeps up the number of Sikhs to 3,000 and adds that a considerable body had also gone towards Iskardo. Ahmad Shah, the dispossessed Raja of Baltee, was with the Chinese. The action, which I reported in my letter No. 39 of the 20th instant, appears from further accounts to have been a very trifling one, seven or eight only were killed on either side, but the Chinese lost the Pun Aghin, a partisan leader.
3. My messenger has brought a letter from Gumbo, formerly the treasurer of Ludakh and still the last influential native in that country, to the Bussahir Agent with me and I enclose an English version of it. The same states, the letter was delivered to him in the presence of one of the Lhasa leaders. What Gumbo gives as the saying of the Sikhs about our reverses in Cabool and their alliance with the Dooranees may possibly be an exaggeration,[39] but can

---

39. The first Anglo-Afghan War can be traced to the growing Russian involvement and Persian expansion in Afghanistan and periphery, inducing the British Indian government to establish friendly ties with Ranjit Singh in Punjab and Amirs of Sind. But it failed to sign a treaty with Dost Muhammad, the ruler of Afghanistan, owing to the latter's conflict with the Sikhs over Peshawar. According to the Tripartite Treaty (June 1839), the British and

hardly be his own invention. It is the first I have heard of such expressions, but I am aware that the Sikh soldiery talk as if they suspected, we were more friendly to the Chinese than to them. That the Sikhs however should boast exceedingly, we need not wonder, for besides that they are half barbarous; they have never met us in arms, and their career upon the whole has been a series of successes, but still such sayings show with what anxious jealousy we are watched, and with what joy our disasters are regarded. It is quite probable indeed that such reports may have originated with, or at least be encouraged by the Jammoo Rajas, for we are in the way of their ambition, and they may think, they can give vent to their feelings without our knowledge on a distant frontier. Our name too is great, and if in the presence of their enemy, they proclaim our defeat and their alliance with our conquerors, they may further work for a salutary effect upon the minds of the people of Lhasa, who have some knowledge of us, but none of the Afghans, our reputed vanquisher? If we are thus run down by our oldest friends, these sayings also prove how little we are in India to the goodwill of its princes and leading men. They are obedient and respectful chiefly through fear. They

---

Ranjit Singh agreed to install Shah Shuja as a puppet ruler in Afghanistan. During the first Anglo-Afghan War, the British army (being refused passage through Punjab) marched via Sind and Bolan, succeeding in occupying large parts of Afghanistan and installing Shah Shuja. But the latter failed to consolidate his rule, while the British failed to maintain satisfactory commissariat through unfriendly lands. Afghan soldiery broke out in rebellion (1841) and killed the leading British commanders, forcing the British to sign a humiliating treaty. As the British army retreated towards Peshawar, it was harassed by Afghan tribes. Nearly 120 British soldiers were taken hostage and the rest perished almost to the last man. Dost Muhammad recovered his throne, while the British suffered a loss of 20,000 lives and 15 million pounds sterling. Parshotam Mehra, *A Dictionary of Modern Indian History 1707-1947*, pp. 6-9.

disdain the advantage of civilised rule. They are impatient under our control, and they hail our reverses as opening to themselves a prospect of greatness and a surer and a freer field for their exertions. It is necessary that we closely watch the proceedings of our nearest allies, whether they affect our trade, or supremacy or our reputations.

FDSC No. 87 of 12 October 1842

From Gumbo, ex-Treasurer of Ludakh to the Bussahir Agent with J.D. Cunningham, dated from the Chinese Camp, 14 August 1842

The Sikhs both in writing and in talking, and in the presence of both of Vizeer Zoorkang and Vizeer Shutta have said, "Our friends are the Doorranees and we do not agree that the English should mediate between us and you. The Doorranees have killed many 'lacs' of English, they have made about 1,000 of them as prisoners, and have taken 800 guns from them. In one day the Doorranees "made the faces of the English black."

If from your side, a person of authority comes, we may then hope that our affairs will be then settled. If no one comes, the name and honour of our Rajas will be lost.

It is said, a Sikh force has come to Pittee – ascertain whether such is the case. If a force has come, a portion of the reinforcement on their way from Lhasa will go to that quarter.

FDSC No. 46 of 19 October 1842

From J.D. Cunningham To G.R. Clerk
Shalkur on the Pittee river
18 September 1842

Subject: Chinese force defeated by the Sikhs in Ludakh

1. A respectable servant of the Raja of Bussahir, whom I had sent in June last ostensibly to make some purchases in Leh, returned to me yesterday. He is also the person alluded to in the letter to Gumbo, the late treasurer of Ludakh, forwarded with my Despatch No. 41 of the 31st ultimo. He says that he was detained in the Sikh camp by Vizeer Hurree Chand and for no avowed reason until after active hostilities had commenced against the Chinese, but he was told by men around the Diwan [Hurree Chand] and by the soldiers generally that until it was seen, whether the man sent by the young Raja of Ludakh to me with letters (see my despatch of 13th June) returned and also whether he returned with assistance from us, he must remain where he was. This may show the suspicions of all powerful states, however honourable in their dealings, natural to the Sikhs and other orientals, or it may show that the Ludakhees had been diligent in spreading rumours that we would aid them to restrain the Sikhs.
2. The Sikh force in the field might amount to 1,800 men; it had five small guns with it and latterly it had encamped opposite to the Lhasa troops as already reported to you. A few men were left to garrison the new fort of Leh – a party of 100 men was stationed in Noomra [Nubra] on the Yarkand road – a considerable body stated to amount to 2,000 men had gone direct from Cashmere to Iskardo, a small party perhaps 300 men had crossed from Kishtwar into Zanskar, and as I have before mentioned, a force of perhaps 700 men had arrived in Pittee. The above appears to have been the amount and disposition of the Sikh troops north of the Himalayas towards the end of August.
3. The Lhasa force might amount to 7,000 or 8,000 men in all, composed however of the peasantry of the country of men,

who had never before been in arms, and the distrust of their leaders, may be presumed from the fact, that they thought proper to form an entrenched camp in the presence of an enemy numerically very inferior, and for the present to have confined themselves to the defensive. The Chinese had one gun with them, which they took from the Vizeer Zorawar Singh in December last.

4. The Sikhs sent Vakeels to the Chinese leaders requesting that they would evacuate the country, restore the young Raja and continue the trade in shawl wool, tea etc. on the old footing. The Chinese replied that the Sikhs must quit Ludakh first and give up all claims upon it. When you are gone, the Chinese added, and the young Raja in the possession of his country, the old trade will be reviewed, but not before several such endeavours would seem to have been made to restore Ludakh without having recourse to arms – but all this desire for a peaceful settlement would also to have been on their part only. The Chinese sending no persons to treat and contenting themselves with replies to propositions of the Sikhs.
5. Seeing that no arrangement could be made, the Sikh leaders, Diwan Hurree Chand and Vazeer Rutnoo, were determined to have recourse to arms, and on 27 August 1842 they attacked the Chinese entrenched camp. On 28th the Sikhs lost two commandants and on the 29th Vazeer Rutnoo was wounded in the breast (appears to be wrong), it is believed 'mortally.' The loss of Sikhs in common men was also severe. In the above account the dates may not be exact.
6. My messenger stayed for some days in the Ruopshu [Rupshu] district, about half a way between this and Leh, or rather he was desired to stay by the Commanders of a Chinese detachment stationed there about – until the result of the fighting should be known. On the 12th instant (September 1842), it was reported that the Sikhs had sent people to say they were still desirous of coming to terms and that if the Chinese would depute officers to treat with Diwan Hurree Chand it would be well. One of the Lhasa Vizeers by name Shutta and Gumbo, the late treasurer of Ludakh, left the camp for this purpose, but they were seized

by the Sikhs who had concealed some men near the place of meeting. The above, I may observe, is the Chinese account of the captivity of their two leaders.

7. On the night following, the Lhasa Vizeer Zoorkang seems to have resolved on falling back and to have accordingly commenced his retreat to Tasheegong (near Garoo). As soon as this news reached the commander of the detachment in the Roopshoo [Rupshu] district, he also broke up his camp and retired in haste. My accounts of what took place after my man left the Sikh force are necessarily obscure, but I would infer that the Sikhs were gradually making the Chinese entrenched camp untenable and that the Lhasa Vizeer, distrusting the courage of his men and apprehensive of being straitened for supplies, resolved on a retreat to the neighbourhood of his magazines.
8. I do not think this reverese of the Chinese will at once determine them to abandon the cause of the Raja of Ludakh and, if it has been accompanied by any treachery on the part of the Sikhs, they may be more resolved than ever on confining that people to the south of the Himalayas – otherwise the manifest superiority of the soldiers of the plains in courage and in equipment over native Tibetans might have induced the Lhasa authorities to listen to terms less unfavourable to the Sikhs than they had hitherto insisted on.
9. The above circumstances added to the tenor of Vizeer Zoorkang's letters to me, to the probability that the Lamas, the spiritual guides of the Chinese Emperor, have urged him to expel and punish the oppressors of their brethern and to the general impression of the people about a seven years war show, I think, that Chinese are resolved on attaining their objects.
10. If the Sikhs treacherously seized two men deputed to treat with them, they may not care to disavow their act and if they confess it to you or should I thereafter ascertain to my satisfaction that Vizeer Shutta and the treasurer Gumbo were so seized, I think we should insist on their immediate release. Since the death of Runjeet Singh, the Sikh

Government has been kept together chiefly by our forbearance, and we had also been accepted as mediators between them and the Chinese some time before the event in question, and we must be informed of more or less with the proceedings of the Sikh authorities. Further, we ourselves are at war with China,[40] partly on account of the seizure of an ambassador by his deputies – and propriety demands and consistency seems both to require that we should cause the release of those of a similar quality treacherously seized by our allies, after their case has been put into our hands.

11. The Sikhs may possibly try to justify their act by saying two persons whom they had sent to treat were detained by the Chinese in December last, but the Chinese version of

---

40. This war was caused by conflicting interests over trade. Till the middle of the 1820s, China enjoyed a favourable balance of international trade, receiving gold and silver in exchange for its goods. The next decade witnessed a phenomenal reversal of the trend. This was caused by East India Company's import of opium, which increased from 10,000 chests in 1830 to 40,000 chests in 1839. The number of consumers varied from 18 million taels during 1823-31 to 30 million taels during 1834-38. What was disturbing, the annual outflow of silver rose to nearly 5 million dollars. In 1836 the British sold opium worth 18 million dollars. The situation was complicated by the arbitrary trade regulations of the Chinese, the termination of the Company's monopoly over Canton trade and the entry of the British government in the uneasy scenario. Matters were precipitated by the Chinese ban on opium traffic and destruction of opium stocks. In the ensuing Opium War, the British forces overwhelmed Chinese opposition in the ports south of the Yangtze. By the Treaty of Nanking (29 August 1842), the British secured an indemnity of 6 million pounds, the cession of the island of Hong Kong, free access to several ports, the termination of monopolistic role of Ko-hong group of Chinese merchants and equality in official correspondence. A supplementary treaty (18 October 1843) settled the tariffs, allowed the British warships to anchor at five ports to protect its commerce and gave Britain the most favourable nation treatment. Immanuel C.Y. Hsu, *The Rise of Modern China*, Oxford University Press, New York, (Sixth Edition), 2000, pp. 168-190.

this story is that under pretence of coming to terms, Zorawar Singh gained time and made sudden move against the Lhasa troops. They may "also say that Gumbo is their own subject so deliver up him on that account," but he (Gumbo) was at any rate an open enemy and made use of no treachery towards them, nor do I think any excuse should avail them with us after we were accepted as a party to the settlement. Even if the Chinese were formally as faithless as the Sikhs are now said to have been, were the Sikhs as independent of us as the Chinese are, the case might be somewhat different and we might merely refuse to mediate, but the Punjab has of late become except in name,[41] little more than a British dependency and our own honour may be involved in the proceedings of the Sikhs. Perhaps indeed only in our own estimation, but nevertheless in a manner binding upon us.

12. Ahmad Shah, the rightful Raja of Iskardo, was with the Chinese headquarters, when the Sikhs began their attack. The young Raja of Ludakh, his brother and his mother are now at the Mansarovar Lake on a pilgrimage.

---

41. Such a situation began to develop after the death (27 June 1838) of Ranjit Singh, which was followed by wide fissures in the ruling family as well as the nobles. The resultant political instability and maladministration in the kingdom was marked by a series of conspiracies and murders. Kharak Singh (r. June 1839 – November 1840) grappled with the opposition from his step brother Sher Singh and prime minister Dhian Singh. As prince Naunihal Singh gathered the reigns of power, the king's favourite Chet Singh Bajwa was murdered and members of the Missar family were imprisoned. The authority of Dhian Singh was curtailed and relations with the British took a turn for the worse. In the wake of Kharak Singh's death (5 November 1840), Naunihal Singh died in an accident while returning from the funeral. The new ruler Sher Singh overcame the opposition of Chand Kaur and secured the support of the Dogra brothers, but failed to impose discipline on the disgruntled army or suppress the intrigues of the Sandhawalias. It was during this phase that Zorawar Singh invaded Ladakh and Western Tibet.

FDSC No. 94 of 26 October 1842

From G.R. Clerk	To T.A. Maddock
Agent to the GG	Secretary to the GOI
North West Frontier	With the GG
31 August 1842	

Subject: Mediation of the British in the Ludakh Dispute

1. I have the honour to transmit a copy, with a translation, of a Purwanah from the Durbar which was yesterday read to me by Rai Kishan Chand, the Maharaja's Agent in attendance upon me.
2. Rai Kishan Chand did previously read to me the first three of these stipulations in a former Purwanah addressed to him. The fourth is now added and is a proper stipulation. But on that occasion, I observed to the Rai and required him to convey my reply accordingly to Raja Dhean Singh that I considered his first and second objects, if reasonably modified by a direct mediator, as practicable, but the third not so. Rai Kishan Chand however gave me to understand that in his opinion, if the third stipulation ever came to be discussed, it would be found that the Sikh claims on this score could be reduced to the recovery of such property of theirs as was still forthcoming. I lost no time in apprising Lieutenant Cunningham of these intentions, as soon as I discussed them on my first reading these three stipulations.
3. Some of the victories alluded to in Maharaja's memo seem exaggerated.
4. Raja Dhean Singh would not thus sue for the intervention of a British Agent without the sanction of his brother, Goolab Singh, nor would either have so soon turned their minds to this course of moderation, but from an inclination to respect the advice conveyed to them by me, which they know to have come from the Head of the Government of India
5. I hold Lieutenant Cunningham in readiness to proceed as he may be directed by the Governor General. From his present station of Shalkur on the Spitti river, he is not prominent enough to act in any degree as a mediator, but I

am of the opinion that through the little intercourse he has hitherto had with the Chinese authorities, he has been cautious, on the part of the latter. This is owing to his caution, and that they are not to be trusted, and that he should not enter any territory which they occupy. There is a road open to Lieutenant Cunningham for two months to come to get to Leh or to Raja Goolab Singh's headquarters via Kishtwar, without requiring any protection from the Chinese. Should Lieutenant Cunningham proceed to Leh or run to the west of Ludakh in this capacity, it would be advisable, I think that he should previously communicate to the Lhasa Vizeer, purpose of his deputation, and I am inclined to anticipate that the Vizeer would be glad of it.

FDSC No. 95 of 25 October 1842

Subject: Translation of a Purwanah issued by the Lahore Darbar to Rai Kishan Chand, its Vakeel, dated 1 Bhadon 1899 (corresponding with 15 August 1842)

To Rai Kishan Chand

You are hereby directed to represent to Clerk at a proper time that under the auspices of God, and owing to the virtue of the true friendship subsisting between the two high Governments, there are about 9,000 fighting men under the orders of Raja Goolab Singh in the different parts of the Ludakh country. About 1,500 of these together with a Hill Battalion are encamped 30 coss beyond Ludakh (Leh). Dewan Hurree Chand at the head of 1,500 men to support the above advanced party was encamped about 5 coss in their rear, while on the other side about 5,000 Lhasa troops were encamped opposite to them. On 31 July 1842 (15 Sawan 1899) the Lhasa troops, having assembled from different positions, made a night attack on the advanced party at about 3 o'clock in the morning. The Commandant of the Hill Battalion on this side being a vigilant Commander had picquet beyond the campment on the alert, while half the troops were sleeping on their arms, and the other half off duty. The Lhasa troops suddenly fell upon them. The picquet announced the approach of the army by firing on matchlock and the Commandant of the Khalsa troops immediately sounded the bugle and beat to arms, while the enemy had actually entered the lines.

An obstinate and severe action took place, but the Khalsa troops with great bravery repulsed the enemy by dawn of the day and following them up killed about 200 of them and 16 horses, and put the rest to flight beyond the Lhasa encampment. The Khalsa troops however did not stop here. They still pursued the enemy to a bridge on the river which was situated about 4 *coss* behind the camp and killed about 200 more, and it being difficult for their unwieldy post to cross the bridge, about 200 of them were drowned in the river, while about 400 men with three or four noted officers surrendered themselves as prisoners of war. Thus four minor affairs and one great battle have already been fought in which the Lhasa troops have always been overpowered and fled, and in these several battles about 1,500 of their men have been killed and about 900 are prisoners with the Khalsa and under the goodness of Providence all the old boundaries of Ludakh are now repossessed by the Khalsa.

You had reported that Clerk says, the remaining of Lieutenant Cunningham on the Bussahir frontier has now for its object merely the adjustment of the boundaries between the Khalsa and Lhasa authorities. You know that the Lhasa troops have always been routed and put to flight in five successive battles that have taken place, and you may now without any hesitation, report to Clerk at a proper time according to the friendship that if Cunningham, consistently with the treaties, may adjust this case in accordance with the 4 Articles that have already been specified, which are now repeated, so much the better otherwise his detention there may be considered as only a trouble to friends. The 4 Articles are as follows:

1. To preserve the old boundaries of the Ludakh country, as possessed by the ancient Rajas.
2. To continue the import of shawl wool and tea as usual towards Cashmere.
3. To restore in original or its value, the property, cash and things, small guns and baggage that were plundered on the death of Vizeer Zorawar Singh.
4. To release the prisoners mutually.

You ought to report these things to Clerk, and we are waiting to hear from you. Consider this urgent.

FDSC No. 61 of 24 May 1843

From J.C. Erskine	G.R. Clerk
Sub Commissioner, NWF	Envoy to the Court of Lahore
Simla	
1 April 1843	

Subject: Treaty between Thibet and the Sikhs

1. I have the honour to forward translation of a Treaty of Peace between the Chinese and the Sikhs dated 28 Assoge 1899 Sambut (17 October 1842) copies of which in the Bhoty and Bedechuree characters had been sent by the Raja of Bussahir.
2. The Raja informs me that a copy of this treaty was stuck up on one of the temples of Garoo, and a copy of it taken by his Bussahirees, recently returned from thence, where they had proceeded with the customary yearly presents from Bussahir to Garpon.
3. The Raja of Bussahir further states that since the conclusion of peace, the Chinese troops have returned to Lhasa.

FDSC No. 62 of 24 May 1843

Translation of a treaty of peace and amity concluded between the Chinese and the Sikhs, subsequently to the death of Vizeer Zorawar Singh, signed by Kaloon Zoorkang on the part of the former, and Rutnoo Wuzeer and Dewan Hurry Chand on the part of the latter:

The following chiefs here assembled in the city of Le [Leh] on 28 Assuge 1899 Sambut, corresponding with 17 October 1842 viz. Kaloon Zoorkang and Dewar Jeesy on the part of the Chinese and Shah Gholam on the part of the ruler of Lahore, and Rutnoo Wuzeer and Hurry Chand on the part of Raja Goolab Singh, besides others of inferior note belonging to both parties. It was mutually agreed that a treaty of amity and peace should be concluded between the Chinese and Sikhs, the conditions of which as undermentioned were recorded in writing in the presence of the chiefs aforesaid, and likewise Sibchu Tuapun Peesy and Lamba Wuzeer, both confidential advisers of the Viceroy of Lhasa.

Art. 1. That the boundaries of Ludak and Lhassa shall be constituted as formerly, the contracting parties engaging to confine themselves within their respective boundaries, the one to refrain from any act of aggression on the other.

Art. 2. That in conformity with ancient usage, Tea and Pashm Shawl Wool shall be transmitted by the Ludak road.

Art. 3. Such persons as may in future proceed from China to Ludak or from Ludak to China, not to be obstructed on road.

Art. 4. That no renewal of the war between the chiefs of Raja Goolab Singh and those of the Viceroy of Lhassa shall take place.

Art. 5. That the above mentioned conditions shall remain in force without interruption and, whatever customs formerly existed, shall not be removed and continue to prevail.

Art. 6. It is understood that in signing the above treaty, the contracting parties are bound to a true and faithful observance of all the provisions thereof, by the solemn obligations attached to the Holy Place called 'Gengri to the lake of Shanta Lari and to the temple of Kojoon Chu in China.'

True Translation
(J.C. Erskine)

FDSC No. 42 of 11 January 1843

From J.D. Cunningham To G.R Clerk
Shalkur on Spittee river
24 September 1842

1. I have the honour to transmit for your information (Encl. No. 1) the translation of a letter by one of the Governors of Garoo to the Bussahir Vazeer, respecting the seizure of the Lhassa Commander by the Sikhs. A letter of a similar tenor was received along with it, written in the name of the various functionaries of Lhassa in Garoo and the local authorities of the neighbouring districts have anxiously written to the Bussahir Agent with me to know whether I can restrain the Sikhs and confine them to Ludakh.
2. I have told the Bussahir Vazeer or Agents to reply to these communications in general terms viz. to the effect that the Sikhs as well as the Chinese are an independent people—that the dispute is between them and the Ludakhees etc. only, and that we do not without good cause interfere in the affairs of others, that however we are not indifferent to the proceedings in these countries, that we wish them peace and prosperity, that perhaps our good offices may not be pleasing to the other party, further that the Governor General of India had arrived in the Hills, and that I might shortly learn what his friendly intentions were. I thought, I could say so much with propriety, as we had offered and the Sikhs had accepted our mediation. To the Garpon, the Bussahir Agent also acknowledged that their traders had met with no impediments.
3. I have not yet learnt whether the Sikh leaders are moving on Garoo, or whether they are for the present content with their success and three days ago the Ccommander of the forces in Pittee had not heard anything of their proceedings excepting so much, as I told him. In my letter No. 42 of the 18th instant, I mentioned that two persons of rank only had been seized, but subsequent account

and the letter of the Garpon lead me to think that all the principal men have been killed or made prisoners and that the Lhassa force at once took to flight.

4. It has occurred to me that the Lhassa deputies in this quarter, or their deputies in that city may have concealed from their superiors the real state of affairs with the Sikhs and that buoyed up by their first success, they may have hoped to add without difficulty and to their own honour a new Province to the Empire or to reestablish an oppressed king in his independence. They may have talked largely of their victory in December last, but now seeing they cannot effect their objects and that the Sikhs are masters, they may wish to save themselves from utter ruin personally, by our aid. They know that we silently confined the Sikhs last year, they may think that we will also this year confine them to Ludakh on the North and East and we may suppose that our second intervention although solicited will be studiously concealed from the Emperor by those whom we had rescued from a dilemma. The letter of the Gorpon implies a desire to be relieved from a difficulty by some other means than their own, and we know that the Chinese Governors can garble the truth, exaggerate successes and even explain a defeat into a victory. Thus the expulsion of the Sikhs from Garoo might be enlarged on and the reestablishment of the Ludakh Raja might be boldly asserted, while English mediation would be left untold.
5. We should also remember that the people bordering on India are unprepared with the superiority of our government, while the less warlike, if not all of them, would gladly hail our supremacy partly by way of change and partly because they felt some real gains. All conquered people have some objections to their rulers and their hope is in a new master. The Garpon and others may desire our intervention in the expectation that it will lead to our Dominion and put an end to the jealous despotism of the Chinese.
6. All this however is mere speculation and, even if true, it is of little moment. We should do what we think best

and what our greatness and our position require at our hands without much reference to the wishes or feelings of those about us. If we think it proper, we should restrain the heedless ambition of the Sikhs and although the Chinese may in the abstract applaud that kind of dexterity and want of faith, which have deprived them of their leaders, it is nevertheless incumbent on us, of a higher honour and purer morality, to reprobate such conduct on the part of the Sikhs, our allies.

Enclosure No. 1

From Chogn Garpun (one of the Joint Governors of Garoo) to the Vazeer of Bussahir, Garoo, dated 17 September 1842

The Chinese army sometime ago took up a position in the neighbourhood of Leh and had several engagements with the Sikhs. Although each force was sent to its other reencampment and the chiefs (on both sides) met by themselves to settle the terms of peace. The Sikhs, forgetful of the consequences, killed some of the Lhassa authorities and made the Vizeer Zoorkang and four others of rank prisoners. Such appears to be the truth. Whensoever we may report these things to the rulers of Lhassa mighty force will follow.

If reparation is not made in this case and circumstances reach the ear of the great king (Gerrongwah Chinpoch, the Lhassa Raja, the temporal minister of the Supreme Lama) the affairs will take root and vast large army innumerable as the stars of heaven and equipped for a war of five or six years, compared with the present affairs, will indeed be different.

During the present year, the traders of Bussahir experienced no difficulties and returned without inconvenience into their own territory. Now however your people should be circumspect.

FDSC No. 88 of 11 January 1843

Extract from Punjaub Intelligence

From G.R. Clerk	T.A. Maddock
Agent GG, NWFA	Secretary to the GOI
Lahore	
11 December 1842	

Sending herewith an extract of Kashmeer intelligence.

Subject: Return of Ludakh army to Kashmeer

5 December 1842

Intelligence was received from Cashmeer that Dewan Hurree Chand returned with the Ludakhee army to Cashmeer and that on account of the difference of the climate about 1,000 men out of 5,000 have lost their lives on the way from Ludakh. The force had left Cashmeer with the Dewan for Jammoo, all these troops are more or less sick owing to the long march. About 500 men only had been left to guard the Iskardo fort and all the rest had returned. It appears that Raja Goolab Singh, instead of leaving Raja Ahmad Shah at the fort of Iskardo, would confine him with his sons at Jammoo and that no confidence could be placed from the Lhassa authorities. If the Raja would release Ahmad Shah, and after presenting him with khillats and concluding a treaty with him,[42] he would reinstate him as the chief of Iskardo, all differences with Lhassa would cease.

---

42. The word *khilat* denoted a dress of honour presented by a superior to an inferior on ceremonial occasions. But the meaning was often extended to the whole of a ceremonial present of that nature, whatever it might consist of. Literally, it meant "what a man strips from his person." Among the later Mughals, there were five degrees of *khilat* i.e. those of three, five, six or seven pieces. As a mark of special favour, they might consist of clothes that the emperor had actually worn. In 1786 it was recorded that Warren Hastings sent *khilats* or robes of honour (the most public and distinguished mode of acknowledging merit known in India) to ministers in testimony of his approbation of their services. However, in Russian the word has been degraded to mean the long loose gown which formed the most common dress in Turkistan. Henry Yule and A.C. Burnell, *Hobson-Jobson: The Definitive Glossary of British India,* Ed., Kate Teltscher, Oxford University Press, Oxford, 2013, p. 298.

FDSC No. 61 of 9 November 1842

From J.D. Cunningham To G.R. Clerk
27 September 1842

1. Regarding the dispersion of the Lhasa force and the seizure of its leaders, I have just learnt some more particulars, of which I think, it is well to inform you.
2. The Lhassa Vezeers seem to have been inert, to have had so little confidence in their men, or to have trusted so entirely to the speedy setting in of winter, that they not only entrenched themselves as I have before mentioned, but allowed all the commanding positions in the neighbourhood to be quietly occupied by the Sikhs. The Sikhs then dammed up a narrow position of the ravine low down, in which the Chinese had entrenched themselves. Their camp was thus gradually flooded, and when the water was thus about knee deep, the Lhassa Vezeer Zoorkang informed the Sikhs that he was willing to treat. He himself together with an inferior Vezeer named Peshee or Shutta and one of the Garpons (or Governors of Garoo) went to meet the Sikh leaders. The Sikhs said, they could soon come to terms with the Lhassa authorities themselves, but the Ludakhees had an interest in working against the Sikhs and they therefore must be given up before any negotiations could be entered into. The Lhassa Vezeer is said to have sent for Gumbo, called the Treasurer, and Guodoop Tenzin, who sometime ago was made Rája of Leh by the late Zorawar Singh. The story there goes that the Sikhs secretly brought their men to the neighbourhood, fell upon the small party of the Lhassa Vezeer, killed some and wounded and made others prisoners (among the wounded is said to be Zoorkang himself) and then as secretly assaulted the camp and made two other inferior Vezeers of Lhassa prisoners, and put the whole of the troops to flight.
3. The above story is derived from a Ludakhee, who was in the Chinese camp, the day before the Lhassa Vezeer proposed to come to terms, and who then went to the

Chinese outpost distant a day's journey, where the horses of the force were kept, and where his services lay. The account of the seizure of the chiefs he heard from one of Zoorkang's servants who had escaped; his master was made prisoner. No implicit reliance therefore can be placed on any portion of this statement, excepting on the superior military arrangements of the Sikhs, and on their sudden seizure of men, who were treating with them in good faith, the one as creditable as the other as dishonourable.

4. A few of our Kumaonee subjects have lately returned from Leh, whither they had gone to purchase the "churrus" of Yarkand, which seems to be produced in that district in greater plenty and excellence than our own hills. These men were charged a duty (by the Sikhs) on such articles as they took with them into the town, and brought away with them on their return. Each party of traders likewise paid a personal tax. I have before informed you (see particularly my letter No. 25 of 8 May 1842) that, by an old agreement between the Raja of Ludakh and Bussahir, the subjects of the latter traded free to the possessions of the former and that the Sikhs, sometime after their occupation of Leh, had imposed first the usual tax, then half of it on Kunawurees.

5. It may be argued that the Sikhs as an independent people and as the actual masters of Ludakh had a perfect right to place such restrictions as they pleased on those who traded to that country – and also perhaps on our trade itself, although the restrictions went as far as to prohibit shawl wool being taken to Kunawar. The Raja of Bussahir however is our tributary and the relations of Lahore with the British Government, by leaving it no other ally, can hardly be said to have it independent in the proper sense of the term. It seems to me therefore that the Sikhs should at least have informed us of their intention to tax such of our subjects as had hitherto traded free and that as they did not do so, we should at least express to them our serious displeasure. In the early part of the summer, when the Chinese were masters of the town of Leh, our subjects traded on the old footing – that is free.

6. From the Mansarovar Lake, I have the following

intelligence about parties of Gorkhas. Towards the end of July, a hundred men arrived, and a month afterwards, about 50 others reached that neighbourhood. Both parties came ostensibly to bathe, but the first party had also letters for the Lhassa Vezeer Zoorkang and, it was understood, they had offered their services on condition that the district of Poorung (South of Lake) should be ceded to them. The Lhassa Vezeer is reported to have answered that he had at that time no authority to obtain the assistance of the Nepalese.

7. The first party is no doubt the same as that mentioned by Lushington in his letter of 16 August 1842, and although the story about the cession of a district is mere hearsay, I think it right to mention it, as I believe a suspicion of Government is that the Sikhs and Nepalese desired to approximate their dominions on the North side of Himalayas. But as the offer of service in question was made to a subordinate authority, it may have proceeded from a party of adventurers and not from the Kathmandoo Durbar.
8. Since writing the above, I have heard that the Sikhs had agreed to release the Chinese leaders on the delivery of the Ludakh Raja, his brother, mother etc. and that the young man, now on a pilgrimage to the Mansarovar Lake, had accordingly been sent for. This is a report only, but whether true or not, the quiet way in which it and other things are mentioned show, either that the Lhassa leaders are in the extremity of fear and have little honour or spirit individually, or that Chinese views of upright dealing are much on a par with those of the Sikhs.

FDSC No. 43 of 11 January 1843

From G.R. Clerk
Envoy at the Court of Lahore
21 October 1842 with the GG

To T.A. Maddock
Secretary to the GOI

1. I have received a copy (annexed) from J.D. Cunningham No. 46 of today's date forwarding a letter from one of the Garpons of Garoo, addressed to the Bussahir Vezeer, which is further confirmatory of the late intelligence of a pacification between the Sikhs and Chinese.
2. I have for some time thought that the opinion held and expressed by the British Government in regard to this war was operating to moderate the views of both the parties and I feel quite satisfied that the Sikhs or rather the Jammoo Rajas have been greatly influenced in their late anxiety to adjust peacefully all differences on the border of Ludakh by a deference to the wishes on this subject conveyed to them from the Governor General.

FDSC No. 45 of 11 January 1843

Translation of a letter from one of the Garpons or Governors of Garoo to the Bussahir Vezeer at Shalkur in attendance upon Lt. J.D. Cunningham. Dated Tasheegong on the Indus, 2 October 1842

Your messengers have arrived with your letter, the perusal of which has given me much pleasure. You write that if the dispute between the Sikhs and Chinese continues, you will be sorry, as your wish is that peace should be in these countries.

Of a truth our two houses are one, and as you are desirous that hostilities be at an end, I now inform you that through the favour of Goongma Chooyon, peace has been made, and that our ryots are released from their troubles and made happy.[43] You need no longer be full of anxiety.

43. Originally ryot was an Arabic word which, according to its etymology, meant a herd at pasture. For native Indians, it denoted a subject, while its specific Anglo-Indian application is to a tenant of the soil i.e. an individual occupying land as a farmer or cultivator. In contrast to the noble (raees), it meant a person who was the protected one, a subject or a commoner. During the second half of the nineteenth century, it was used in this particular sense and not in that of a tenant. Under the Ryotwari System, the settlement of land revenue was made by the government with the individual peasant, not with the village community or landlord or middleman. Henry Yule and A.C. Burnell, *Hobson-Jobson: The Definitive Glossary of British India*, pp. 447-448.

FDSC No. 41 of 11 January 1843

From J.D. Cunningham To G.R. Clerk
Simla
19 October 1842

Subject: Conclusion of Peace between the Sikhs and the Chinese

1. On the night of 5 October 1842 just before leaving Shalkur, I heard that the peace had been concluded and that the Lhassa Vezeer was to be released by the Sikhs, as the present report is corroborative of what I then learnt, it may be substantially true.
2. The greater part of the Sikh force in Spittee had proceeded towards Leh on the 5th instant under Baba Luchman Singh and about 300 men have been left to protect the valley under Lala Hargovind.

FDSC No. 64 of 21 December 1842

From J.D. Cunningham Late on a deputation to the Frontier of Tibet Simla 28 October 1842	To G.R. Clerk The Envoy to the Court of Lahore

Subject: Peace concluded between the Chinese and the Sikhs on Ludakh

1. I learn from my Munshee at Shalkur that Jeewan Singh, the Agent placed with me by Raja Dhian Singh, had received a letter from Dewan Hurree Chand, the Sikh Commander in Ludakh, to the effect that peace had been made with the Lhassa authorities on the 10th Asuj (24 September 1842) and that they, the Vezeer Zoorkang and others had accordingly been released. It would further appear that Raja Goolab Singh had given up his intention of proceeding to Leh in consequence of this settlement of affairs and also that orders had been issued for the withdrawal of a considerable portion of the troops sent into Ludakh during the summer.
2. Some men sent to gain intelligence had also returned from Garoo to my encampment at Shalkur, and their stories corroborate the various reports of terms of one kind or another having been come to by the Sikhs and Chinese. These men however relate that they found a considerable portion of eastern Ludakh still occupied by detachments, but as the Vezeer Zoorkang was a prisoner at that time, this is not to be wondered at.
3. It is scarcely necessary for me to observe that any terms come to by the Lhassa Vezeer while in confinement may be respected. The handwritten text has been accepted by his superiors, and that the present peace can only be regarded as a suspension of hostilities, until it is confirmed by the Emperor himself.

B. No. 131 II Lr-84 (No. 4) of 3 September 1842

From R.N.C. Hamilton
Secretary to the Government
North West Province

To G.R. Clerk
Agent to the GG, NWFA

Forwards the correspondence received from the Lieutenant Governor of Delhi, containing intelligence of a considerable body of Sikhs troops upon the frontier of the Bussahir State.

Raja Mohinder Singh wrote to the Subathu Agent on 14 August 1842, that he has been informed that 3,000 Sikhs have assembled at Spittee in the fort of Dunkur and that the Zamindars of the Parganah Spittee are consequently in a state of great alarm and wish to enter his territory.[44] Therefore Raja Mohinder Singh wants to know whether he is permitted to do so or not.

In reply to this, the Subathu Agent wrote that as the persons who wanted to enter the Raja's territory were only villagers or agriculturists or traders, seeking asylum, and were not in possession of arms or munitions of war, and were not connected with either the Sikhs or Chinese, he has no objection to Raja's giving them asylum.

Raja Mohinder Singh further writes to the Subathu Agent on 14 August 1842, that Raja Jodh Beer (Kooloo) being taken ill has returned home, that Baba Luchman Dass and Lala Doonee

---

44. A hill cantonment of the British in Simla District, Sabathu was situated on a table land at the extremity of the Simla range with an elevation of 4,500 feet above sea level and overlooking the Gambhir river. It lay above the old road from Kalka to Simla, 9 miles from Kasauli and 23 from Simla station. Sabathu has been held by the British as a military post since the close of the Anglo-Gurkha war in 1816. A detachment of the British infantry regiment was usually stationed here. There was a small fort above the parade ground, formerly of military importance, but later on used as a store. The American Presbyterian Mission maintained a school and an asylum for lepers was supported by voluntary contributions. In 1901, its population was 2,177. *Imperial Gazetteer of India (Provincial Series): Punjab,* Vol. I, Superintendent of Government Printing, Calcutta, 1908, pp. 346-347.

Chand have arrived in Spittee with 1,000 troops, and 500 matchlocks have been taken from Kooloo and 400 from Roodur Chund and Jodh Beer of Kooloo. Raja Mohinder Singh says that he has also been asked to furnish 500 matchlocks, but he has not yet responded to the call. Moreover Geyaroo Wuzeer is stationed at Parganah Lahool to forward on commissariat and ordnance stores.

B. No. 131 II Lr-103 (No. 6) of 5 October 1842

From R.N.C. Hamilton	To G.R. Clerk
Secretary to the Government	Agent to the GG
North West Province	NWF Agency

Forwards copies of correspondence received from the Agent, Lieutenant Governor of Delhi regarding an engagement between the Sikh forces and the Zamindars of Dunkur and Peenee in which 13 of the former were killed by matchlocks; the Sikh troops were reinforced from the Dunkur garrison, whereupon a panic immediately seized the Zamindars who were engaged in the conflict. The Zamindars being worsted flew across into the Bussahir territory with their families and sought refuge there.

The Raja of Bussahir was informed by Lala Doonee Chund, confidential Agent of Raja Goolab Singh of Jammoo, that Lala Doonee Chund would pursue Zamindars in the Bussahir territory.

Hamilton requests Clerk to see that the Bussahir frontier is not violated by the Sikhs.

B. No. 154 Lr-62 (No. 422) of 9 October 1842

From G.R. Clerk	To R.N.C. Hamilton
Agent, NWF Agency	Secretary to Goverment
	North West Province

Refers to Hamilton's letter regarding the apprehension of the Raja of Bussahir that the Sikh Commandant Doonee Chund may penetrate from Kooloo into his territory to punish the Zamindars of Dunkur and Peene, who have taken refuge there. Clerk states that he will lose no time in directing the Durbar to warn its officers on the frontier against any violation of the Bussahir provinces.

3

Appendices

(A) Chinese Intervention in Tibet

Chinese influence in Tibet may be traced to the developments in the first quarter of the eighteenth century. In 1720, Emperor Kang-hsi, the Manchu ruler of China, dispatched three military expeditions to Tibet and, thus, succeeded in expelling the Dzungar Mongols from the country and installing the seventh Dalai Lama, Kelzang Gyatso. A Manchu resident was placed in Lhasa along with a garrison of 300 Chinese troops, while communication was ensured by stationing small detachments of soldiers on the Lhasa-Chamdo-Botang-Tachienlu road.[1] In Tibet, a new form of government headed by a council of four ministers, two seniors and two juniors, was assigned the task of internal administration. But a dissension in the ministerial council triggered a long period of strife which was fed by differences over the sect of Nying-ma-pa. In the middle of 1728, Emperor Yung-cheng sent a military force to protect the Dalai Lama and put an end to the civil war. The Manchus not only reorganized their garrison in Lhasa, but also appointed two residents (Ambans) who were to act as direct representatives of the Manchu sovereign in Tibet. The Ambans continued to be stationed in Lhasa till 1911. By 1728 Miwang Pholhanas, a member of the ministerial council, emerged as the sole ruler of Tibet and steered an efficient administration for nineteen years i.e. till 1747. His collaboration with the Manchus provided the

1. George N. Patterson, 'Tibet', in Guy Wint, (ed.), *Asia: A Handbook*, Anthony Blond, London, 1965, pp. 111.

grounds for Manchu and later on Chinese claims of overlordship over Tibet. His son and successor Gyumey Namgyal sought to shake off the Manchu yoke. He demanded the withdrawal of the Manchu garrison as well as the Ambans, besides creating a regular army and renewing contact with the Dzungars. The Ambans conspired to murder him and, in retaliation, the Tibetans killed the Ambans along with a hundred Chinese soldiers. The Dalai Lama assumed full temporal and spiritual powers over the Tibetan administration with the help of the ministerial council (Kashag). In view of the public complaints regarding the exploitation of local populace at the hands of the Chinese army (1751), the Tibetan regime negotiated with the Ambans and secured withdrawal of most Chinese soldiers, leaving a garrison with 1500 men. Manchus, in an attempt to build bridges with the Tibetan regime, obtained Tibetan cooperation in building two monasteries at Jebol, hosted Panchen Lama's visit to China (1780) and permitted Dzungar refugees to live in their former territories. Subsequently, the Regent of the eighth Dalai Lama maintained outward courtesy towards the Ambans, but did not encourage them to take interest in the Tibetan affairs. The Manchus tried to undermine the Regent's position by inviting (1786) him to China, providing an opportunity to the Ambans to regain their influence.[2]

The role of the Chinese in Tibet came to the centre stage during the Gurkha invasion (1788) of Tibet. The root cause of the conflict lay in differences over trade and currency, which were intensified by Tibetan support to Sikkim and Panchen Lama's property. When the Gurkhas occupied a few districts on their border with Tibet, the Chinese Emperor Chien-lung dispatched an army to restore the original position on the border. While this army was on its way, the Tibetans succeeded in driving out the Gurkhas from Shekar and Saga, while four districts remained in the hands of their opponents. The Chinese army not only delayed its advance and avoided actual fighting, but also forced the Tibetans to negotiate with the Gurkhas as pleaders and accept a humiliating settlement. Not only this, the

2. Tespon W.D. Shakabpa, *Tibet: A Political History*, Yale University Press, New Haven and London, 1967, pp. 146-156.

Chinese persuaded both parties, Tibetans and Nepalese, to send their envoys to Peking in order to thank the Manchu emperor for his good offices. According to Tibetan sources, the Chinese had been more of a hindrance than help in the war against Nepal. In fact, the Chinese were so ashamed of their conduct that they took the original treaty away with them and removed the portion bearing their seals before showing it to the Manchu emperor. The Chinese commander of this particular army, feeling the guilt of his failure to perform his responsibilities and misconduct of his subordinates, committed suicide after returning to his country.

In 1791 Tibet faced a fresh bout of Gurkha aggression which, coupled with pressure and treachery, threatened the town of Shigatse. The Manchu Amban adopted a timid attitude and advised the Dalai Lama to withdraw to Chamdo in the Kham for safety. While the Lhasa officials removed valuables to a safer place, the abbots of three monasteries promised to protect the Dalai Lama and upbraided the Kashag for the panic. They expressed strong opposition to the advice of Manchus, whose actions in the recent past proved that they could not protect the interest of Tibet. This bold stance strengthened the morale of the Tibetan army, which drove the Gurkhas back to Nyanang and Kyirong. At this juncture, a large Chinese army of 13,000 men arrived in Tibet under a Manchu general, while the Tibetans brought 10,000 strong into the field. The joint forces entered Nepal and defeated the Gurkhas who could offer only token resistance. In the ensuing negotiations, Nepal had no choice but to accept the Tibetan demands. The Manchus registered their participation in the Tibetan expedition against Nepal by erecting a stone pillar at the foot of the Potala Palace in Lhasa. During the course of the war, the populace of Lhasa protested against the exploitation and interference of the Ambans in Tibetan affairs and, while demanding their withdrawal, asserted that the imperial army had done more damage than the Gurkhas and that the Tibetans would have driven out the enemy without any outside help. Bowing to the popular sentiment and to placate the Tibetans, the Ambans were recalled to China. Having become wiser from the experience, Emperor Chien-lung increased the power of the Ambans, who would henceforth receive the petitions formerly submitted directly to him. At the same time, imperial troops were stationed at Shigatse and Dingri to guard against Nepalese incursions.[3]

In the words of a Tibetan scholar, "The main base for later Chinese claims of sovereignty over Tibet was the sending of military assistance by the Manchu Emperor, Chien-lung, to Tibet to drive out the Gurkhas. It is to be noted, however, that the Manchus supplied imperial troops as an ally of long standing and that the imperial troops did not enter Tibet to attack Tibetans or to conquer their country. The 'patron-lama' relationship between the Dalai Lama and the Manchu Emperor was predicated on the mutual responsibilities of each. The patron was to provide temporal assistance; the lama spiritual guidance. When the Manchus were strong in China, as they were during the reigns of Kang-hsi and Chien-lung, the Emperor fulfilled his obligations as imperial patron by sending troops into Tibet against the Dzungars first and then against the Gurkhas. When the Manchus began to decline in power during the nineteenth century, they were no longer able to supply temporal assistance to the Tibetans; consequently, no imperial troops were involved in the Dogra war of 1841-42 or the second Gurkha war of 1855-56. The decline of Manchu power in China led to a degeneration of control exercised by the Ambans in Lhasa to the point where again they were little more than political observers."[4]

In spite of the fact that the Tibetan government provided relief to those who lived along the routes taken by the Chinese army during its onward and return march against the Gurkhas, the people complained to the Regent of the Dalai Lama and the Manchu Emperor against the Tibetan officials collaborating with the Chinese and also demanded permanent withdrawal of the Ambans and the Lhasa garrison. Chia-ching, the new Manchu ruler (1796-1820), acting on a report of two investigators, recalled several imperial officers and reduced the Lhasa garrison to 250 men. The Tibetan government reciprocated by taking stern measures against the leaders of the protest movement, besides arresting high ranking Tibetan officials accused of colluding

3. Ibid., pp. 158-168.
4. Ibid., pp. 169-170.

with the Ambans. The Manchu rulers sent fresh investigators to Lhasa in 1805, resulting in the dismissal and banishment of two Ambans. During the first quarter of the nineteenth century, the political influence of the Manchus in Tibet continued to decline. However, a conscious attempt was made to exert influence through religious channels. The Ambans tried to impose the selection of the Dalai Lama through a lottery system in the place of the traditional methods hitherto adopted by the Tibetans. The Manchu attempt remained unsuccessful owing to strong opposition from the Tibetans.[5]

(B) Companions of Zorawar Singh

In his adventures and conquests, Wazir Zorawar Singh was supported by many able and brave officers and soldiers who made supreme sacrifices. Till now they remain unknown and unsung heroes. It would be a befitting tribute to them by recounting their achievements which hitherto had not attracted the notice of writers. However, it may be mentioned that the scanty sources, which are available on the subject, do not throw much light on their role and only sketchy references are found about them. In many cases, only their names are given and there is no mention of their background or native place. Therefore, it is difficult to construct a detailed and connected account about their activities. Yet, it is hoped that for a keen student of history who may be interested in the subject, this information would prove as the sheet anchor. Some of the important persons were as follows:

Colonel Mehta Basti Ram

Mehta Basti Ram, who was a close confidant of Wazir Zorawar Singh and a Colonel in the Dogra army, needs a detailed treatment. Information about him has been pieced together from various sources, though the following account still remains sketchy. He was a native of Kishtwar. When Zorawar Singh invaded Ladakh for the first time in the summer of 1834, the

5. Ibid., pp. 170-176.

Dogras fought many pitched battles in Lower Ladakh at places such as Suru, Kartse, Langkartse and Pashkym. The Tri-Sultans, who ruled over some of these places, fought few battles and then escaped towards Sod, which was an important village on the road leading towards Leh. Salam Khan, the Qiladar of Sod, had strongly fortified the fort and fought bravely for about ten days and kept the invaders at bay. During these days nearly 40 Dogra soldiers were killed and many more were wounded. At long last, Mehta Basti Ram, an enterprising and intrepid officer that he was, prepared for fresh action. In the early hours of one morning, he advanced at the head of a body of 500 soldiers and, supported by the covering fire of his battery, assaulted the fort. By daybreak the invaders took possession of it and made many hundred Ladakhis their prisoners.

Another occasion when Mehta Basti Ram displayed his ingenuity and valour was the Dogra conquest of Baltistan. As we already know, after the conquest of Ladakh, Wazir Zorawar Singh invaded Baltistan. Marching from Kargil and crossing the Indus from its right side, the invaders moved towards Marol whence, in order to follow the then usual road to Skardu, they were required to cross the Indus to its left side. But the Balti and Ladakhi rebels had destroyed the bridge near Marol. Further, a strong Balti army had been posted there to oppose the assailants. Under these circumstances, the invaders continued to march for days together along the right bank of the Indus, but there was no way out. Further, during their march, they were forced to cross very high snow-clad mountains and deep ravines quite frequently. The invading army continued to march for nearly four weeks. Though the chief of Kharmang (Karthakhsho), who was a feudatory of King Ahmad Shah of Skardu, submitted, yet the condition of the Dogras became quite critical. There was no way in sight for them to cross the Indus, while provisions and fuel had run short in the Dogra camp. Mian Nidhan Singh, at the head of about 5,000 soldiers, was sent to collect the supplies. When they were about fifteen miles away from the main Dogra army, the Baltis lured them into an ambuscade. In a pitched battle, Mian Nidhan Singh and all of his soldiers except 400 were killed by the Baltis. The survivors returned to the main army with great difficulty and told their woeful tale to Zorawar Singh. The invaders were now indeed in a very precarious condition. The winter was in full swing and the heavy fall of snow had closed all the passes from behind, thereby snapping their supply lines. Alexander Cunningham, the younger brother of J.D. Cunningham, who visited the area in 1846-48 i.e. about seven years after this episode, described the pitiable condition of the invaders in the following words:

"With an impassable river in their front, and certain starvation both from cold and hunger, whether they retreated or remained in their present position, the majority of the troops paid no attention to orders, and of the few who still obeyed, none did so with alacrity. The Dogra army had halted in this position for fifteen days, exposed to frost by night and to hunger by day. Many had sought shelter from the snow amongst the overhanging rocks and there they sat listless and vacant, and utterly indifferent whether they should be cut off by the sword of the enemy or be frozen to death by the cold."[6]

But courage and skill of Mehta Basti Ram, the hero of Sod, again saved the Dogras. At the dead of a night, he led a party of about 50 daring soldiers and moved along the river Indus to reconnoiter if it could be easily bridged at some place. At last, at one place near the Wanko pass, the Dogras made an ice bridge over the river with the help of Ali Sher Khan, the ruler of Kharmang and Dards, the local tribesmen of Deh.[7] This enabled them to cross the river. Near the Wanko pass, also known among the locals as the 'bloody battle field,' a pitched battle was fought in which the Baltis were routed and their leader Wazir Ghulam Hussain was killed.[8] This victory proved a turning point in the Dogra conquest of Baltistan as it facilitated an easy march towards Skardo. At Marwan, the next important place on this road, Wazir Zorawar Singh handsomely rewarded Mehta Basti Ram and about thirty of his companions for the bravery

6. Alexander Cunningham, *Ladakh: Physical, Statistical and Historical*, Sagar Publications, New Delhi, (Reprint), New Delhi, 1970, pp. 347-348.
7. A.H. Francke, *A History of Western Tibet*, S.W. Partridge, London, 1907, p. 157.
8. Hashmatullah Khan, *Tarikh-i-Jammu*, Lucknow, 1939, p. 367.

exhibited by them in the recent military action and for laying an ice bridge over the Indus. They were given golden bracelets (*karahs*) and cash awards.[9]

Another contribution of Mehta Basti Ram could be seen in Western Tibet when it was invaded by the Dogras. At many places such as Gartok, Rudok and Tirtha Puri, Tibetan treasure fell into the hands of the invaders. The latter also plundered the rich Gompas and the prosperous traders. All this treasure was put in the hands of Mehta Basti Ram, who took steps to carry it to Leh and then onwards to Jammu.[10] Another achievement of Mehta Basti Ram was the defense of Taklakot fort, which was conquered after a feeble resistance on 6 September 1841. It was the last important Tibetan post which was situated about 15 miles from the border of Nepal. Taklakot or Takla Khar, meaning 'Tiger's Fortress,' was situated at an elevated place and was like a huge mound. The dwellings were excavated in the centre and the sides were loopholed for defensive purposes. The fort was supplied with provisions and water. A garrison of nearly 300 soldiers was placed under the charge of Mehta Basti Ram. After the occupation of this fort, the Dogra conquest of West Tibet was complete.

As the *de facto* ruler of the conquered territories, Wazir Zorawar Singh issued a general order (*hukam namah*), directing the people to pay him taxes, which heretofore they had been paying to the Tibetan authorities.[11] The Bhotias, the inhabitants of Kumaun and Garhwal, who were British citizens, were also taxed as in the past. They were provided with the necessary facilities so that they could carry trade with the Hunias, their counterparts on the other side of the Himalayan crest. There were some complaints of highhandedness meted out to the Bhotias and the trading community and it caused a commotion

---

9. Alexander Cunningham, op. cit., p. 349.
10. See the deposition of two of the deserters (Gulzar Khan and Aukhoo Khan) from Zorawar Singh's army which was taken by G.T. Lushington, Commissioner of Kumaun on 8 October 1841. *FDSC, Consultations*, 6 December 1841, No. 57. Also see, Appendix D of the present volume.
11. *FDS Proceedings*, 11 October 1841, No. 50.

among them. In order to alley their fears, Wazir Zorawar Singh sent Mehta Basti Ram to meet G.T. Lushington, the Commissioner of Kumaun. The Dogra officer met the latter at village Kala Pani situated about ten miles in the Byans Parganah of the Kumaun district. Mehta Basti Ram observed that their ruler i.e. Raja Gulab Singh was helping the British in Peshawar and Hazara sectors in their war against the Afghans. Therefore, there should not be any differences between the two powers in this particular sector also. The issue pertaining to the imposition of cesses on the Hunias was amicably settled.

After returning to Taklakot, Mehta Basti Ram further strengthened the fortifications and stocked the fort with more provisions and water. However, in November a large Tibetan army descended down from Lhasa and surrounded Zorawar Singh and his troops. He called for help from all quarters, including Mehta Basti Ram. The latter had also tried to join Zorawar Singh but, finding the way blocked by the enemy, he had to return to the Taklakot fort. Similarly, Zorawar Singh also endeavoured to reach Taklakot, but he was surrounded by a large Tibetan army who blocked the paths. Heavy snowfall further increased the difficulties of the Dogras. Mehta Basti Ram, who was also beleaguered, made a couple of sorties which enabled him to set things right in the fort. The citadel, where natural strength was combined with ample stock of provisions, enabled Mehta Basti Ram to hold out for about a month. However, he was quite anxious to know the fate of Zorawar Singh and his troops. To procure intelligence about his comrades, he dispatched two men who brought the details of the catastrophe which had befallen Zorawar Singh and his army. Mehta Basti Ram had already expended his ammunition in his recent sorties and there was no hope of support from any side. Having been reduced to a very difficult situation, he sent fifteen soldiers to Lushington and begged for assistance in the name of Raja Gulab Singh and the Dogras. Since the British attitude in this war was that of neutrality, he could not get any help.

Mehta Basti Ram realized that it was impossible to reach Leh under these trying conditions. As a last resort, the Mehta undertook a desperate step. Leaving behind camp fires burning and some horses tied and leading a party of about 250 soldiers, he made a valiant attempt to cross the Lipu Lakh pass (16,750 feet) and sought refuge in the British territory. In this task, his previous knowledge of the locale and terrain (when he had met Lushington at Kala Pani) proved helpful. The Lipu Lakh pass and the surrounding hills were under five to six feet of snow. After four painful days of toil and suffering, they reached Gorbea which happened to be the first village in the British territory. It may not be out of place to mention here that while crossing the snow covered mountains, the Dogras suffered much. After reaching the British territory, many of them sold their belongings—swords, helmets and armour—for a handful of grain, just to keep their bodies and souls together. Some of these implements of war, which had been collected by the Rajbar of Askot, were seen by Charles A. Sherring when he visited this area in the summer of 1905. The Rajbar of Askot, who was said to have provided generous help to the refugees, was given a commendatory certificate by the British Commissioner of Kumaun on 18 October 1842.[12]

When Mehta Basti Ram and his companions reached Almorah, they were treated nicely by the British authorities. They were provided with medical facilities and other necessaries of life. Many of the Dogra soldiers were much worn out and emaciated. Some of them suffered from grievous wounds and were maimed for life. G.T. Lushington, the Commissioner of Kumaun, remarked that successful crossing of the Lipu Lakh pass at a time when it had the maximum snow, bore witness to the hardihood, perseverance and stamina of Colonel Mehta Basti Ram and his followers. After a few days of rest and medical treatment at Almorah, the Colonel and those of his associates, who were in a position to walk, were safely conducted to Punjab by the British authorities. This party reached Ferozepur on 16 February 1842, whence they went to their homes in the Jammu Hills. After some time, Raja Gulab Singh appointed Mehta Basti Ram as the Thanedar (Chief Administrator) of Ladakh in recognition of his services. In 1846, a rebellion broke out in

12. For details, see, Charles A. Sherring, *Western Tibet and British Borderland*, p. 197.

Zanskar, which Mehta Basti Ram immediately suppressed with a strong hand.[13] Thereafter peace was rarely disturbed in this area.

Regarding the promotion of trade in Ladakh, Pandit Manphool, Extra Assistant Commissioner of Trade, Lahore, wrote that there were many fiscal obstructions to trade under the government of Maharaja Gulab Singh and oppression of Mehta Basti Ram towards the traders, who passed through Ladakh from all directions. However, the custom duties levied at Leh did not affect the traders of Punjab and Yarkand. They remained the same as were imposed by Zorawar Singh after his conquest of Ladakh in 1834. These duties were very light in comparison to those levied in other parts of the Maharaja's dominion. The only exception was a small cess of 2 percent by the name of 'Chungee' on the goods sold in the state by weight and 1 percent known as 'Shoomaree' on the goods sold by number.[14] However, it may be mentioned that Mehta Basti Ram did not have any control on the Customs Department. The custom duties and extra cesses were farmed out to a contractor, Partap Shah Khatri, who was a native of Rawalpindi in the Punjab. Pandit Manphool further remarked that Mehta Basti Ram's extensive commercial speculations both on account of the Maharaja's Government and himself materially interfered with the prosperity and freedom of trade in Ladakh.[15]

Mehta Basti Ram also acted as the Maharaja's commercial agent in Ladakh and, as such, he took a prominent part in the trade of shawl wool, tea, salt and sulphur which were imported from Chang Thang. Pandit Manphool further writes that Mehta Basti Ram ran his private business also. He had a firm of his own in Leh in the name of Ram Jee, his nephew (sister's son). His wife, his adopted son and his nephew (brother's son) also

---

13. A.H. Francke, *A History of Western Tibet*, p. 162.
14. R.H. Davies, *Report on the Trade and Resources of the Countries on the North-Western Boundary of British India*, Government Press, Lahore, 1862; Memo by Pandit Manphool, Extra Assistant Commissioner on trade between the British Territories (Punjab) and the Countries with and beyond the dominion of Maharaja of Kashmir, Appendix XXIV.
15. Ibid.

traded separately for him. They purchased and sold goods at their own prices to traders from all directions. Goods at arbitrary prices were forced upon traders in lieu of cash advances or payments to the traders of Ladakh and Chang Thang for the purchase of shawl wool, tea and salt. "No trader can dare decline his officers, or those of his relatives, for fear of being molested and oppressed by Bustee Ram in various ways." It has been observed that had Bustee Ram contented himself with acting as an agent only, all perhaps would have been right, as it used to be under the Gyalpos; but Bustee Ram is also the greatest private merchant in Ludakh. Armed with power, political as well as commercial, and authorized (as it is believed) also to trade for himself, an avaricious and unscrupulous man like him cannot be expected to lose any opportunity of enriching himself at the expense of his master, and the mercantile community, at such a great mart as Le."

In short, Mehta Basti Ram played a prominent role in the Dogra conquest of Ladakh, Baltistan and West Tibet. As mentioned earlier, the fort of Sod in lower Ladakh which had been fortified by the Tri-Sultans and regarded impregnable by the Ladakhis, was demolished by Mehta Basti Ram and his troops. Again, when Zorawar Singh invaded Baltistan, it was his ingenuity and courage which extricated the Dogras from a very difficult situation. With the help of the Dards, he built an ice bridge over the Indus and this enabled the Dogras to cross the river. He was placed in-charge of the treasure which was acquired from various places in West Tibet. However, the most important of his assignments was the charge of the Taklakot post. From here he was sent on a diplomatic mission to G.T. Lushington, Commissioner of Kumaun, so as to sort out issues pertaining to taxes levied on the British subjects who traded with the Tibetans. Last of all, when Mehta Basti Ram safely returned to Jammu after the defeat and death of Zorawar Singh in West Tibet, he was appointed the Thanedar of Ladakh. Unlike many other Dogra officers, he was fortunate in escaping and went on to enjoy the patronage of Maharaja Gulab Singh. During his administration of Ladakh, however, he appears to have become quite an avaricious person and amassed wealth, not always resorting to fair means.

Wazir Lakhpat Rai

Wazir Lakhpat Rai did not fight in Zorawar Singh's army, yet he was responsible for suppressing the Balti revolt after the death and defeat of Zorawar Singh and his army in West Tibet. Like Diwan Hari Chand and Wazir Ratnu who restored peace in Ladakh, Lakhpat Rai restored normalcy in Baltistan. It is for this reason that his name has been included in the present list. He was originally the Prime Minister of Raja Tegh Singh of Kishtwar. The latter incurred the wrath of Maharaja Ranjit Singh by giving shelter to Shah Shuja, the ex-ruler of Afghanistan, who had escaped from Maharaja's captivity. The Maharaja asked Raja Gulab Singh to conquer Kishtwar and teach a lesson to its ruler. When the Dogras invaded Kishtwar, Lakhpat Rai assisted them. Soon the Raja took him into his service. Thereafter, Lakhpat Rai served his new master most faithfully and, thus, became a high ranking officer in the Dogra kingdom. Many times Lakhpat Rai was sent on important expeditions. When the Baltis revolted after the fateful end of Zorawar Singh, Lakhpat Rai was sent at the head of a strong force of 3,000 soldiers to establish order in Baltistan. He moved from Kishtwar to Baltistan via Suru and Kargil. He reached Skardu by forced marches, but not without fighting many battles on the way. Many of the rebels were hanged and not a few were made prisoners. A strong garrison of 300 soldiers was stationed in the Skardu fort. Muhammad Shah, a protégé of Raja Gulab Singh, whom the rebels had made a prisoner, was got released and restored to his previous position. Taking with him many arch rebels of Baltistan, Lakhpat Rai returned to Jammu. He was killed in 1846 while quelling the resistance of Shaikh Imamuddin, the Sikh Governor of Kashmir.[16]

Bhagwan Singh Kishtwaria

He played a prominent part in the Dogra invasion for conquering Ladakh and Baltistan. After the latter's subjugation,

16. See, K.M. Pannikar, *Founding of Kashmir State: Gulab Singh 1792-1858*, Allen & Unwin, London, 1953; pp. 168-69; Hashmatullah Khan, *Tarikh-i-Jammu*, pp. 413-14.

Zorawar Singh demolished King Ahmad Shah's fort at Skardu and constructed a new structure in its place. Bhagwan Singh Kishtwaria was placed at the head of a strong contingent of 300 Dogra soldiers in the fort.

Sardar Rai Singh

He was Zorawar Singh's second in command who, along with hundreds of Dogra troops, fought against the Tibetans for about three days (10 to 12 December 1841). It was the last battle near Do-Yo in which Zorawar Singh was killed. Most of the information about what transpired after this episode was given by Mehta Basti Ram to G.T. Lushington, Commissioner of Kumaun, on 13 January 1842. In fact, the Mehta narrated these details after his escape from Taklakot to Almorah. Sardar Rai Singh and his soldiers intended to join Mehta Basti Ram at Taklakot which was about one day's march. However, he could not do that due to heavy snowfall and a large Tibetan force blocking the passage. Sardar Rai Singh was induced by the Lhasa Commander to surrender his arms, stores and baggage in return for food and free passage to Ladakh for himself and his soldiers. However, according to Mehta Basti Ram, these conditions were violated by the Lhasa Chief, and the Sikh followers were left to die of cold and starvation. After this encounter, about 700 invaders were made prisoners-of-war and taken to Lhasa. However, thereafter we do not hear anything about Sardar Rai Singh. Nor do we find his name in the list of Dogra prisoners-of-war who, in 1856, were liberated from Tibet with the help of the Nepalese Durbar and Major Ramsay, the then British Resident at Kathmandu.

Mian Magna Ram

He was the bother-in-law (wife's brother) of General Zorawar Singh. After the Dogra conquest of West Tibet, Magna Ram was appointed the Thanedar (administrator) of Leh. When the Tibetan army descended down in large numbers in November-December 1841, Zorawar Singh's wife and many other ladies had gone to the Kailash Parbat on pilgrimage and for holy bath. It was Magna Ram who safely escorted his sister and her companions back to Leh. In J.D. Cunningham's reports, her name has been mentioned several times. The Thanedar made the requisite arrangements to safely escort the party of women from Leh to Kishtwar. A.H. Francke, the German Moravian Missionary, noted that even after sixty years of Zorawar Singh's death, the Ladakhi folklore preserved a song sung by the local women comprising the bitter memories of the Dogra invasion as well as the journey of the Dogra women. In particular, this song asserted that just as Zorawar Singh widowed the local women of Leh, his wife also returned home as a widow.[17] After the defeat and expulsion of the Dogras from West Tibet, Magna Ram fortified the fort of Leh and held on while it was repeatedly assaulted by the Ladakhis and Tibetans. Thus, it was he who, despite heavy odds, fought bravely and protected the Leh fort till the arrival of the expeditionary force under Wazir Ratnu and Diwan Hari Chand.

Mian Awtara Kishtwaria

Mehta Basti Ram informs us that Mian Awtara Kishtwaria was a relative of General Zorawar Singh. He was the Commandant of the Kardam Kot, a post situated about one day's journey from Do-Yo (where Zorawar Singh had been killed) on the route leading towards the Mansarowar Lake. Before the final assault on the main Dogra army at Do-Yo, the Tibetans besieged this post in order to prevent Mian Awtara from rendering any help to the Dogra invaders. In the battle that ensued, Mian Awtara was put to the sword along with nearly one hundred of his soldiers.

Some Other Names

During the second invasion of Ladakh during the summer of 1835, General Zorawar Singh and his army had to face very stiff resistance from the Ladakhis. The latter had gathered in large numbers and in a well contested battle which was fought near Langkartse the Ladakhis were killed in large numbers, though losses on the side of the Dogras were comparatively less. But their three brave leaders – Uttam Padhiar, Hazru Wazir

17. A.H. Francke, *A History of Western Tibet*, p. 169.

of Una and Surtu (probably Surat Singh Rana) were killed in this battle.

After the death and defeat of General Zorawar Singh and his army in West Tibet, some of his soldiers escaped safely into Kinnaur sector also. H. Lushington , then Officiating Political Agent, Subathu, reported that thirteen sepoys,[18] a remnant of Sikh garrison of Churit, who effected their escape when that post fell into the hands of the Tibetans , had taken shelter in the British territory. He sought sanction of the Lieutenant Governor, North Western Province, to his advancing a sum of seventeen rupees for their subsistence and to enable them to reach from Simla to Lahore in safety.[19] The Lieutenant Governor agreed and sanctioned this amount.

(C) Ladakhi and Tibetan Texts of the Agreement

Ladakhi Letter of Agreement 1842

The following is a translation of the original letter written in Tibetan:

Shri Khalsaji Apsarani Shri Maharajah; Lhasa representative Kalon Surkhang; investigator Dapon Peshi, commander of forces; Balana, the representative of Gulam Kahandin; and the interpreter Amir Shah, have written this letter after sitting together. We have agreed that we have no ill feelings because of the past war. The two kings will henceforth remain friends forever. The relationship between Maharajah Gulab Singh of Kashmir and the Lama Guru of Lhasa (Dalai Lama) is now established. The Maharajah Sahib, with God (Kunchok) as his witness, promises to recognize ancient boundaries, which should be looked after by each side without resorting to warfare. When the descendants of the early kings, who fled from Ladakh

18. Our sources do not provide the names of these soldiers and their whereabouts.
19. H. Lushington, Officiating Political Agent, Subathu to T.T. Metcalfe, Agent, Lieutenant Governor, North Western Province, Delhi, 12 May 1842, *Ambala Division Records*, Series, No. VII/4/ (i), Bundle No. 8, Punjab State Archives, Patiala.

to Tibet, now return, they will be restored to their former stations. The annual envoy from Ladakh to Lhasa will not be stopped by Shri Maharajah. Trade between Ladakh and Tibet will continue as usual. Tibetan government traders coming into Ladakh will receive free transport and accommodations as before, and the Ladakhi envoy will, in turn, receive the same facilities in Lhasa. The Ladakhis take an oath before God (Kunchok) that they will not intrigue or create new troubles in the Tibetan territory. We have agreed, with God as witness, that Shri Maharajah Sahib and the Lama Guru of Lhasa (Dalai Lama) will live together as members of the same household. We have written the above on the second of Assura, Sambat 1899 (September 17, 1842).

Sealed by the Wazir, Dewan, Balana, and Amir Shah.

Tibetan Letter of Agreement, 1842

The following is a translation of the original Tibetan letter:

This agreement is made in the interests of the friendship between the Lhasa authorities and Shri Maharajah Sahib and Maharajah Gulab Singh. On the thirteenth day of the eighth month of the Water Tiger year (September 17, 1842), the Lhasa representative Kalon Surkang, investigator Dapon Peshi, Shri Raja Sahib Dewan Hari Chand and Wazir Ratun Sahib, the representative of Shri Maharajah Sahib, sat together amicably with Kunchok (God) as witness. This document has been drawn up to ensure the lasting friendship of the Tibetans and the Ladakhis. We have agreed not to harm each other in any way, and to look after the interests of our own territories. We agree to continue trading in tea and cloth on the same terms as in the past, and will not harm Ladakhi traders coming into Tibet. If any of our subjects stray into your country, they should not be protected. We will forget past differences between the Lhasa authority and Shri Maharajah. The agreement arrived at today will remain firmly established forever. Kunchok (God), Mount Kailash, Lake Manasarovar, and Khochag Jowo have been called as witnesses to this treaty.

Sealed by Kalong Surkhang and Dapon Peshi.[20]

20. Tsepon W.D. Shakabpa, *Tibet: A Political History*, pp. 327-328.

(D) Deposition of Two Deserters from Zorawar Singh's Army FDSC No. 57 of 6 December 1841

From G.T. Lushington
Commissioner of Kumaun
N.W. Province Camp Bareilly

To Asstt. Secretary
to the Lt. Governor,

1. I have the honour to forward for information of the honourable the Lieutenant Governor translations of depositions taken from two of Zorawar Singh's followers who joined my camp of Beans on 8 October 1841, declaring that they were deserters, and whom I brought with me to this place. I should mention that three persons came over in all to my camp in Beans on that day. The whole three are Mahommedans of Peshawar and as the third party does not appear to understand him [?] assistance [sense not clear], speaking only Pushto as he asserts, I have not been able to take his deposition.
2. Whether these persons are in reality deserters may perhaps be doubted, but the fact of their being mere mercenaries of Peshawar and of the Mahommedan religion renders it not unlikely that they are so. When they joined my Camp, they professed to be in the greatest alarm lest the Sikh envoy or his followers should discover them when he came to visit me and should ask me to send them back, the consequence of which they declared would be the loss of their hands and ears. The Beans Zameendars moreover informed me that these three persons had been pursued by Zorawar Singh's Sawars as far as our frontier which however they had entered two or three hours before their pursuers and the latter then turned back.
3. There is little of importance in these depositions which was not already known to us, but the fact of Zorawar Singh's having been dispatched on his late mission by Raja Dhyan Singh and Goolab Singh and of his having been in constant communication with the latter by Daks carried by Sawars, appears to be established if any credit

can be assigned to these depositions. I shall be obliged by your informing me, whether in the opinion of His Honour that will be expedient to detain these persons any longer at Almorah, whether they should be forwarded to the Governor General's Agent at Umbala for further examination and disposal.

Postscript: Copies of this letter and enclosures will be sent to Mr. Clerk and Kathmandoo.

Deposition of Two of Zorawar Singh's Sipahees Taken at Almorah on 27 October 1841 by me (G.T. Lushington)

No. 1

Name Gulzar Khan, son of Shooke Mansoor, caste Mohammedan, m. Ramalee Tillah, Peshawar, age 25 years, profession Sipahee.

1. **When did you first join the Sikhs for service?**
   Six years ago. Three years I served with Raja Gulab Singh who used to pay me regularly 4 rupees per month. I have been further three years with Zorawar Singh, but have received no pay; nothing but rations.
2. **What service did you perform?**
   I was employed in grounding (cis) fighting etc. In short, whatever orders were given me I performed.
3. **When did you first arrive in Ludakh?**
   Three years ago.
4. **When did you leave it?**
   About six months ago.
5. **Of what strength was the force which marched from Ludakh under Zorawar Singh?**
   In round numbers about three thousand.
6. **Of whom was it composed?**
   Of these 500 were by profession Sipahees, the rest Zameendars; some of the latter Baltee, about 5,000 (cis) and the rest were Kishtwaree Hindus of the Thakur caste. The Baltee people were Mohammedans.

7. **How many Pathans and how many Rajputs?**
   About 500 Pathans of Cabool and other places and the rest of Baltee, the Hindus were Kishtwarees.
8. **When you marched from Ludakh, where was Goolab Singh?**
   At Lahore, Dhyan Singh was also there.
9. **Had any quarrel arisen previously to your march between the Sikhs and Hunias?**
   A quarrel had arisen about tea and wool Pushum. The Singh said, "Take these things only to Cashmere and do not send them to Loodhiana." On this war ensued.
10. **By what route did the Hunias send Pushum to Loodhiana?**
    I do not know.
11. **What is the relationship between Goolab Singh and Zorawar Singh?**
    There is no relationship. Zorawar Singh is the servant of Goolab Singh.
12. **By whose orders did Zorawar Singh come to Taklakot?**
    By Goolab Singh's and Dhyan Singh's orders. They said, "We will supply troops and money. Take the country. They supplied him every thing. Troops, arms and money.
13. **What pay does Zorawar Singh get?**
    One hundred rupees is his money stipend and he has the Ryasee country in jagir. It is under his orders and he pays tribute to Goolab Singh.
14. **How many Ladakhis were there with the force?**
    About 250. Employed in carrying baggage on yaks.
15. **How many days were you from Ladakh to Gartok?**
    Seventeen days. After about ten days we reached Gartok; a fight took place immediately on our arrival.
16. **Did any engagement take place previously?**
    No. Only at Garoo.
17. **How many Hunias were there at Garoo?**
    About 100 fighting men and the rest had fled.
18. **Did they offer much resistance?**

Some shells were fired. Four of our Pathans were killed and two of the Hunias. They were all inside the fort. The next day they all came out and surrendered themselves to us.

19. **How many days did you remain at Garoo?**
Two months.

20. **Did the Dak arrive regularly at your Camps from Goolab Singh?**
Yes. He sent orders that he would dispatch what ever was required in the way of guns, troops etc.

21. **Was Garoo plundered?**
The Wazir put a guard over the khazana under Bustee Ram with 60 men. The Sipahees got no booty. In exchange for the four Pathans who were killed, Zorawar Singh levied a fine of 100 horses, 15,000 rupees and 100 goats from the Gartok people.

22. **Was there any Hunia Sardar at Garoo?**
There was a Suniar from Lhasa in the fort. The Wazir told him, he should in future be his Thanadar as he was before of the Lhasa people and ordered him to invite the Zameendars back and restore confidence in them.

23. **Why were the goats taken by Zorawar Singh?**
The Wazir placed them in his own khazana and gave them back to parties who paid for them.

24. **Is there any other Sardar besides Zorawar Singh at Taklakot?**
Zorawar Singh is the only Sardar on the part of Goolab Singh, but he has 4 to 5 of his own Sardars under him.

25. **Who are they?**
Mugnu, Thanadar of Ludakh, Miyan Utara Kishtwaria with 100 matchlocks; Rai Singh Rajput with 60 matchlocks; Bustee Ram, the treasurer and commissioner.

26. **Who is Bustee Ram?**
He is a respectable man and is allowed to sit in court.

27. **Had you seen any fighting at Taklakot?**
The Lhasa Amil fled about hour before day break upon

which the Zameendars came to Zorawar Singh, who immediately stationed Bustee Ram in the fort with a strong guard. The Wazir appropriated all the gold, silver, salt, grain and horses he could find. Shortly after this 5 Gurkha soldiers came to make inquiries and subsequently a Nepalese Jamadar and 10 men arrived. The Jamadar said, "Come with us to Lhasa, we will pay expenses." Zorawar Singh refused saying Goolab Singh had sent a purwana to summon him back and he should return to Jammu. He also said, "I hear that a Sahib has come to Beans; after seeing him, I should depart."

28. **Were there any Gosains in the army?**
Two. One young and one old.

29. **What service do they perform?**
Nothing; they are fed and allowed horses to ride on by the state.

30. **Who are they?**
Hindustanis, not Punjabees.

31. **Who was your Jamadar?**
A Khanzadah; he had 23 men under him.

32. **Do you wish to return to your country?**
No. Not to the Sikhs. We wish to enter the British service.

33. **Will you get employment in your own country?**
We have no means of reaching there.

34. **Who commanded the party which went to Rudok and what occurred there?**
Magna Thanadar, the brother-in-law of the Wazir. Two of the Sikhs were killed on that occasion; and two or three of Rudok wallas. No treasure was found; only ten horses and grain for two years consumption.

35. **Why did you stop the trade of our people?**
We did not stop it. They did not come there owing to the state of alarm.

36. **Were any of our people seized or molested on their way?**
I never heard or seen any thing of that sort.

No. 2

Name Aukhoo Khan, son of Tooruhbar,
Pathan of Peshawar, profession Sipahee.

1. **When did you first join the Sikhs for service?**
   6. years. 3 with Goolab Singh and 3 with Zorawar Singh.
2. **When did you first arrive in Ladakh?**
   3 years ago. Left it in September.
3. **What was the strength of the force which marched from Ladakh under Zorawar Singh?**
   About 3,000.
4. **How many regular Sipahees were there in the force?**
   120 Rajputs, 100 Pathans and thirty Kishtwarees.
5. **Had any quarrel arisen previously to your march between the Sikhs and Hunias?**
   No. Without asking, Zorawar Singh attacked Takla Kot.
6. **Is Zorawar Singh related to Goolab Singh?**
   No Zorawar Singh is of another country and not related.
7. **By whose orders did Zorawar Singh come?**
   By Goolab Singh's.
8. **What does Zorawar Singh get?**
   Riyasi Shahr is his possession.
9. **How many Ladakhis were there?**
   About 20 matchlocks; the rest were the coolies.
10. **How many Baltee people?**
    About 500.
11. **How many days were you from Ladakh to Garoo?**
    About 10. The country is a plain, the whole way fit for horses.
12. **Where did you get supplies?**
    Some were brought with us and some came from Ladakh.
13. **Where was the first fight?**
    At Garoo.
14. **How many Hunias were there?**
    About 200 armed with guns and swords etc. On both sides firing took place. 4 of our Pathans were killed. The Hunias

were at that time in the fort. Some of them were killed. After that, a truce was concluded and the fort surrendered.

15. **How long were you at Gartok?**
22 days.

16. **Did Dak come to Garoo regularly from Goolab Singh to Zorawar Singh?**
Yes. Sawars brought it.

17. **Did you get any loot of Garoo?**
No. Zorawar Singh fined the Hunias 15,000 rupees as jurmana.

18. **Was there any Hunia Sardar there?**
He had gone to Takla Kot.

19. **Is there any other Sardar on the part of Goolab Singh besides Zorawar Singh?**
Zorawar Singh is the sole commander. There is a Sahib with Goolab Singh at Jammu and other Sardars at Jammu, but none on the part of Goolab Singh with our army except Zorawar Singh.

20. **Did you lose any men at Takla Kot?**
No.

21. **Was any resistance offered?**
One day, a few shots were fired. 5 or 6 Hunias were killed and the rest fled; also the Hunia Sardar. A few Hunias remained behind. 4 or 5 of the chiefs were seized and put in rooms by Zorawar Singh.

22. **Did you get any plunder at Takla Kot?**
No. Zorawar Singh appropriated all that was found. I heard that there was a good deal of gold, also grain and salt in the fort, but I did not see it with my own eyes.

23. **Why did you leave Zorawar Singh?**
Because we did not get pay or sufficient food and wanted to enter your service.

24. **Did any Goorkhas come to visit Zorawar Singh while at Takla Kot?**
3 Sipahees came in the first instance and next a Jamadar and 10 men.

25. **What occurred between them and the Wazir?**
The Jamadar offered to assist, as friends of Zorawar Singh would go into Lhasa. Zorawar Singh refused saying that a Dak had arrived from Goolab Singh to summon him back to Ladakh. It came about six days before we left. Zorawar Singh gave out that after seeing the Sahib, he should return to Ladakh.

26. **Did Zorawar Singh go to Manasarovar?**
The whole army came by it.

27. **Was it very cold at Takla Kot?**
Yes, excessively so.

28. **Where did you get the horses which were with the army?**
Some were plundered from Baltees, some from Garoo and some from Takla Kot.

29. **Has a fort been built at Takla Kot?**
Yes. 24 paths [?] high and about 40 paths [?] broad as long as this house (meaning my house).

30. **Had the Hunia Zamindars returned to Takla Kot when you fled?**
Some of them had returned; not all.

31. **Who were the people whose tongues were cut out at Takla Kot by Zorawar Singh and what offence had they committed?**
They were Cashmiris and had come with us from Ladakh. The offence of which they were accused was the killing of a Chinese cow. None of the Hunias of the place have been put to death.

True Translation

Sd.
(G.T. Lushington)
Commissioner

Note: The above examination was taken separately in my presence and neither of the parties knew what questions would be asked. The statement appears to correspond in all material points.

(E) Spellings of Place Names

Spellings used at present	Spellings used by J.D. Cunningham
1. Bashahr	Bushahar, Bissihir, Bassahar, Bushihir
2. Braham Putra	Burram Putra
3. Churit	Choorut, Choorit
4. Chumurty	Chumurting, Chumurtung, Choommooty
5. Garo	Garoo, Garroo, Gartop, Gardokh, Gartokh, Ghertope
6. Gulab Singh	Goolab Singh
7. Jammu	Jammoo
8. Kabul	Cabool, Cabul, Caubal
9. Kashmir	Kashmeer, Cashmir
10. Kinaur	Kunawar, Kunnawar, Kinnaur
11. Kulu	Koolloo, Kooloo
12. Ladakh	Ludakh
13. Parganah	Pargannah, Purganaa, Purgunnah
14. Pathan	Putans
15. Rupshu	Roopshoo, Ruopshu
16. Shalkhar	Shialkur, Shyalkur, Shalkur
17. Shipki	Shipkee
18. Spiti	Spittee, Spite, Pittee
19. Taklakot	Taklaghour, Takla Ghat, Taklaghur

Bibliography

1. Aitchison, C.U., *Treaties, Engagements and Sanads Relating to India and Neighbouring Countries*, Vol. XIV, Central Publishing Branch, Government of India, Calcutta, 1933.
2. *Ambala Division Records*, Series VII, Bundle No. 8, Punjab State Archives, Patiala.
3. Bal, S.S., 'Cunningham's Attempt to Get Himself Rehabilitated in the Political Service,' in Harbans Singh and N. Gerald Barrier, (ed.), *Essays in Honour of Dr. Ganda Singh*, Punjabi University, Patiala, 1976.
4. Chopra, Barkat Rai, *Kingdom of the Punjab 1839-45*, Vishveshwaranand Institute, Hoshiarpur, 1969.
5. Cunningham, Alexander, *Ladakh: Political, Statistical and Historical*, Sagar Publications, New Delhi, Reprint, 1970.
6. Cunningham, Joseph Davey, *A History of the Sikhs*, ed., H.L.O. Garret and R.R. Sethi, S. Chand & Co., Delhi, Reprint, 1955.
7. Das, Sarat Chandra, *Journey to Lhasa and Central Tibet*, Manjusri Publishing House, New Delhi, 1970.
8. Datta, C.L., *The Raj and the Simla Hill States: Socio-economic Problems, Agrarian Disturbances and Paramountcy*, ABS Publications, Jalandhar, 1997.
9. ———, *General Zorawar Singh: His Life and Achievements in Ladakh, Baltistan and Tibet*, Deep & Deep Publications, New Delhi, 1984.
10. ———, *Ladakh and Western Himalayan Politics: 1819-1848*, Munshiram Manoharlal, New Delhi, 1973.
11. ———, 'Significance of Shawl Wool Trade in Western Himalayan Politics,' *Bengal: Past and Present*, Vol. LxxxiX, Part 1, Serial No. 167, 1970.
12. Davies, R.H., *Report on the Trade and Resources of the Countries on the North West Boundary of British India*, Government Press, Lahore, 1862.

13. Fisher, M., W.M. Rose and R.A. Huttenback, *Himalayan Battleground: Sino-Indian Rivalry in Ladakh*, Frederick A. Praeger, New York and London, 1963.
14. Francke, A.H., *A History of Ladakh*, (with Critical Introduction and Annotation by S.S. Gergan and F.M. Hassnain, Sterling Publishers, New Delhi, 1977.
15. ———, *A History of Western Tibet: One of the Unknown Empires*, S.W. Partridge, London, 1907.
16. *Gazetteer of the Simla Hill States: Bashahr State Gazetteer 1910*, Indus Publishing House, New Delhi, Reprint, 1995.
17. *Gazetteer of the Kangra District: Kulu, Lahaul and Spiti 1997*, Indus Publishing House, New Delhi, Reprint, 1994.
18. Hasrat, Bikrama Jit, *Life and Times of Ranjit Singh: A Saga of Benevolent Despotism*, V.V. Research Institute, Hoshiarpur, 1977.
19. Hsu, C.Y., *The Rise of Modern China*, Oxford University Press, New York, Sixth Edition, 2000.
20. Hutchison, J. and J. Ph. Vogel, *History of the Panjab Hill States*, 2 Vols., Low Price Publications, New Delhi, 2008.
21. *Imperial Gazetteer of India, Provincial Series, Punjab*, Vol. II, Superintendent of Government Printing, Calcutta, 1908.
22. Irvine, William, *The Army of the Indian Moghuls: Its Organization and Administration*, Eurasia Publishing House, New Delhi, Reprint, 1962.
23. Khan, Hashmatullah, *Tarikh-i-Jammu*, Lucknow, 1939.
24. Lamb, Alastair, *Britain and Chinese Central Asia: The Road to Lhasa*, Routledge & Kegan Paul, London, 1961.
25. Macdonald, David, *Cultural Heritage of Tibet*, Light and Life Publishers, New Delhi, n.d.
26. Mehra, Parshotam, *A Dictionary of Modern Indian History, 1707-1947*, Oxford University Press, Delhi, 1985.
27. Moorcroft, William and George Trebeck, *Travels in the Himalayan Provinces of Hindustan and the Punjab, in Ladakh and Kashmir, in Peshawar, Kabul, Kunduz and Bokhara*, Vol. II, Sagar Publications, New Delhi, Reprint, 1971.
28. Pannikar K.M., *The Founding of the Kashmir State: A Biography of Maharaja Gulab Singh (1792-1858)*, Allen & Unwin, London, 1953.
29. Patterson, George N., 'Tibet,' in Guy Wint, (ed.), *Asia: A Handbook*, Anthony Blond, London, 1965.
30. Petech, L., 'Tibetan-Ladakhi-Moghul War of 1681-83,' *Indian Historical Quarterly*, Vol. XXIII, September 1947.
31. Quarter Master General, Intelligence Bureau, (ed.), *Gazetteer of Kashmir and Ladak*, Vivek Publishing House, Delhi, Reprint, 1974.

(First published in 1890 by the Superintendent of Government Printing, Calcutta).

32. Rose, Leo E., *Nepal: Strategy for Survival*, Oxford University Press, Bombay, 1971.
33. Thomson, Thomas, *West Himalayas and Tibet: A Narrative on Ladakh and Mountains of Northern India*, Cosmo Publications, New Delhi, Reprint, 1978.
34. Muhiuddin, Momin, *The Chancellary and Persian Historiography under the Mughals*, Iran Society, Calcutta, 1971.
35. Rizvi, Janet, *Ladakh: Crossroads of High Asia*, Oxford University Press, Delhi, 1983.
36. *Secret Consultations of the Foreign Department*, (unpublished documents including the reports of J.D. Cunningham, referred to in this volume as FDSC), National Archives of India, New Delhi, 1841-1842.
37. Shakabpa, Tsepon W.D., *Tibet: A Political History*, Yale University Press, New Haven and London, 1967.
38. Sherring, Charles A., *Western Tibet and the Indian Borderland*, Cosmo Publications, New Delhi, Reprint, 1974.
39. Suri, Sohan Lal, *Umdat-ut-Tawarikh*, Daftar III, English Translation, V.S. Suri, S. Chand & Co., New Delhi, 1961.
40. Yule, Henry and A.C. Burnell, *Hobson Jobson: The Definitive Glossary of British India*, ed., Kate Teltscher, Oxford University Press, Oxford, 2013.
41. Yasin, Khwaja, *Dastur-i-Malguzari*, Persian Text and English Translation, S. Hasan Mahmud, Kitab Bhavan, New Delhi, 2000.

Index